**BRITISH
ELECTORAL
FACTS
1832-1987**

OTHER BOOKS IN THIS SERIES

BRITISH
ELECTORAL
FACTS
1832–1987

Compiled and Edited by
F. W. S. CRAIG

Parliamentary Research Services
Dartmouth

First published in 1968 under the title
British Parliamentary Election Statistics
Second Edition 1971
Third Edition under the present title 1976
Fourth edition 1981
Fifth edition 1989

Published by
Parliamentary Research Services
Gower Publishing Company Limited
Gower House
Croft Road
Aldershot
Hants. GU11 3HR
England

Gower Publishing Company
Old Post Road
Brookfield
Vermont 05036
USA

British Library Cataloguing in Publication Data

Craig, F.W.S.
  British electoral facts 1832-1987.
  1. Great Britain. *Parliament—*
  Elections---Statistics
  1. Title
  324.941'08   JN1037

  ISBN 0-900178-30-2

Typeset by *LITHOSET, Chichester, West Sussex*

Printed in Great Britain by
Billing & Sons Ltd, Worcester

For my wife Phyllis —
1968-1988 and five editions

CONTENTS

PREFACE

Since this book first appeared in 1968 it has undergone a number of important changes in design and content. This fifth edition incorporates several new tables and appendices, some suggested by users of the previous editions and I am grateful to them for their many helpful comments. The publication in 1987 of my book *Chronology of British Parliamentary By-Elections 1833-1987* has enabled me to reduce the number of pages devoted to by-election statistics and accommodate new tables in other sections.

The book still maintains the original aim of providing an accurate reference source to British election statistics in a single volume and makes no claim to be a study of voting behaviour or voting by regions. It does however provide the basic facts and figures most likely to be required by the psephologist, librarian, journalist or politician and many others seeking information on British elections.

I could not have compiled this book without the co-operation of numerous individuals, government departments, political parties, libraries, etc. and I would especially like to thank Leslie Raphael for his many useful suggestions and his contributions to some of the new tables.

When in the autumn of 1968 the first edition was published I had no idea that it would lead to the publication of more than 30 new books and new editions of reference books during the next 20 years. Looking back over those years gives me some satisfaction that I have filled a number of gaps in books of reference which had been sadly lacking on library shelves. Every compiler of reference books has a favourite book of which he is especially proud and *British Electoral Facts* would be my choice.

Although the very greatest care has been taken to ensure accuracy, it would be unrealistic to expect that no errors arithmetical or typographical, have slipped through and I hope that readers will let the Publisher know of any they may detect.

Parliamentary Research Services   F.W.S. CRAIG

December 1988

INTRODUCTORY NOTES

COALITION CANDIDATES 1918-1922 In the majority of tables, official Coalition candidates are not distinguished from other candidates of the same party. The only exception is in respect of the five Coalition Labour candidates at the General Election of 1918 who could not be classed with other Labour candidates as they were not endorsed by the Labour Party. The Coalition prefix has only been used for official candidates of the Coalition, *i.e.* those who received the 'coupon', a letter signed by Lloyd George and Bonar Law which was sent to approved nominees.

CO-OPERATIVE PARTY From the General Election of 1922, all Co-operative Party candidates have been endorsed by the Labour Party and sought election as 'Labour and Co-operative'. No distinction is made in the tables between these joint candidates and other Labour candidates.

ELECTORATE As a result of the Representation of the People Act, 1969, those becoming 18 years of age during the period covered by the annual Electoral Register now have the date on which they attain their 18th birthday inserted in the Register and they can vote from that date.

This change in the registration procedure meant that it was no longer possible to know the exact electorate in a constituency on a particular date without asking Electoral Registration Officers to go through each register and deduct the number of post-election "dated names" from the total electorate. This was a laborious task which caused delays in the obtaining of electorate figures and frequently resulted in Electoral Registration Officers providing estimated rather than exact figures.

In 1974, Parliamentary Research Services initiated discussions with the Office of Population Censuses and Surveys, the Home Office, the Press Association, the British Broadcasting Corporation, Independent Television News and a number of interested academics in an attempt to find an acceptable formula for calculating electorates on a particular date. As a result the following formula was used by the media in calculating the electorate from the General Election of October 1974.

Total number of "dated names" on the Register multiplied by the fraction

$$\frac{\text{Number of days from February 17 to Polling Day (both dates inclusive)}}{364 \text{ (or 365 in a Leap Year)}}$$

The following is an example of the calculation:—

Electorate at 16 February	64,162
Number of "dated names"	757
Total	64,919

Using the Electorate Calculator on page 80 and assuming polling day was October 1 the formula would be:

$$757 \times \frac{227}{364} \ (0.623626) = 472.084882 \ \text{(truncate)}$$

The estimated electorate at October 1 would be:

$$64,162 + 472 = 64,634$$

The figures for electorate given in this book for General Elections and subsequent by-elections from 1974 have been calculated using the above formula.

ENGLAND Prior to April 1, 1974, the term 'England' *excludes* Monmouthshire.

GAINS AND LOSSES When compiling the tables of gains and losses, a gain or loss has been recorded on the basis of the incumbent's party allegiance at the time of the Dissolution or by-election. This means that where an MP changed from one party to another or became an Independent during a Parliament and did not resign immediately, his seat was from then on considered to be held by his new party. A detailed list of changes of party allegiance since 1900 will be found in *British Political Facts,* 6th edition, by David Butler and Gareth Butler, pp. 234-239.

INDEPENDENT LABOUR PARTY From 1900 until August 1932, the Independent Labour Party (ILP) was affiliated to the Labour Party and as their candidates normally received endorsement they are treated as official Labour candidates in the tables. There were however four by-elections where ILP candidates went forward without Labour Party endorsement and they have therefore been classed as ILP and not Labour candidates.

INDEPENDENTS AND MINOR PARTIES The columns headed 'Others' include all Independents and candidates of minor parties and organisations.

LIBERALS AND NATIONAL LIBERALS 1922-1923 In the majority of tables, no distinction is made between (Asquith) Liberal and (Lloyd George) National Liberal candidates. The two groups merged in November 1923 to fight the forthcoming General Election as a united party.

MULTI-MEMBER SEATS Percentage figures of votes cast and turnout have been adjusted to allow for the multi-member seats which existed prior to 1950. In calculating the percentage of votes, the total votes in multi-member constituencies have been divided by the number of votes which each elector was allowed. In two-member seats each elector had two votes; in three member constituencies prior to 1868 each elector had three votes but from 1868 this was reduced to two votes; in the four-member constituency of the City of London, prior to 1868 each elector had four votes but this was reduced to three votes from 1868.

In calculating turnout prior to 1885, votes in multi-member seats have been counted as one quarter, one third or one half votes which makes no allowance for electors using fewer than the votes allowed to them. The turnout percentages produced are therefore a slight underestimate of the number of electors voting as distinct from the number of votes cast.

From 1885 onwards figures of the actual number of electors voting in multi-member seats were, with a few exceptions, generally available and have been used in calculating the turnout.

NATIONAL LIBERAL AND CONSERVATIVE CANDIDATES In the majority of tables, no distinction is made between joint National Liberal and Conservative candidates and other Conservative candidates. In May 1947, recommendations were issued by Lord Woolton, on behalf of the Conservative Party, and Lord Teviot, on behalf of the National Liberal Organization, which advocated that the two parties should come together in constituencies and form combined associations under a mutually agreed title. Immediately following the 1950 election, a Liberal-Unionist Group was formed in the House of Commons by those MPs elected under the auspices of joint local associations. Owing to local circumstances and preferences, the actual 'labels' used by candidates varied from one constituency to another but for the sake of uniformity the designation National Liberal and Conservative (NL & C) has been used throughout this book.

In May 1968 the National Liberal Council was disbanded.

NORTHERN IRELAND Until the General Election of February 1974, no distinction has been made between Unionist, Labour (provided they were endorsed by the Labour Party in London) and Liberal candidates in Northern Ireland and Conservative/Unionist, Labour and Liberal candidates in Great Britain.

From the General Election of February 1974, candidates of the Ulster Unionist Council, Northern Ireland Labour Party and the Ulster Liberal Party have been classed as 'Others' in all the tables. This reflects the changed political situation in Ulster which makes it unrealistic to continue the former method of classification.

SOURCES Unless otherwise stated, all statistics have been compiled from *British Parliamentary Election Results, 1832-1983* (5 volumes) and *Britain Votes 4* compiled and edited by F.W.S. Craig.

The Introductory Notes to these volumes include full details of the original sources used.

Statistics relating to elections in Ireland from 1832-1922 for which detailed constituency results are not included in *British Parliamentary Election Results* have been based on Dr Brian Walker's book *Parliamentary Election Results in Ireland 1801-1922*.

SPEAKER OF THE HOUSE OF COMMONS The Speaker of the House of Commons takes no active part in an election campaign and since 1950 (when the Speaker requested that he be given no party 'label') has sought re-election as 'The Speaker' and not as a party candidate. It would however be unrealistic to include votes cast for the Speaker among 'Others' as clearly the majority of electors voting for him do so on a political basis. Therefore, throughout the tables the Speaker has been regarded as a candidate of the party he represented before his appointment.

STATE OF PARTIES AFTER GENERAL ELECTIONS Throughout this book the state of parties in the House of Commons following a General Election reflects the position *after* the double and treble elections had been decided but *prior* to changes caused by election petitions.

UNIVERSITY SEATS From 1918 in the university constituencies returning more than one member, General Elections were conducted by Proportional Representation (single transferable vote). In compiling the tables, figures of first preference votes have been used.

WALES Prior to April 1, 1974, the term 'Wales' *includes* Monmouthshire.

ABBREVIATIONS

PARTIES

AP	Anti-Partitionist (candidate of the Anti-Partition of Ireland League of Great Britain)
APNI	Alliance Party of Northern Ireland
BEP	British Empire Party
BLP	Belfast Labour Party (subsequently Northern Ireland Labour Party)
BM	British Movement
BNP	British National Party
BSP	British Socialist Party
C	Conservative and Unionist Party
CFMPB	Campaign for a More Prosperous Britain
Ch	Chartist
CNP	Cornish Nationalist Party
Co	Coalition
Com	Communist Party of Great Britain
Const	Constitutionalist
Co-op	Co-operative Party
CP	Christian Pacifist
CPE	Communist Party of England (Marxist-Leninist)
Crf	Crofter
CW	Common Wealth Movement
CW Land P	Commonwealth Land Party
CWLP	Commonwealth Labour Party
Dem Lab	Democratic Labour
Dem P	Democratic Party (1942-45)
DP	Democratic Party (1969-71)
EFP	European Federal Party
ENP	English National Party
EP	Ecology Party (formerly People Movement, subsequently Green Party)
EP/WFLOE	Ecology Party/Women for Life on Earth joint candidate
FP	Fellowship Party
FTACMP	Free Trade Anti-Common Market Party
GP	Green Party (formerly Ecology Party)
HLL	Highland Land League
HP	Humanist Party
HR	Irish Home Ruler
ICRA	Irish Civil Rights Association
IDA	Independent Democratic Alliance
IIP	Irish Independence Party
ILP	Independent Labour Party
IMG	International Marxist Group

xvii

Ind . . . . Independent (indicates an unofficial candidate when
                      placed before a party abbreviation)
INDEC. . . . . . Independent Nuclear Disarmament Election Committee
Irish LP . . . . Labour Party (Dublin)
L . . . . Liberal Party
Lab . . . . . . Labour Party
Lab/Co-op . . . Labour Party/Co-operative Party joint candidate
LC . . . . . . Liberal Conservative
L/Lab . . . . . Liberal/Labour
Loyalist . . . . Independent Loyalist (candidate of the League of
                      Empire Loyalists)
LPP. . . . . . Liverpool Protestant Party
LU . . . . . . Liberal Unionist Party
MGC . . . . . Mudiad Gweriniaethol Cymru (Welsh Republican Movement)
MK . . . . . . Mebyon Kernow (Sons of Cornwall) — Cornish Nationalist
                      Movement
MRLP . . . . . Monster Raving Loony Party
N . . . . . . Irish Nationalist/Anti-Partitionist
Nat . . . . . . National
Nat DP. . . . . National Democratic Party
Nat P . . . . . National Party (1917-21)
Nat Pty . . . . Nationalist Party (formerly National Front Constitutional
                      Movement)
NBP. . . . . . New Britain Party
NIEP . . . . . Northern Ireland Ecology Party
N Dem P . . . . National Democratic Party
NDP. . . . . . National Democratic and Labour Party
NF . . . . . . National Front
NFDSS . . . . National Federation of Discharged and Demobilized
                      Sailors and Soldiers
NI Ind Lab . . . Northern Ireland Independent Labour Party
NI Lab. . . . . Northern Ireland Labour Party
NIP. . . . . . National Independence Party
NL . . . . . . National Liberal (candidate of Lloyd George's National
                      Liberal Council, 1922-23 or of the National Liberal
                      Organization (Liberal National Organization, 1931-48),
                      1931-68)
N Lab . . . . . National Labour Organization
N Lab P . . . . National Labour Party (1981-)
NL & C . . . . National Liberal and Conservative (joint candidate of the
                      Conservative Party and the National Liberal Organization)
NLP . . . . . National Labour Party (1958-60)
NP . . . . . . New Party
NSP. . . . . . National Socialist Party
OSM . . . . . Orkney and Shetland Movement
PAL . . . . . Party of Associates with Licensees
Pat P . . . . . Patriotic Party
PC . . . . . . Plaid Cymru (pronounced *Plide Cumree*) — Welsh
                      (Nationalist) Party
People . . . . . People Movement (subsequently Ecology Party)

Prog	. Progressive
Prot U	. Protestant Unionist Party (subsequently Ulster Democratic Unionist Party)
R	. Irish Repealer
RA	. Radical Alliance
Rep	. Irish Republican
Rep C	. Republican Clubs (subsequently Republican Clubs — The Workers Party)
Rep C/TWP . . .	. Republican Clubs — The Workers Party (formerly Republican Clubs)
Rep LP	. Republican Labour Party
Rev CP	. Revolutionary Communist Party
RF	. Red Front (candidate of the Revolutionary Communist Party)
SCLP	. Scottish Labour Party
SCPGB	. Social Credit Party of Great Britain
SD	. Social Democrat (candidate of the Campaign for Social Democracy)
S Dem P . . .	. Social Democratic Party (formerly Social Democratic Federation) (1907-1911)
SDF	. Social Democratic Federation (subsequently Social Democratic Party)
SDLP	. Social Democratic and Labour Party
SDP	. Social Democratic Party (1981-)
SF	. Sinn Fein (pronounced *Shin Fane*) — Irish Republican Organisation
SLP	. Socialist Labour Party
SLRL	. Scottish Land Restoration League
SNP	. Scottish National Party
Soc	. Socialist
SPGB	. Socialist Party of Great Britain
SPLP	. Scottish (Parliamentary) Labour Party
SPP	. Scottish Prohibition Party
SSF	. Scottish Socialist Federation
SU	. Socialist Unity
SUTCLP . . .	. Scottish United Trades Councils Labour Party
SWRC	. Scottish Workers Representation Committee
TWP	. The Workers Party (formerly Republican Clubs — The Workers Party)
UACM	. United Anti-Common Marketeers
UCP	. United Country Party
UDP	. United Democratic Party
UDUP	. Ulster Democratic Unionist Party (formerly Protestant Unionist Party)
UM	. Union Movement
Unity	. Opposition Unity (candidate in Northern Ireland opposed to the Government and sponsored by various organisations)
UPNI	. Unionist Party of Northern Ireland
UDUP	. Ulster Democratic Unionist Party (formerly Protestant Unionist Party)
UPUP	. Ulster Popular Unionist Party
UU	. Ulster Unionist (candidate of the Ulster Unionist Council)
UUUC	. United Ulster Unionist Council
UUP	. United Ulster Unionist Party

VNP.	. . . . .	Vectis (Isle of Wight) Nationalist Party
VUPP	. . . . .	Vanguard Unionist Progressive Party
WFLOE	. . .	Women for Life on Earth
Wk P	. . . .	Workers Party
WP	. . . . .	Women's Party
WR	. . . . .	Wessex Regionalist
WRP	. . . .	Workers Revolutionary Party

MISCELLANEOUS

Bt	. . . . .	Baronet
CLP	. . . .	Constituency Labour Party
Dr	. . . . .	Doctor of Medicine
GLC	. . . .	Greater London Council
HM	. . . . .	His/Her Majesty
Hon.	. . . .	Honourable
MEP	. . . .	Member of the European Parliament
Metro	. . . .	Metropolitan
MP	. . . . .	Member of Parliament
Rev	. . . . .	Reverend
UK	. . . . .	United Kingdom
Unopp	. . . .	Unopposed

Table 1.01 GENERAL ELECTION 1832

	Total Votes	%*	Candidates	Unopposed	Elected
ENGLAND					
C	193,442	29.2	228	32	117
L	474,542	70.8	488	81	347
Total	667,984	100.0	716	113	464
WALES					
C	7,466	53.4	19	10	14
L	6,348	46.6	21	12	18
Total	13,814	100.0	40	22	32
SCOTLAND					
C	9,752	21.0	28	4	10
L	44,003	79.0	70	12	43
Total	53,755	100.0	98	16	53
IRELAND					
C	28,030	32.1	69	16	28
L	29,013	33.3	55	4	33
R	31,773	34.6	51	14	42
Total	88,816	100.0	175	34	103
UNIVERSITIES					
C	2,594	76.2	6	4	6
L	813	23.8	2	0	0
Total	3,407	100.0	8	4	6
UNITED KINGDOM					
C	241,284	29.4	350	66	175
L	554,719	66.7	636	109	441
R	31,773	3.9	51	14	42
Total	827,776	100.0	1,037	189	658

*Adjusted to allow for multi-member seats. See Introductory Notes.

Table 1.02 GENERAL ELECTION 1835

	Total Votes	%*	Candidates	Unopposed	Elected
ENGLAND					
C	209,964	42.6	278	77	200
L	281,576	57.4	380	100	264
Total	491,540	100.0	658	177	464
WALES					
C	10,210	63.9	21	11	17
L	5,119	36.1	19	11	15
Total	15,329	100.0	40	22	32
SCOTLAND					
C	15,733	37.2	33	8	15
L	28,307	62.8	52	15	38
Total	44,040	100.0	85	23	53
IRELAND					
C	25,362	42.4	69	19	35
L	34,866	57.6	87	28	68
Total	60,228	100.0	156	47	103
UNIVERSITIES					
C	–	–	6	6	6
Total	–	–	6	6	6
UNITED KINGDOM					
C	261,269	42.6	407	121	273
L	349,868	57.4	538	154	385
Total	611,137	100.0	945	275	658

*Adjusted to allow for multi-member seats. See Introductory Notes.

Table 1.03   GENERAL ELECTION 1837

	Total Votes	%*	Candidates	Unopposed	Elected
ENGLAND					
C	321,124	48.9	348	80	239
L	347,549	51.1	352	60	225
Total	**668,673**	**100.0**	**700**	**140**	**464**
WALES					
C	11,616	52.8	25	11	19
L	10,144	47.2	20	6	13
Total	**21,760**	**100.0**	**45**	**17**	**32**
SCOTLAND					
C	18,569	46.0	35	7	20
L	22,082	54.0	49	15	33
Total	**40,651**	**100.0**	**84**	**22**	**53**
IRELAND					
C	26,694	41.5	70	19	30
L	38,370	58.5	88	34	73
Total	**65,064**	**100.0**	**158**	**53**	**103**
UNIVERSITIES					
C	1,691	90.1	6	4	6
L	186	9.9	1	0	0
Total	**1,877**	**100.0**	**7**	**4**	**6**
UNITED KINGDOM					
C	379,694	48.3	484	121	314
L	418,331	51.7	510	115	344
Total	**798,025**	**100.0**	**994**	**236**	**658**

*Adjusted to allow for multi-member seats. See Introductory Notes.

Table 1.04 GENERAL ELECTION 1841

	Total Votes	%*	Candidates	Unopposed	Elected
ENGLAND					
C	272,755	53.1	374	147	277
L	236,813	46.8	277	62	187
Ch	307	0.1	4	0	0
Total	509,875	100.0	655	209	464
WALES					
C	4,102	53.2	24	16	21
L	3,605	46.8	16	8	11
Ch	0	0.0	1	0	0
Total	7,707	100.0	41	24	32
SCOTLAND					
C	9,793	38.3	35	16	22
L	16,356	60.8	40	13	31
Ch	385	0.9	3	0	0
Total	26,534	100.0	78	29	53
IRELAND					
C	19,664	40.1	59	27	41
L	17,128	35.1	55	30	42
R	12,537	24.8	22	12	20
Total	49,329	100.0	136	69	103
UNIVERSITIES					
C	—	—	6	6	6
Total	—	—	6	6	6
UNITED KINGDOM					
C	306,314	50.9	498	212	367
L	273,902	46.9	388	113	271
Ch	692	0.1	8	0	0
R	12,537	2.1	22	12	20
Total	593,445	100.0	916	337	658

*Adjusted to allow for multi-member seats. See Introductory Notes.

Table 1.05   GENERAL ELECTION 1847

	Total Votes	%*	Candidates	Unopposed	Elected
ENGLAND					
C & LC	170,407	42.1	319	149	239
L	230,656	57.2	297	92	222
Ch	2,848	0.7	9	0	1
Total	**403,911**	**100.0**	**625**	**241**	**462**
WALES					
C & LC	11,114	89.5	22	15	20
L	1,394	10.5	13	12	12
Total	**12,508**	**100.0**	**35**	**27**	**32**
SCOTLAND					
C & LC	3,509	18.3	23	16	20
L	20,092	81.7	48	21	33
Total	**23,601**	**100.0**	**71**	**37**	**53**
IRELAND					
C & LC	11,258	34.0	49	33	40
L	5,935	20.2	33	11	25
R	14,128	43.6	51	18	36
Others	661	2.2	4	0	2
Total	**31,982**	**100.0**	**137**	**62**	**103**
UNIVERSITIES					
C & LC	9,193	88.2	9	0	6
L	1,234	11.8	2	0	0
Total	**10,427**	**100.0**	**11**	**0**	**6**
UNITED KINGDOM					
C & LC	205,481	42.2	422	213	325
L	259,311	53.9	393	136	292
Ch	2,848	0.6	9	0	1
R	14,128	3.1	51	18	36
Others	661	0.2	4	0	2
Total	**482,429**	**100.0**	**879**	**367**	**656**

*Adjusted to allow for multi-member seats. See Introductory Notes.

Table 1.06 GENERAL ELECTION 1852

	Total Votes	%*	Candidates	Unopposed	Elected
ENGLAND					
C & LC	232,407	40.5	332	109	244
L	334,121	59.2	334	56	216
Ch	1,541	0.3	4	0	0
Total	**568,069**	**100.0**	**670**	**165**	**460**
WALES					
C & LC	7,212	54.7	25	14	20
L	5,251	45.3	17	7	12
Total	**12,463**	**100.0**	**42**	**21**	**32**
SCOTLAND					
C & LC	6,955	27.4	31	18	20
L	21,015	72.6	43	15	33
Total	**27,970**	**100.0**	**74**	**33**	**53**
IRELAND					
C & LC	61,672	46.3	66	15	40
L	70,495	53.7	94	17	63
Total	**132,167**	**100.0**	**160**	**32**	**103**
UNIVERSITIES					
C & LC	3,235	100.0	7	4	6
Total	**3,235**	**100.0**	**7**	**4**	**6**
UNITED KINGDOM					
C & LC	311,481	41.4	461	160	330
L	430,882	58.4	488	95	324
Ch	1,541	0.2	4	0	0
Total	**743,904**	**100.0**	**953**	**255**	**654**

*Adjusted to allow for multi-member seats. See Introductory Notes.

Table 1.07 GENERAL ELECTION 1857

	Total Votes	%*	Candidates	Unopposed	Elected
ENGLAND					
C & LC	168,705	31.7	255	102	185
L	355,913	68.2	362	112	275
Ch	614	0.1	1	0	0
Total	**525,232**	**100.0**	**618**	**214**	**460**
WALES					
C & LC	3,586	34.6	19	15	17
L	7,892	65.4	17	12	15
Total	**11,478**	**100.0**	**36**	**27**	**32**
SCOTLAND					
C & LC	4,060	15.2	19	13	14
L	31,999	84.8	49	25	39
Total	**36,059**	**100.0**	**68**	**38**	**53**
IRELAND					
C & LC	61,741	43.6	52	14	42
L	67,935	47.8	77	27	48
Others	12,099	8.6	19	4	13
Total	**141,775**	**100.0**	**148**	**45**	**103**
UNIVERSITIES					
C & LC	1,620	80.7	6	4	6
L	388	19.3	2	0	0
Total	**2,008**	**100.0**	**8**	**4**	**6**
UNITED KINGDOM					
C & LC	239,712	33.1	351	148	264
L	464,127	65.1	507	176	377
Ch	614	0.1	1	0	0
Others	12,099	1.7	19	4	13
Total	**716,552**	**100.0**	**878**	**328**	**654**

*Adjusted to allow for multi-member seats. See Introductory Notes.

Table 1.08   GENERAL ELECTION 1859

	Total Votes	%*	Candidates	Unopposed	Elected
ENGLAND					
C & LC	152,591	32.9	286	129	209
L	307,949	67.1	330	109	251
Ch	151	0.0	1	0	0
Total	**460,691**	**100.0**	**617**	**238**	**460**
WALES					
C & LC	2,767	63.6	18	14	17
L	1,585	36.4	18	14	15
Total	**4,352**	**100.0**	**36**	**28**	**32**
SCOTLAND					
C & LC	2,616	33.6	17	11	13
L	5,174	66.4	44	34	40
Total	**7,790**	**100.0**	**61**	**45**	**53**
IRELAND					
C & LC	35,258	38.9	67	36	53
L	57,409	61.1	73	26	50
Total	**92,667**	**100.0**	**140**	**62**	**103**
UNIVERSITIES					
C & LC	—	—	6	6	6
Total	**—**	**—**	**6**	**6**	**6**
UNITED KINGDOM					
C & LC	193,232	34.3	394	196	298
L	372,117	65.7	465	183	356
Ch	151	0.0	1	0	0
Total	**565,500**	**100.0**	**860**	**379**	**654**

*Adjusted to allow for multi-member seats. See Introductory Notes.

Table 1.09 GENERAL ELECTION 1865

	Total Votes	%*	Candidates	Unopposed	Elected
ENGLAND					
C	291,238	41.0	308	94	213
L	406,978	59.0	359	88	251
Total	**698,216**	**100.0**	**667**	**182**	**464**
WALES					
C	1,600	26.0	16	12	14
L	4,565	74.0	21	15	18
Total	**6,165**	**100.0**	**37**	**27**	**32**
SCOTLAND					
C	4,305	14.6	17	7	11
L	43,480	85.4	51	30	42
Total	**47,785**	**100.0**	**68**	**37**	**53**
IRELAND					
C	41,497	44.4	59	27	45
L	51,532	55.6	83	28	58
Total	**93,029**	**100.0**	**142**	**55**	**103**
UNIVERSITIES					
C	7,395	76.5	6	2	6
L	2,266	23.5	2	0	0
Total	**9,661**	**100.0**	**8**	**2**	**6**
UNITED KINGDOM					
C	346,035	39.8	406	142	289
L	508,821	60.2	516	161	369
Total	**854,856**	**100.0**	**922**	**303**	**658**

*Adjusted to allow for multi-member seats. See Introductory Notes.

Table 1.10 GENERAL ELECTION 1868

	Total Votes	%*	Candidates	Unopposed	Elected
ENGLAND					
C	803,637	40.2	334	54	211
L	1,192,098	59.7	412	46	244
Others	969	0.1	1	0	0
Total	**1,996,704**	**100.0**	**747**	**100**	**455**
WALES					
C	29,866	37.9	20	4	10
L	52,256	62.1	29	10	23
Total	**82,122**	**100.0**	**49**	**14**	**33**
SCOTLAND					
C	23,985	17.5	20	3	7
L	125,356	82.5	70	23	51
Total	**149,341**	**100.0**	**90**	**26**	**58**
IRELAND					
C	38,767	41.9	53	26	37
L	54,461	57.9	85	41	66
Others	188	0.2	2	0	0
Total	**93,416**	**100.0**	**140**	**67**	**103**
UNIVERSITIES					
C	7,063	55.4	9	4	6
L	4,605	44.6	4	1	3
Total	**11,668**	**100.0**	**13**	**5**	**9**
UNITED KINGDOM					
C	903,318	38.4	436	91	271
L	1,428,776	61.5	600	121	387
Others	1,157	0.1	3	0	0
Total	**2,333,251**	**100.0**	**1,039**	**212**	**658**

*Adjusted to allow for multi-member seats. See Introductory Notes.

Table 1.11 GENERAL ELECTION 1874

	Total Votes	%*	Candidates	Unopposed	Elected
ENGLAND					
C	905,239	46.2	387	100	280
L	1,035,268	53.8	355	26	171
Others	2	0.0	1	0	0
Total	**1,940,509**	**100.0**	**743**	**126**	**451**
WALES					
C	31,574	39.1	23	5	14
L	57,768	60.9	32	7	19
Total	**89,342**	**100.0**	**55**	**12**	**33**
SCOTLAND					
C	63,193	31.6	36	6	18
L	148,345	68.4	61	16	40
Total	**211,538**	**100.0**	**97**	**22**	**58**
IRELAND					
C	91,702	40.8	54	7	31
L	39,778	18.4	39	1	10
HR	90,234	39.6	80	10	60
Others	2,934	1.2	3	0	0
Total	**224,648**	**100.0**	**176**	**18**	**101**
UNIVERSITIES					
C	—	—	7	7	7
L	—	—	2	2	2
Total	**—**	**—**	**9**	**9**	**9**
UNITED KINGDOM					
C	1,091,708	43.9	507	125	350
L	1,281,159	52.7	489	52	242
HR	90,234	3.3	80	10	60
Others	2,936	0.1	4	0	0
Total	**2,466,037**	**100.0**	**1,080**	**187**	**652**

*Adjusted to allow for multi-member seats. See Introductory Notes.

Table 1.12 GENERAL ELECTION 1880

	Total Votes	%*	Candidates	Unopposed	Elected
ENGLAND					
C	1,205,990	43.7	390	47	197
L	1,519,576	56.2	372	19	254
Others	1,107	0.1	2	0	0
Total	2,726,673	100.0	764	66	451
WALES					
C	41,106	41.2	22	1	4
L	59,403	58.8	32	9	29
Total	100,509	100.0	54	10	33
SCOTLAND					
C	74,145	29.9	43	0	6
L	195,517	70.1	60	12	52
Total	269,662	100.0	103	12	58
IRELAND					
C	99,607	39.8	57	4	23
L	56,252	22.7	32	1	15
HR	95,535	37.5	81	10	63
Total	251,394	100.0	170	15	101
UNIVERSITIES					
C	5,503	49.2	9	6	7
L	5,675	50.8	3	0	2
Total	11,178	100.0	12	6	9
UNITED KINGDOM					
C	1,426,351	42.0	521	58	237
L	1,836,423	55.4	499	41	352
HR	95,535	2.6	81	10	63
Others	1,107	0.0	2	0	0
Total	3,359,416	100.0	1,103	109	652

*Adjusted to allow for multi-member seats. See Introductory Notes.

Table 1.13 GENERAL ELECTION 1885

	Total Votes	%*	Candidates	Unopposed	Elected
ENGLAND					
C	1,675,757	47.5	440	1	213
L	1,809,665	51.4	452	4	238
N	3,489	0.1	2	0	1
Others	40,990	1.0	26	0	4
Total	**3,529,901**	**100.0**	**920**	**5**	**456**
WALES					
C	79,690	38.9	29	0	4
L	119,231	58.3	34	4	29
Others	5,766	2.8	2	0	1
Total	**204,687**	**100.0**	**65**	**4**	**34**
SCOTLAND					
C	151,137	34.3	55	0	8
L	238,627	53.3	70	5	51
Others	57,124	12.4	32	0	11
Total	**446,888**	**100.0**	**157**	**5**	**70**
IRELAND					
C	111,503	24.8	70	2	16
L	30,022	6.8	14	0	0
N	307,119	67.8	92	19	85
Others	2,822	0.6	10	0	0
Total	**451,466**	**100.0**	**186**	**21**	**101**
UNIVERSITIES					
C	2,840	53.7	8	7	8
L	2,453	46.3	2	1	1
Total	**5,293**	**100.0**	**10**	**8**	**9**
UNITED KINGDOM					
C	2,020,927	43.5	602	10	249
L	2,199,998	47.4	572	14	319
N	310,608	6.9	94	19	86
Others	106,702	2.2	70[1]	0	16[2]
Total	**4,638,235**	**100.0**	**1,338**	**43**	**670**

*Adjusted to allow for two-member seats. See Introductory Notes.

[1] Including 5 SLRL, 3 SDF.

[2] Namely: W. Abraham (Glamorganshire, Rhondda—Ind L/Lab); Sir R. Anstruther, Bt. (St. Andrews Burghs—Ind L); J.M. Cameron (Wick Burghs—Ind L); Sir G. Campbell (Kirkcaldy Burghs—Ind L); Dr. G.B. Clark (Caithness—Ind L/Crf); C.A.V. Conybeare (Cornwall, Camborne—Ind L); J. Cowen (Newcastle upon Tyne—Ind L); Hon. W.J.W. Fitzwilliam (Peterborough—Ind L); G. Fraser-Mackintosh (Inverness-shire—Ind L/Crf); G.J. Goschen (Edinburgh, East—Ind L); Sir G. Harrison (Edinburgh, South—Ind L); Dr. R. Macdonald (Ross and Cromarty—Ind L/Crf); D.H. Macfarlane (Argyll—Ind L/Crf); C.S. Parker (Perth—Ind L); Sir E.W. Watkin, Bt. (Hythe—Ind L); J. Wilson (Edinburgh, Central—Ind L).

Table 1.14 GENERAL ELECTION 1886

	Total Votes	%*	Candidates	Unopposed	Elected
ENGLAND					
C & LU	1,193,289	52.6	432	105	332
L	1,087,065	47.2	347	23	123
N	2,911	0.1	1	0	1
Others	1,791	0.1	3	0	0
Total	2,285,056	100.0	783	128	456
WALES					
C & LU	60,048	46.1	24	2	8
L	70,289	53.9	32	10	26
Total	130,337	100.0	56	12	34
SCOTLAND					
C & LU	164,314	46.4	63	2	27
L	193,801	53.6	68	7	43
Total	358,115	100.0	131	9	70
IRELAND					
C & LU	98,201	50.4	35	3	17
L	1,910	1.0	1	0	0
N	94,883	48.6	97	66	84
Total	194,994	100.0	133	69	101
UNIVERSITIES					
C & LU	5,034	84.7	9	6	9
L	516	13.8	1	0	0
N	111	1.5	2	0	0
Total	5,661	100.0	12	6	9
UNITED KINGDOM					
C & LU	1,520,886	51.4	563	118	393[1]
L	1,353,581	45.0	449	40	192
N	97,905	3.5	100	66	85
Others	1,791	0.1	3	0	0
Total	2,974,163	100.0	1,115	224	670

*Adjusted to allow for two-member seats. See Introductory Notes.

[1] Including approximately 77 Liberal Unionists.

Table 1.15 GENERAL ELECTION 1892

	Total Votes	%*	Candidates	Unopposed	Elected
ENGLAND					
C & LU	1,788,108	51.1	441	22	261
L	1,685,283	48.0	426	9	190
N	2,537	0.1	1	0	1
Others	29,891	0.8	18	1	4
Total	**3,505,819**	**100.0**	**886**	**32**	**456**
WALES					
C & LU	78,038	37.2	29	0	3
L	141,465	62.8	34	4	31
Total	**219,503**	**100.0**	**63**	**4**	**34**
SCOTLAND					
C & LU	209,944	44.4	68	0	19
L	256,944	53.9	70	0	51
Others	8,242	1.7	11	0	0
Total	**475,130**	**100.0**	**149**	**0**	**70**
IRELAND					
C & LU	79,263	20.6	59	11	21
L	4,327	1.1	2	0	0
N	308,972	78.1	133	9	80
Others	611	0.2	1	0	0
Total	**393,173**	**100.0**	**195**	**20**	**101**
UNIVERSITIES					
C & LU	3,797	80.9	9	7	9
Others	897	19.1	1	0	0
Total	**4,694**	**100.0**	**10**	**7**	**9**
UNITED KINGDOM					
C & LU	2,159,150	47.0	606	40	313[1]
L	2,088,019	45.1	532	13	272[2]
N	311,509	7.0	134	9	81[2]
Others	39,641	0.9	31[3]	1	4[4]
Total	**4,598,319**	**100.0**	**1,303**	**63**	**670**

*Adjusted to allow for two-member seats. See Introductory Notes.

[1] Including approximately 45 Liberal Unionists.

[2] Including 9 'Parnellites'.

[3] Including 3 SPLP, 3 SUTCLP, 2 SDF, 1 joint SSF and SUTCLP.

[4] Namely: J.W. Burns (Battersea and Clapham, Battersea—Ind Lab); J.K. Hardie (West Ham, South—Ind Lab); Sir E.W. Watkin, Bt. (Hythe—Ind L); J.H. Wilson (Middlesbrough—Ind Lab).

Table 1.16 GENERAL ELECTION 1895

	Total Votes	%*	Candidates	Unopposed	Elected
ENGLAND					
C & LU	1,521,938	51.9	442	106	343
L	1,369,598	46.7	342	8	112
ILP	40,056	1.1	21	0	0
N	2,089	0.1	1	0	1
Others	5,675	0.2	9	0	0
Total	**2,939,356**	**100.0**	**815**	**114**	**456**
WALES					
C & LU	103,802	42.2	31	0	9
L	144,216	56.8	34	2	25
Others	2,677	1.0	2	0	0
Total	**250,695**	**100.0**	**67**	**2**	**34**
SCOTLAND					
C & LU	214,403	47.4	68	4	31
L	236,446	51.7	66	1	39
ILP	4,269	0.8	7	0	0
Others	608	0.1	1	0	0
Total	**455,726**	**100.0**	**142**	**5**	**70**
IRELAND					
C & LU	54,629	26.0	38	13	19
L	15,006	7.1	5	0	1
N	150,870	66.9	104	46	81
Total	**220,505**	**100.0**	**147**	**59**	**101**
UNIVERSITIES					
C & LU	—	—	9	9	9
Total	**—**	**—**	**9**	**9**	**9**
UNITED KINGDOM					
C & LU	1,894,772	49.1	588	132	411[1]
L	1,765,266	45.7	447	11	177
ILP	44,325	1.0	28	0	0
N	152,959	4.0	105	46	82[2]
Others	8,960	0.2	12[3]	0	0
Total	**3,866,282**	**100.0**	**1,180**	**189**	**670**

*Adjusted to allow for two-member seats. See Introductory Notes.

[1] Including approximately 71 Liberal Unionists.
[2] Including 12 'Parnellites'.
[3] Including 4 SDF.

Table 1.17   GENERAL ELECTION 1900

	Total Votes	%*	Candidates	Unopposed	Elected
ENGLAND					
C & LU	1,421,195	52.4	441	139	332
L	1,218,525	45.6	302	12	121
Lab	53,100	1.4	13	0	1
N	2,044	0.1	1	0	1
Others	13,628	0.5	6	0	1
Total	2,708,492	100.0	763	151	456
WALES					
C & LU	63,932	37.6	21	1	6
L	105,837	58.5	33	10	27
Lab	9,598	3.9	2	0	1
Total	179,367	100.0	56	11	34
SCOTLAND					
C & LU	237,217	49.0	70	3	36
L	245,092	50.2	66	0	34
Others	3,921	0.8	3	0	0
Total	486,230	100.0	139	3	70
IRELAND					
C & LU	45,614	32.2	28	11	19
L	2,869	2.0	1	0	1
N	89,011	57.4	100	58	81
Others	11,899	8.4	6	0	0
Total	149,393	100.0	135	69	101
UNIVERSITIES					
C & LU	—	—	9	9	9
Total	—	—	9	9	9
UNITED KINGDOM					
C & LU	1,767,958	50.3	569	163	402[1]
L	1,572,323	45.0	402	22	183
Lab	62,698	1.3	15	0	2
N	91,055	2.6	101	58	82[2]
Others	29,448	0.8	15[3]	0	1[4]
Total	3,523,482	100.0	1,102	243	670

*Adjusted to allow for two-member seats. See Introductory Notes.

[1] Including approximately 68 Liberal Unionists.
[2] Including 5 Independents.
[3] Including 1 SWRC.
[4] Namely: Sir J. Austin, Bt. (Yorkshire, Osgoldcross—Ind L).

Table 1.18 GENERAL ELECTION 1906

	Total Votes	%*	Candidates	Unopposed	Elected
ENGLAND					
C & LU	2,050,800	44.3	435	3	122
L	2,255,358	49.0	421	14	306
Lab	288,285	5.3	43	0	26
N	2,808	0.1	1	0	1
Others	60,358	1.3	28	0	1
Total	4,657,609	100.0	928	17	456
WALES					
C & LU	65,949	33.8	20	0	0
L	128,461	60.2	34	12	32
Lab	11,865	3.5	2	0	1
Others	4,841	2.5	1	0	1
Total	211,116	100.0	57	12	34
SCOTLAND					
C & LU	225,802	38.2	69	0	10
L	336,400	56.4	70	1	58
Lab	16,897	2.3	4	0	2
Others	17,815	3.1	8	0	0
Total	596,914	100.0	151	1	70
IRELAND					
C & LU	63,218	47.0	23	6	15
L	26,572	19.7	9	0	3[1]
Lab	4,616	3.4	1	0	0
N	32,223	23.9	85	73	81
Others	8,052	6.0	5	1	2
Total	134,681	100.0	123	80	101
UNIVERSITIES					
C & LU	16,302	60.6	9	4	9
L	4,266	19.4	2	0	0
Others	5,203	20.0	3	0	0
Total	25,771	100.0	14	4	9
UNITED KINGDOM					
C & LU	2,422,071	43.4	556	13	156[2]
L	2,751,057	49.4	536	27	399[1]
Lab	321,663	4.8	50	0	29
N	35,031	0.7	86	73	82
Others	96,269	1.7	45[3]	1	4[4]
Total	5,626,091	100.0	1,273	114	670

*Adjusted to allow for two-member seats. See Introductory Notes.

[1] Including 'Russellite' candidates in Ireland.

[2] Including approximately 25 Liberal Unionists.

[3] Including 8 SDF, 5 SWRC.

[4] Namely: W. O'Brien (Cork City—Ind N); T.H. Sloan (Belfast, South—Ind C); J.W. Taylor (Durham, Chester-le-Street—Ind Lab); J. Williams (Glamorganshire, Gower—Ind L/Lab). Taylor's candidature had for technical reasons not been endorsed by the Labour Representation Committee but he joined the Parliamentary Labour Party upon election.

Table 1.19 GENERAL ELECTION 1910 (January)

	Total Votes	%*	Candidates	Unopposed	Elected
ENGLAND					
C & LU	2,645,914	49.3	453	5	233
L	2,291,062	43.0	405	1	188
Lab	403,358	6.9	62	0	33
N	2,943	0.1	1	0	1
Others	44,768	0.7	19	0	1
Total	5,388,045	100.0	940	6	456
WALES					
C & LU	116,769	31.9	33	0	2
L	195,288	52.3	29	0	27
Lab	60,496	14.9	5	0	5
Others	5,090	0.9	2	0	0
Total	377,643	100.0	69	0	34
SCOTLAND					
C & LU	260,033	39.6	70	0	9
L	354,847	54.2	68	0	58
Lab	37,852	5.1	10	0	2
Others	7,710	1.1	4	0	1
Total	660,442	100.0	152	0	70
IRELAND					
C & LU	68,982	32.7	29	8	19
L	20,339	9.6	7	0	1
Lab	3,951	1.9	1	0	0
N	123,704	54.1	104	55	81
Others	3,553	1.7	1	0	0
Total	220,529	100.0	142	63	101
UNIVERSITIES					
C & LU	12,709	61.3	9	6	9
L	4,621	22.3	2	0	0
Others	3,411	16.4	1	0	0
Total	20,741	100.0	12	6	9
UNITED KINGDOM					
C & LU	3,104,407	46.8	594	19	272[1]
L	2,866,157	43.5	511	1	274
Lab	505,657	7.0	78	0	40
N	126,647	1.9	105	55	82[2]
Others	64,532	0.8	27[3]	0	2[4]
Total	6,667,400	100.0	1,315	75	670

*Adjusted to allow for two-member seats. See Introductory Notes.

[1] Including approximately 32 Liberal Unionists.
[2] Including 11 Independents.
[3] Including 9 S Dem P, 1 SPP.
[4] Namely: A.C. Corbett (Galsgow, Tradeston—Ind L); S. Storey (Sunderland—Ind C).

Table 1.20 GENERAL ELECTION 1910 (December)

	Total Votes	%*	Candidates	Unopposed	Elected
ENGLAND					
C & LU	2,035,297	48.8	436	54	233
L	1,849,098	44.4	362	14	187
Lab	300,142	6.4	44	2	34
N	2,458	0.1	1	0	1
Others	11,630	0.3	8	0	1
Total	4,198,625	100.0	851	70	456
WALES					
C & LU	81,100	33.8	20	0	3
L	117,533	47.9	30	10	26
Lab	47,027	17.8	7	1	5
Others	1,176	0.5	1	0	0
Total	246,836	100.0	58	11	34
SCOTLAND					
C & LU	244,785	42.6	57	1	9
L	306,378	53.6	67	11	58
Lab	24,633	3.6	5	0	3
Others	1,947	0.2	3	0	0
Total	577,743	100.0	132	12	70
IRELAND					
C & LU	56,408	28.6	26	9	17
L	19,003	9.6	7	0	1
N	129,262	60.3	105	53	83
Others	2,925	1.5	2	0	0
Total	207,598	100.0	140	62	101
UNIVERSITIES					
C & LU	2,579	58.1	9	8	9
L	1,857	41.9	1	0	0
Total	4,436	100.0	10	8	9
UNITED KINGDOM					
C & LU	2,420,169	46.6	548	72	271[1]
L	2,293,869	44.2	467	35	272
Lab	371,802	6.4	56	3	42[2]
N	131,720	2.5	106	53	84[2]
Others	17,678	0.3	14[3]	0	1[4]
Total	5,235,238	100.0	1,191	163	670

*Adjusted to allow for two-member seats. See Introductory Notes.

[1] Including approximately 36 Liberal Unionists.
[2] Including 10 Independents.
[3] Including 2 S Dem P, 1 SPP.
[4] Namely: F. Bennett-Goldney (Canterbury—Ind C).

Table 1.21   GENERAL ELECTION 1918

	Total Votes	%*	Candidates	Unopposed	Elected
ENGLAND					
Co C	3,097,350	38.9	318	40	295
Co L	962,871	11.6	95	12	82
Co Lab	39,715	0.3	4	1	3
Co NDP	121,673	1.6	15	0	8
Co Ind	9,274	0.1	1	0	1
(Total Co)	(4,230,883)	(52.5)	(433)	(53)	(389)
C	317,281	3.7	34	0	20
L	1,172,700	14.7	232	2	25
Lab	1,811,739	22.6	291	6	42
Co-op	37,944	0.5	7	0	1
N	8,225	0.1	2	1	1
Nat P	94,389	1.2	26	0	2
NDP	20,200	0.2	7	0	0
NFDSS	12,329	0.1	5	0	0
Others	345,188	4.4	114	1	5
Total	**8,050,878**	**100.0**	**1,151**	**63**	**485**
WALES					
Co C	20,328	3.9	2	0	1
Co L	207,377	39.2	19	4	17
Co NDP	22,824	4.3	1	0	1
(Total Co)	(250,529)	(47.4)	(22)	(4)	(19)
C	39,264	7.4	6	0	3
L	51,382	9.7	10	2	3
Lab	163,055	30.8	25	5	9
Others	24,804	4.7	8	0	1
Total	**529,034**	**100.0**	**71**	**11**	**35**
SCOTLAND					
Co C	336,530	30.8	34	1	28
Co L	221,145	19.1	28	7	25
Co Lab	14,247	1.3	1	0	1
Co NDP	12,337	1.1	2	0	0
(Total Co)	(584,259)	(52.3)	(65)	(8)	(54)
C	21,939	2.0	3	0	2
L	163,960	15.0	33	0	8
Lab	265,744	22.9	39	0	6
Co-op	19,841	1.8	3	0	0
NDP	4,297	0.4	1	0	0
Others	66,671	5.6	21	0	1
Total	**1,126,711**	**100.0**	**165**	**8**	**71**
IRELAND					
C	289,213	28.4	36	0	23
N	228,902	22.0	56	0	6
SF	495,345	47.0	100	25	72
Others	25,765	2.6	12	0	0
Total	**1,039,225**	**100.0**	**204**	**25**	**101**

GENERAL ELECTION 1918 (Cont.)

	Total Votes	%*	Candidates	Unopposed	Elected
UNIVERSITIES					
Co C	18,530	45.2	8	0	8
Co L	5,197	12.7	3	0	3
(Total Co)	(23,727)	(57.9)	(11)	(0)	(11)
C	3,757	9.2	4	0	2
L	742	1.8	1	0	0
Lab	5,239	12.8	6	0	0
N	1,070	2.6	2	0	0
SF	1,762	4.3	2	0	1
Others	4,673	11.4	6	0	1
Total	**40,970**	**100.0**	**32**	**0**	**15**
UNITED KINGDOM					
Co C	3,472,738	32.5	362	41	332
Co L	1,396,590	12.6	145[1]	23	127
Co Lab	53,962	0.4	5[2]	1	4
Co Ind	9,274	0.1	1	0	1
Co NDP	156,834	1.5	18	0	9
(Total Co)	(5,089,398)	(47.1)	(531)	(65)	(473)
C	671,454	6.2	83[3]	0	50[4]
L	1,388,784	13.0	276	4	36[5]
Lab	2,245,777	20.8	361	11	57
Co-op	57,785	0.6	10	0	1[6]
N	238,197	2.2	60	1	7
Nat P	94,389	0.9	26	0	2
NDP	24,497	0.2	8	0	0
NFDSS	12,329	0.1	5	0	0
SF	497,107	4.6	102	25	73[7]
Others	467,101	4.3	161[8]	1	8[9]
Total	**10,786,818**	**100.0**	**1,623[10]**	**107**	**707**

*Adjusted to allow for two-member seats. See Introductory Notes.

[1] Excluding 14 candidates who received the 'coupon' (the endorsement given to officially approved candidates) but repudiated it.

[2] Of the five Coalition Labour candidates, only two were official and received the 'coupon'. They were J.R. Bell (Kingston-upon-Hull, South-West) and J. Parker (Staffordshire, Cannock). They were however incorrectly designated in the official list of Coalition candidates as National Democratic Party and Liberal respectively.

[3] The majority of Conservative candidates supported the Coalition although not all received the 'coupon'. There were also numerous other candidates, among them members of the National Party and National Democratic Party and at least half the Independents, who were certainly not opposed to the Coalition and the figures of votes polled by the official Coalition candidates must underestimate very considerably the number of electors who supported the Coalition.

[4] Including three members of the Ulster Unionist Labour Association who were elected for Belfast constituencies and ran under the title 'Labour-Unionist'.

[5] This is in fact an overestimate of the number of non-Coalition Liberals as nine who had not received the 'coupon' accepted the Coalition Whip upon election. They were: Sir F.D. Blake, Bt. (Northumberland, Berwick-upon-Tweed); G.P. Collins (Greenock); Hon. W.H. Cozens-Hardy (Norfolk, Southern); J. Gardiner (Perthshire and Kinross-shire, Kinross and Western); S.G. Howard (Suffolk, Sudbury); G. Lambert (Devon, South Molton); J.T.T. Rees (Devon, Barnstaple). Sir W.H. Seager (Cardiff, East); E.H. Young (Norwich).

GENERAL ELECTION 1918 (Cont.)

A few other Liberals were, with reservations, general supporters of the Coalition and the number of anti-Coalition Liberals (commonly called 'Free" or 'Asquithian' Liberals) who were prepared to follow Asquith's leadership was estimated by *The Times* in January 1919, to be about fourteen members who could be relied upon to consistently oppose the Coalition Government. The other non-Coalition Liberals at first adopted an independent attitude but as opposition to the Coalition grew, they tended to drift into the Asquith group.

Joined the Parliamentary Labour Party upon election.

The actual number was 69 as four Sinn Fein candidates were returned for two constituencies. They were: E. de Valera (Clare, East and Mayo, East); A. Griffith (Cavan, East and Tyrone, North-West); J.E. MacNeill (Londonderry, and National University); W.L.J. Mellows (Galway, East and Meath, North). The Sinn Fein members did not take their seats in the House of Commons.

Including 4 HLL, 3 BSP, 3 NSP, 3 SLP, 1 SPP, 1 WP.

Namely: R.H. Barker (Yorkshire, Sowerby); N.P. Billing (Hertfordshire, Hertford); H.W. Bottom-ley (Hackney, South); J.J. Jones (West Ham, Silvertown—NSP); F.H. Rose (Aberdeen, North—Ind Lab); Sir O. Thomas (Anglesey—Ind Lab); J.C. Wedgwood (Newcastle-under-Lyme—Ind L); Sir R.H. Woods (Dublin University—Ind C).

Jones, Rose and Sir O. Thomas joined the Labour Party immediately after being elected. Wedg-wood joined the Labour Party in August 1919. Sir O. Thomas resigned from the Labour Party in July 1919. Sir R.H. Woods accepted the Conservative Whip upon election.

The number of persons seeking election was 1,611 owing to the fact that in Ireland nine candidates contested two constituencies each and one contested four constituencies.

Table 1.22   GENERAL ELECTION 1922

	Total Votes	%*	Candidates	Unopposed	Elected
ENGLAND					
C	4,809,797	41.5	406	29	307
L	2,260,423	19.6	271	3	44
NL	950,515	7.6	97	2	31
Lab	3,370,430	28.8	340	2	95
Com	9,693	0.1	2	0	0
N	12,614	0.1	2	1	1
Others	282,958	2.3	38	0	7
Total	**11,696,430**	**100.0**	**1,156**	**·37**	**485**
WALES					
C	190,919	21.4	19	1	6
L	74,996	8.4	11	1	2
NL	230,961	25.8	19	1	8
Lab	363,568	40.8	28	1	18
Others	32,256	3.6	3	0	1
Total	**892,700**	**100.0**	**80**	**4**	**35**
SCOTLAND					
C	379,396	25.1	36	0	13
L	328,649	21.5	48	1	15
NL	288,529	17.7	33	1	12
Lab	501,254	32.2	43	1	29
Com	23,944	1.4	3	0	1
Others	47,589	2.1	5	0	1
Total	**1,569,361**	**100.0**	**168**	**3**	**71**
NORTHERN IRELAND					
C	107,972	55.8	12	9	10
N	90,053	36.3	2	0	2
Others	9,861	7.9	1	0	0
Total	**207,886**	**100.0**	**15**	**9**	**12**
UNIVERSITIES					
C	14,214	54.8	9	3	8
L	4,075	15.7	4	1	1
NL	1,312	5.0	2	0	2
Lab	2,097	8.1	3	0	0
Others	4,255	16.4	4	0	1
Total	**25,953**	**100.0**	**22**	**4**	**12**

GENERAL ELECTION 1922 (Cont.)

	Total Votes	%*	Candidates	Unopposed	Elected
UNITED KINGDOM					
C	5,502,298	38.5	482	42	344
L	2,668,143	18.9	334	6	62[1]
NL	1,471,317	9.9	151	4	53[1]
Lab	4,237,349	29.7	414	4	142
Com	33,637	0.2	5[2]	0	1
N	102,667	0.4	4	1	3
Others	376,919	2.4	51[3]	0	10[4]
Total	**14,392,330**	**100.0**	**1,441**	**57**	**615**

*Adjusted to allow for two-member seats. See Introductory Notes.

[1] Two National Liberals, T.M. Guthrie (Moray and Nairnshire) and J. Hinds (Carmarthenshire, Carmarthen) accepted the Liberal Whip upon election bringing the party's strength up to 64 members.

[2] For details of Communists who secured endorsement as official Labour candidates see Table 7.07.

[3] Including 1 SPP.

[4] Namely: H.T.A. Becker (Richmond—Ind C); J.R.M. Butler (Cambridge University—Ind L); J.M.M. Erskine (Westminster, St. George's—Ind C); G.R. Hall Caine (Dorset, Eastern—Ind C); A. Hopkinson (Lancashire, Mossley); G.W.S. Jarrett (Kent, Dartford—Const); O.E. Mosley (Middlesex, Harrow); G.H. Roberts (Norwich); E. Scrymgeour (Dundee—SPP); Sir O. Thomas (Anglesey—Ind Lab). Becker, Erskine, Hall Caine and Roberts were subsequently granted the Conservative Whip.

Table 1.23 GENERAL ELECTION 1923

	Total Votes	%*	Candidates	Unopposed	Elected
ENGLAND					
C	4,732,176	39.8	444	24	221
L	3,572,335	29.9	362	3	123
Lab	3,549,888	29.7	350	1	138
N	10,322	0.1	2	1	1
Others	62,364	0.5	8	0	2
Total	**11,927,085**	**100.0**	**1,166**	**29**	**485**
WALES					
C	178,113	21.1	19	0	4
L	299,314	35.4	31	3	11
Lab	355,172	42.0	27	2	19
Others	12,469	1.5	1	0	1
Total	**845,068**	**100.0**	**78**	**5**	**35**
SCOTLAND					
C	468,526	31.6	52	0	14
L	422,995	28.4	59	4	22
Lab	532,450	35.9	48	0	34
Com	39,448	2.4	4	0	0
Others	37,908	1.7	4	0	1
Total	**1,501,327**	**100.0**	**167**	**4**	**71**
NORTHERN IRELAND					
C	117,161	49.4	12	8	10
N	87,671	27.3	2	0	2
Others	37,426	23.3	2	0	0
Total	**242,258**	**100.0**	**16**	**8**	**12**
UNIVERSITIES					
C	18,565	58.1	9	3	9
L	6,837	21.4	5	1	2
Lab	2,270	7.1	2	0	0
Others	4,285	13.4	3	0	1
Total	**31,957**	**100.0**	**19**	**4**	**12**
UNITED KINGDOM					
C	5,514,541	38.0	536	35	258
L	4,301,481	29.7	457	11	158
Lab	4,439,780	30.7	427	3	191
Com	39,448	0.2	4[1]	0	0
N	97,993	0.4	4	1	3
Others	154,452	1.0	18[2]	0	5[3]
Total	**14,547,695**	**100.0**	**1,446**	**50**	**615**

*Adjusted to allow for two-member seats. See Introductory Notes.

[1] For details of Communists who secured endorsement as official Labour candidates see Table 7.07.

[2] Including 1 BLP, 1 SPP.

[3] Namely: G.M.L. Davies (University of Wales—CP); A. Hopkinson (Lancashire, Mossley); R.H. Morris (Cardiganshire—Ind L); O.E. Mosley (Middlesex, Harrow); E. Scrymgeour (Dundee—SPP). Davies and Mosley joined the Labour Party shortly after the election and Morris was granted the Liberal Whip.

Table 1.24 GENERAL ELECTION 1924

	Total Votes	%*	Candidates	Unopposed	Elected
ENGLAND					
C	6,460,266	47.7	440	13	347
L	2,388,429	17.6	280	2	19
Lab	4,467,236	32.8	414	2	109
Com	39,416	0.3	6	0	1
Const	185,075	1.4	12	0	7
N	—	—	1	1	1
Others	21,136	0.2	6	0	1
Total	13,561,558	100.0	1,159	18	485
WALES					
C	224,014	28.4	17	0	9
L	244,828	31.0	21	1	10
Lab	320,397	40.6	33	7	16
Total	789,239	100.0	71	8	35
SCOTLAND					
C	688,299	40.7	56	0	36
L	286,540	16.6	34	3	8
Lab	697,146	41.1	63	0	26
Com	15,930	0.7	2	0	0
Others	29,193	0.9	1	0	1
Total	1,717,108	100.0	156	3	71
NORTHERN IRELAND					
C	451,278	83.8	12	2	12
SF	46,457	9.9	8	0	0
Others	21,639	6.3	2	0	0
Total	519,374	100.0	22	2	12
UNIVERSITIES					
C	30,666	57.9	9	1	8
L	8,940	16.9	4	0	3
Lab	4,308	8.1	4	0	0
Others	9,086	17.1	3	0	1
Total	53,000	100.0	20	1	12
UNITED KINGDOM					
C	7,854,523	46.8	534	16	412
L	2,928,737	17.8	339	6	40[1]
Lab	5,489,087	33.3	514	9	151
Com	55,346	0.3	8	0	1
Const	185,075	1.2	12[2]	0	7
N	—	—	1	1	1
SF	46,457	0.2	8	0	0
Others	81,054	0.4	12[3]	0	3[4]
Total	16,640,279	100.0	1,428	32	615

*Adjusted to allow for two-member seats. See Introductory Notes.

[1] Including F.E. Guest (Bristol, North) whose name was originally given in the list of Constitutionalist candidates. In the final list his name was omitted and although supported officially by the local Conservative Association he ran as a Liberal.

GENERAL ELECTION 1924 (Cont.)

[2] Of the twelve who ran as Constitutionalists, six [W.L.S. Churchill (Essex, Epping); J.E. Davis (Durham, Consett); Sir H. Greenwood, Bt. (Walthamstow, East); C.E. Loseby (Nottingham, West); A.H. Moreing (Cornwall, Camborne); J.L. Sturrock (Tottenham, North)] were ex-Liberals, most of whom subsequently joined the Conservative Party.

The other six candidates [W. Allen (Stoke-on-Trent, Burslem); J.H. Edwards (Accrington); A. England (Lancashire, Heywood and Radcliffe); H.C. Hogbin (Battersea, North); Sir T. Robinson (Lancashire, Stretford); J. Ward (Stoke-on-Trent, Stoke)] were Liberals and their names appear to have been included in the official list of Liberal candidates.

Those elected were: (Conservatives)—Churchill, Sir H. Greenwood, Bt. and Moreing. (Liberals)— Edwards, England, Sir T. Robinson and Ward.

[3] Including 1 NI Lab, 1 SPP.

[4] Namely: Dr. E.G.G. Graham-Little (London University); A. Hopkinson (Lancashire, Mossley); E. Scrymgeour (Dundee—SPP).

Table 1.25 GENERAL ELECTION 1929

	Total Votes	%*	Candidates	Unopposed	Elected
ENGLAND					
C	7,177,551	38.8	469	2	221
L	4,340,703	23.6	422	0	35
Lab	6,850,738	36.9	467	0	226
Com	15,377	0.1	12	0	0
N	−	−	1	1	1
Others	117,876	0.6	17	0	2
Total	**18,502,245**	**100.0**	**1,388**	**3**	**485**
WALES					
C	289,695	22.0	35	0	1
L	440,911	33.5	34	0	9
Lab	577,554	43.9	33	0	25
Com	8,143	0.6	3	0	0
PC	609	0.0	1	0	0
Total	**1,316,912**	**100.0**	**106**	**0**	**35**
SCOTLAND					
C	792,063	35.9	65	0	20
L	407,081	18.1	45	0	13
Lab	937,300	42.3	66	0	36
Com	27,114	1.1	10	0	0
SNP	3,313	0.2	2	0	0
Others	76,070	2.4	4	0	2
Total	**2,242,941**	**100.0**	**192**	**0**	**71**
NORTHERN IRELAND					
C	354,657	68.0	10	1	10
L	100,103	16.8	6	0	0
N	24,177	6.6	3	2	2
Others	31,116	8.6	3	0	0
Total	**510,053**	**100.0**	**22**	**3**	**12**
UNIVERSITIES					
C	42,259	55.4	11	1	8
L	19,940	26.2	6	0	2
Lab	4,825	6.3	3	0	0
Others	9,200	12.1	2	0	2
Total	**76,224**	**100.0**	**22**	**1**	**12**
UNITED KINGDOM					
C	8,656,225	38.1	590	4	260
L	5,308,738	23.5	513	0	59[1]
Lab	8,370,417	37.1	569	0	287
Com	50,634	0.2	25	0	0
N	24,177	0.1	4	3	3
PC	609	0.0	1	0	0
SNP	3,313	0.0	2	0	0
Others	234,262	1.0	26[2]	0	6[3]
Total	**22,648,375**	**100.0**	**1,730**	**7**	**615**

*Adjusted to allow for two-member seats. See Introductory Notes.

[1] Including Sir W.A. Jowitt (Preston) who joined the Labour Party one week after the election.
[2] Including 1 SPP.
[3] Namely: Dr. E.G.G. Graham-Little (London University); N. Maclean (Glasgow, Govan—Ind Lab); Sir R.H.S.D.L. Newman, Bt. (Exeter); Miss E.F. Rathbone (Combined English Universities); Sir T. Robinson (Lancashire, Stretford); E. Scrymgeour (Dundee—SPP).
Maclean was re-admitted into the Parliamentary Labour Party in February 1930.

Table 1.26 GENERAL ELECTION 1931

	Total Votes	%*	Candidates	Unopposed	Elected
ENGLAND					
C	10,453,349	57.8	427	31	398
L	1,007,510	5.8	85	1	19
Nat	100,193	0.6	4	0	4
NL	632,155	3.4	28	3	23
N Lab	292,688	1.5	17	0	11
(Total Nat)	(12,485,895)	(69.1)	(561)	(35)	(455)
Ind L	31,989	0.2	2	0	0
Lab	5,464,425	30.2	428	2	29
Com	21,452	0.1	15	0	0
NP	20,721	0.1	16	0	0
Others	58,552	0.3	10	0	1
Total	18,083,034	100.0	1,032	37	485
WALES					
C	240,861	22.1	14	0	6
L	157,472	14.5	10	0	4
NL	75,717	7.0	5	2	4
N Lab	24,120	2.2	1	0	1
(Total Nat)	(498,170)	(45.8)	(30)	(2)	(15)
Ind L	71,539	6.6	4	0	4
Lab	479,547	44.1	30	4	16
Com	17,754	1.6	3	0	0
NP	11,300	1.0	2	0	0
PC	1,136	0.1	1	0	0
Others	9,100	0.8	2	0	0
Total	1,088,546	100.0	72	6	35
SCOTLAND					
C	1,056,768	49.5	56	3	48
L	205,384	8.6	14	3	7
NL	101,430	4.9	8	2	8
N Lab	21,803	1.0	1	0	1
(Total Nat)	(1,385,385)	(64.0)	(79)	(8)	(64)
Lab	696,248	32.6	57	0	7
Com	35,618	1.4	8	0	0
NP	3,895	0.2	5	0	0
SNP	20,954	1.0	5	0	0
Others	32,229	0.8	1	0	0
Total	2,174,329	100.0	155	8	71
NORTHERN IRELAND					
C	149,566	56.1	12	8	10
(Total Nat)	(149,566)	(56.1)	(12)	(8)	(10)
Lab	9,410	5.0	1	0	0
N	123,053	38.9	3	0	2
Total	282,029	100.0	16	8	12
UNIVERSITIES					
C	5,381	18.9	9	7	8
L	2,229	7.9	2	1	2
N Lab	2,759	9.7	1	0	0
(Total Nat)	(10,369)	(36.5)	(12)	(8)	(10)
NP	461	1.6	1	0	0
PC	914	3.2	1	0	0
Others	16,691	58.7	3	0	2
Total	28,435	100.0	17	8	12

GENERAL ELECTION 1931 (Cont.)

	Total Votes	%*	Candidates	Unopposed	Elected
UNITED KINGDOM					
C	11,905,925	55.0	518	49	470
L	1,372,595	6.5	111	5	32
Nat	100,193	0.5	4	0	4
NL	809,302	3.7	41[1]	7	35
N Lab	341,370	1.5	20	0	13
(Total Nat)	(14,529,385)	(67.2)	(694)	(61)	(554)
Ind L	103,528	0.5	6[2]	0	4
Lab	6,649,630	30.9	516[3]	6[4]	52[5]
Com	74,824	0.3	26	0	0
N	123,053	0.3	3	0	2
NP	36,377	0.2	24	0	0
PC	2,050	0.0	2	0	0
SNP	20,954	0.1	5	0	0
Others	116,572	0.5	16[6]	0	3[7]
Total	**21,656,373**	**100.0**	**1,292**	**67**	**615**

*Adjusted to allow for two-member seats. See Introductory Notes.

[1] Although standing as National Liberals and using a separate election organisation, the National Liberal candidates had their names included in the official list of Liberal Party candidates and those elected were claimed by the Liberal Party as their members. It appears that it was not until after the Liberal Party withdrew its support from the National Government in September 1932, that the party finally accepted that National Liberals could no longer be classed with Liberals who had stood without the National prefix.

[2] Of the Liberal candidates opposed to the National Government, the four who secured election (the Lloyd George family group) took their seats on the Opposition Benches in the House of Commons and were subsequently joined by the other Liberal M.P.s who decided to cross the floor and go into opposition when the new Parliamentary Session opened on November 21, 1933. D. Lloyd George never again sat on the Liberal Benches from the time of the 1931 election until his elevation to the Peerage in 1945. He always occupied the corner seat on the Opposition (Labour) Front Bench.

[3] Including 25 candidates who did not receive official endorsement. Of this number, 24 were members of the ILP (including 19 official ILP nominees, the remaining 5 although members of the ILP were the nominees of trade unions and Constituency Labour Parties) and refused to sign a form accepting the Standing Orders of the Parliamentary Labour Party, a condition of endorsement which was introduced just prior to the election. The remaining case of a candidate not receiving endorsement was at Glasgow, Hillhead where the candidate, although adopted by the Constituency Labour Party, was refused endorsement on the grounds that neither local finance or organisation warranted the adoption of a candidate. The total votes polled by the 25 non-endorsed candidates were 324,893.

[4] Including 1 unendorsed.

[5] Including six unendorsed members: G. Buchanan (Glasgow, Gorbals); D. Kirkwood (Dumbarton Burghs); J. McGovern (Glasgow, Shettleston); J. Maxton (Glasgow, Bridgeton); R.C. Wallhead (Merthyr Tydfil, Merthyr), J.C. Wedgwood (Newcastle-under-Lyme).

McGovern, Maxton and Wallhead formed an ILP Parliamentary Group and were joined by Buchanan and Kirkwood. Wedgwood remained an Independent.

Subsequently Kirkwood, Wallhead and Wedgwood re-entered the Parliamentary Labour Party.

[6] Including 2 CW Land P, 1 LPP, 1 SPP.

[7] Namely: Sir E.G.G. Graham-Little (London University—Nat Ind); A. Hopkinson (Lancashire, Mossley—Nat Ind); Miss E.F. Rathbone (Combined English Universities).

Table 1.27 GENERAL ELECTION 1935

	Total Votes	%*	Candidates	Unopposed	Elected
ENGLAND					
C	8,997,348	49.4	423	14	329
Nat	13,250	0.1	1	0	0
NL	673,597	3.4	31	2	22
N Lab	303,742	1.6	18	0	6
(Total Nat)	(9,987,937)	(54.5)	(473)	(16)	(357)
L	1,108,971	6.3	132	0	11
Lab	7,054,050	38.5	452	3	116
ILP	18,681	0.1	5	0	0
Others	103,396	0.6	16	0	1
Total	**18,273,035**	**100.0**	**1,078**	**19**	**485**
WALES					
C	204,099	23.4	14	0	6
Nat	35,318	4.1	2	0	1
NL	36,156	4.2	3	1	3
N Lab	16,954	1.9	1	0	1
(Total Nat)	(292,527)	(33.6)	(20)	(1)	(11)
L	157,091	18.0	12	0	6
Lab	395,830	45.4	33	10	18
Com	13,655	1.6	1	0	0
ILP	9,640	1.1	1	0	0
PC	2,534	0.3	1	0	0
Total	**871,277**	**100.0**	**68**	**11**	**35**
SCOTLAND					
C	962,595	42.0	58	1	35
Nat	4,621	0.2	1	0	0
NL	149,072	6.7	9	0	7
N Lab	19,115	0.9	1	0	1
(Total Nat)	(1,135,403)	(49.8)	(69)	(1)	(43)
L	174,235	6.7	16	0	3
Lab	863,789	36.8	63	0	20
Com	13,462	0.6	1	0	1
ILP	111,256	5.0	11	0	4
SNP	25,652	1.1	7	0	0
Total	**2,323,797**	**100.0**	**167**	**1**	**71**
NORTHERN IRELAND					
C	292,840	64.9	12	6	10
(Total Nat)	(292,840)	(64.9)	(12)	(6)	(10)
N	101,494	18.3	2	0	2
Rep	56,833	16.8	3	0	0
Total	**451,167**	**100.0**	**17**	**6**	**12**
UNIVERSITIES					
C	39,418	50.7	8	2	7
NL	7,529	9.6	1	0	1
(Total Nat)	(46,947)	(60.3)	(9)	(2)	(8)
L	2,796	3.6	1	0	1
Lab	11,822	15.2	4	0	0
SNP	3,865	5.0	1	0	0
Others	12,348	15.9	3	1	3
Total	**77,778**	**100.0**	**18**	**3**	**12**

GENERAL ELECTION 1935 (Cont.)

	Total Votes	%*	Candidates	Unopposed	Elected
UNITED KINGDOM					
C	10,496,300	47.8	515	23	387
Nat	53,189	0.3	4	0	1
NL	866,354	3.7	44	3	33
N Lab	339,811	1.5	20	0	8
(Total Nat)	(11,755,654)	(53.3)	(583)	(26)	(429)
L	1,443,093	6.7	161	0	21[1]
Lab	8,325,491	38.0	552	13	154
Com	27,117	0.1	2	0	1
ILP	139,577	0.7	17	0	4
N	101,494	0.3	2	0	2
PC	2,534	0.0	1	0	0
Rep	56,833	0.2	3	0	0
SNP	29,517	0.1	8	0	0
Others	115,744	0.6	19[2]	1	4[3]
Total	**21,997,054**	**100.0**	**1,348**	**40**	**615**

*Adjusted to allow for two-member seats. See Introductory Notes.

[1] Including R.H. Bernays (Bristol, North) and the Hon. J.P. Maclay (Paisley) who although elected as Liberals without prefix, supported the National Government. Bernays accepted the National Liberal Whip in October 1936.

[2] Including 1 LPP, 1 SCPGB.

[3] Namely: Sir E.G.G. Graham-Little (London University—Nat Ind); A.P. Herbert (Oxford University); A. Hopkinson (Lancashire, Mossley—Nat Ind); Miss E.F. Rathbone (Combined English Universities).

Table 1.28 GENERAL ELECTION 1945

	Total Votes	% *	Candidates	Unopposed	Elected
ENGLAND					
C	7,575,577	37.0	461	0	159
Nat	105,862	0.5	8	0	1
NL	587,752	2.7	38	0	7
(Total Nat)	(8,269,191)	(40.2)	(507)	(0)	(167)
L	1,913,917	9.4	265	0	5
Lab	9,972,519	48.5	494	1	331
Com	53,754	0.3	15	0	1
CW	106,403	0.5	21	0	1
ILP	6,044	0.0	2	0	0
Others	217,192	1.1	59	0	5
Total	**20,539,020**	**100.0**	**1,363**	**1**	**510**
WALES					
C	241,380	18.1	21	0	3
Nat	11,306	0.9	1	0	0
NL	64,043	4.8	5	0	1
(Total Nat)	(316,729)	(23.8)	(27)	(0)	(4)
L	198,553	14.9	17	0	6
Lab	779,184	58.5	34	1	25
Com	15,761	1.2	1	0	0
PC	14,321	1.1	6	0	0
Others	6,123	0.5	2	0	0
Total	**1,330,671**	**100.0**	**87**	**1**	**35**
SCOTLAND					
C	878,206	37.4	62	0	24
NL	85,937	3.7	6	0	3
(Total Nat)	(964,143)	(41.1)	(68)	(0)	(27)
L	132,849	5.0	22	0	0
Lab	1,144,310	47.6	68	0	37
Com	33,265	1.4	5	0	1
CW	4,231	0.2	2	0	0
ILP	40,725	1.8	3	0	3
SNP	30,595	1.2	8	0	0
Others	39,774	1.7	8	0	3
Total	**2,389,892**	**100.0**	**184**	**0**	**71**
NORTHERN IRELAND					
C	392,450	53.7	12	1	8
(Total Nat)	(392,450)	(53.7)	(12)	(1)	(8)
Lab	65,459	11.4	5	0	0
CWLP	14,096	2.9	1	0	0
N	148,078	18.8	3	0	2
Others	99,682	13.2	3	0	2
Total	**719,765**	**100.0**	**24**	**1**	**12**
UNIVERSITIES					
C	13,486	11.7	3	0	3
Nat	16,011	13.8	1	0	1
(Total Nat)	(29,497)	(25.5)	(4)	(0)	(4)
L	7,111	6.1	2	0	1
Lab	6,274	5.4	2	0	0
PC	1,696	1.5	1	0	0
Others	71,269	61.5	16	0	7
Total	**115,847**	**100.0**	**25**	**0**	**12**

GENERAL ELECTION 1945 (Cont.)

	Total Votes	%*	Candidates	Unopposed	Elected
UNITED KINGDOM					
C	9,101,099	36.2	559	1	197
Nat	133,179	0.5	10	0	2
NL	737,732	2.9	49	0	11
(Total Nat)	(9,972,010)	(39.6)	(618)	(1)	(210)
L	2,252,430	9.0	306	0	12[1]
Lab	11,967,746	48.0	603	2	393
Com	102,780	0.4	21	0	2
CW	110,634	0.5	23	0	1
CWLP	14,096	0.1	1	0	0
ILP	46,769	0.2	5	0	3
N	148,078	0.4	3	0	2
PC	16,017	0.1	7	0	0
SNP	30,595	0.1	8	0	0
Others	434,040	1.6	88[2]	0	17[3]
Total	25,095,195	100.0	1,683	3	640

*Adjusted to allow for two-member seats. See Introductory Notes.

[1] Including G. Lloyd George (Pembrokeshire) who had accepted office in the National (Caretaker) Government and supported Churchill.

[2] Including 5 Dem P, 1 LPP, 1 SPGB.

[3] Namely: C.V.O. Bartlett (Somerset, Bridgwater—Ind Prog); J. Beattie (Belfast, West—Ind Lab); Sir J. Boyd Orr (Combined Scottish Universities); W.J. Brown (Warwickshire, Rugby); Sir E.G.G. Graham-Little (London University—Nat Ind); H.W. Harris (Cambridge University); A.P. Herbert (Oxford University); W.D. Kendall (Lincolnshire, Grantham); K.M. Lindsay (Combined English Universities); D.L. Lipson (Cheltenham—Nat Ind); Rev. Dr. J. Little (Down—Ind C); Sir M. Macdonald (Inverness-shire and Ross and Cromarty, Inverness—Ind L); J.H. Mackie (Galloway—Ind C); J. MacLeod (Inverness-shire and Ross and Cromarty, Ross and Cromarty—Ind L); D.N. Pritt (Hammersmith, North—Ind Lab); Miss E.F. Rathbone (Combined English Universities); Sir J.A. Salter (Oxford University).

Mackie was granted the Conservative Whip in March 1948 and Beattie joined the Irish Labour Party in 1949. Sir M. Macdonald and MacLeod aligned themselves with the National Liberal Party in the House of Commons.

Table 1.29   GENERAL ELECTION 1950

	Total Votes	%	Candidates	Unopposed	Elected
ENGLAND					
C	9,820,068	41.0	466	0	243
NL & C	679,324	2.8	38	0	10
(Total C)	(10,499,392)	(43.8)	(504)	(0)	(253)
L	2,248,127	9.4	413	0	2
Lab	11,050,966	46.2	505	0	251
Com	55,158	0.2	80	0	0
Others	100,805	0.4	26	0	0
Total	**23,954,448**	**100.0**	**1,528**	**0**	**506**
WALES					
C	320,750	21.0	29	0	3
NL & C	97,918	6.4	6	0	1
(Total C)	(418,668)	(27.4)	(35)	(0)	(4)
L	193,090	12.6	21	0	5
Lab	887,984	58.1	36	0	27
Com	9,048	0.6	4	0	0
PC	17,580	1.2	7	0	0
Others	2,184	0.1	2	0	0
Total	**1,528,554**	**100.0**	**105**	**0**	**36**
SCOTLAND					
C	1,013,909	37.2	57	0	26
NL & C	208,101	7.6	11	0	5
(Total C)	(1,222,010)	(44.8)	(68)	(0)	(31)
L	180,270	6.6	41	0	2
Lab	1,259,410	46.2	71	0	37
Com	27,559	1.0	16	0	0
SNP	9,708	0.4	3	0	0
Others	27,727	1.0	13	0	1
Total	**2,726,684**	**100.0**	**212**	**0**	**71**
NORTHERN IRELAND					
C	352,334	62.7	12	2	10
Lab	67,816	12.1	5	0	0
Irish LP	52,715	9.4	2	0	0
N	65,211	11.6	2	0	2
SF	23,362	4.2	2	0	0
Total	**561,438**	**100.0**	**23**	**2**	**12**
UNITED KINGDOM					
C	11,507,061	40.0	564	2	282
NL & C	985,343	3.4	55	0	16
(Total C)	(12,492,404)	(43.4)	(619)	(2)	(298)
L	2,621,487	9.1	475	0	9
Lab	13,266,176	46.1	617	0	315
Com	91,765	0.3	100	0	0
Irish LP	52,715	0.2	2	0	0
N	65,211	0.2	2	0	2
PC	17,580	0.1	7	0	0
SF	23,362	0.1	2	0	0
SNP	9,708	0.0	3	0	0
Others	130,716	0.5	41[1]	0	1[2]
Total	**28,771,124**	**100.0**	**1,868**	**2**	**625**

[1] Including 4 AP, 4 ILP, 2 SPGB, 1 MGC, 1 SCPGB.
[2] Namely: J. MacLeod (Inverness-shire and Ross and Cromarty, Ross and Cromarty—Ind L). He joined the Liberal-Unionist Group in May 1951.

Table 1.30 GENERAL ELECTION 1951

	Total Votes	%	Candidates	Unopposed	Elected
ENGLAND					
C	10,855,287	45.6	463	0	259
NL & C	767,417	3.2	39	0	12
(Total C)	(11,622,704)	(48.8)	(502)	(0)	(271)
L	537,434	2.3	91	0	2
Lab	11,630,467	48.8	506	0.	233
Com	7,745	0.0	5	0	0
Others	27,745	0.1	8	0	0
Total	23,826,095	100.0	1,112	0	506
WALES					
C	421,525	27.6	30	0	5
NL & C	49,744	3.2	3	0	1
(Total C)	(471,269)	(30.8)	(33)	(0)	(6)
L	116,821	7.7	9	0	3
Lab	925,848	60.5	36	0	27
Com	2,948	0.2	1	0	0
PC	10,920	0.7	4	0	0
Others	1,643	0.1	1	0	0
Total	1,529,449	100.0	84	0	36
SCOTLAND					
C	1,108,321	39.9	57	0	29
NL & C	240,977	8.7	13	0	6
(Total C)	(1,349,298)	(48.6)	(70)	(0)	(35)
L	76,291	2.7	9	0	1
Lab	1,330,244	47.9	71	0	35
Com	10,947	0.4	4	0	0
SNP	7,299	0.3	2	0	0
Others	3,758	0.1	4	0	0
Total	2,777,837	100.0	160	0	71
NORTHERN IRELAND					
C	274,928	59.3	12	4	9
Lab	62,324	13.5	4	0	0
Irish LP	33,174	7.2	1	0	1
N	92,787	20.0	3	0	2
Total	463,213	100.0	20	4	12
UNITED KINGDOM					
C	12,660,061	44.3	562	4	302
NL & C	1,058,138	3.7	55	0	19
(Total C)	(13,718,199)	(48.0)	(617)	(4)	(321)
L	730,546	2.6	109	0	6
Lab	13,948,883	48.8	617	0	295
Com	21,640	0.1	10	0	0
Irish LP	33,174	0.1	1	0	1
N	92,787	0.3	3	0	2
PC	10,920	0.0	4	0	0
SNP	7,299	0.0	2	0	0
Others	33,146	0.1	13[1]	0	0
Total	28,596,594	100.0	1,376	4	625

[1] Including 3 ILP, 1 AP, 1 BEP.

Table 1.31   GENERAL ELECTION 1955

	Total Votes	%	Candidates	Elected
ENGLAND				
C	10,586,790	47.8	480	279
NL & C	578,646	2.6	29	14
(Total C)	(11,165,436)	(50.4)	(509)	(293)
L	571,034	2.6	95	2
Lab	10,355,892	46.8	510	216
Com	15,405	0.1	11	0
Others	28,363	0.1	9	0
Total	**22,136,130**	**100.0**	**1,134**	**511**
WALES				
C	383,132	26.7	28	5
NL & C	45,734	3.2	4	1
(Total C)	(428,866)	(29.9)	(32)	(6)
L	104,095	7.3	10	3
Lab	825,690	57.6	36	27
Com	4,544	0.3	1	0
PC	45,119	3.1	11	0
Others	25,410	1.8	1	0
Total	**1,433,724**	**100.0**	**91**	**36**
SCOTLAND				
C	1,056,209	41.5	59	30
NL & C	217,733	8.6	12	6
(Total C)	(1,273,942)	(50.1)	(71)	(36)
L	47,273	1.9	5	1
Lab	1,188,058	46.7	71	34
Com	13,195	0.5	5	0
SNP	12,112	0.5	2	0
Others	8,674	0.3	2	0
Total	**2,543,254**	**100.0**	**156**	**71**
NORTHERN IRELAND				
C	442,647	68.5	12	10
Lab	35,614	5.5	3	0
Irish LP	16,050	2.5	1	0
SF	152,310	23.5	12	2
Total	**646,621**	**100.0**	**28**	**12**
UNITED KINGDOM				
C	12,468,778	46.6	579	324
NL & C	842,113	3.1	45	21
(Total C)	(13,310,891)	(49.7)	(624)	(345)
L	722,402	2.7	110	6
Lab	12,405,254	46.4	620	277
Com	33,144	0.1	17	0
Irish LP	16,050	0.1	1	0
PC	45,119	0.2	11	0
SF	152,310	0.6	12	2
SNP	12,112	0.0	2	0
Others	62,447	0.2	12[1]	0
Total	**26,759,729**	**100.0**	**1,409**	**630**

[1] Including 2 ILP.

Table 1.32 GENERAL ELECTION 1959

	Total Votes	%	Candidates	Elected
ENGLAND				
C	11,037,998	47.7	484	302
NL & C	521,242	2.3	25	13
(Total C)	(11,559,240)	(50.0)	(509)	(315)
L	1,449,593	6.3	191	3
Lab	10,085,097	43.6	511	193
Com	12,204	0.0	10	0
Others	21,635	0.1	13	0
Total	23,127,769	100.0	1,234	511
WALES				
C	441,461	29.6	31	6
NL & C	44,874	3.0	3	1
(Total C)	(486,335)	(32.6)	(34)	(7)
L	78,951	5.3	8	2
Lab	841,450	56.4	36	27
Com	6,542	0.5	2	0
PC	77,571	5.2	20	0
Others	408	0.0	1	0
Total	1,491,257	100.0	101	36
SCOTLAND				
C	1,060,609	39.7	59	25
NL & C	199,678	7.5	11	6
(Total C)	(1,260,287)	(47.2)	(70)	(31)
L	108,963	4.1	16	1
Lab	1,245,255	46.7	71	38
Com	12,150	0.5	6	0
SNP	21,738	0.8	5	0
Others	19,120	0.7	4	1
Total	2,667,513	100.0	172	71
NORTHERN IRELAND				
C	445,013	77.2	12	12
L	3,253	0.6	1	0
Lab	44,370	7.7	3	0
SF	63,415	11.0	12	0
Others	20,062	3.5	1	0
Total	576,113	100.0	29	12
UNITED KINGDOM				
C	12,985,081	46.6	586	345
NL & C	765,794	2.8	39	20
(Total C)	(13,750,875)	(49.4)	(625)	(365)
L	1,640,760	5.9	216	6
Lab	12,216,172	43.8	621	258
Com	30,896	0.1	18	0
PC	77,571	0.3	20	0
SF	63,415	0.2	12	0
SNP	21,738	0.1	5	0
Others	61,225	0.2	19[1]	1[2]
Total	27,862,652	100.0	1,536	630

[1] Including 2 ILP, 1 FP, 1 NI Ind Lab, 1 NLP, 1 SPGB, 1 UM.
[2] Namely: Sir D. Robertson (Caithness and Sutherland—Ind C).

Table 1.33 GENERAL ELECTION 1964

	Total Votes	%	Candidates	Elected
ENGLAND				
C	9,894,014	43.2	500	256
NL & C	212,014	0.9	11	6
(Total C)	(10,106,028)	(44.1)	(511)	(262)
L	2,775,752	12.1	323	3
Lab	9,982,360	43.5	511	246
Com	24,824	0.1	22	0
Others	48,287	0.2	42	0
Total	**22,937,251**	**100.0**	**1,409**	**511**
WALES				
C	398,960	27.6	34	6
NL & C	26,062	1.8	2	0
(Total C)	(425,022)	(29.4)	(36)	(6)
L	106,114	7.3	12	2
Lab	837,022	57.8	36	28
Com	9,377	0.7	5	0
PC	69,507	4.8	23	0
Total	**1,447,042**	**100.0**	**112**	**36**
SCOTLAND				
C	981,641	37.3	65	24
NL & C	88,054	3.3	6	0
(Total C)	(1,069,695)	(40.6)	(71)	(24)
L	200,063	7.6	26	4
Lab	1,283,667	48.7	71	43
Com	12,241	0.5	9	0
SNP	64,044	2.4	15	0
Others	4,829	0.2	5	0
Total	**2,634,539**	**100.0**	**197**	**71**
NORTHERN IRELAND				
C	401,897	63.0	12	12
L	17,354	2.7	4	0
Lab	102,759	16.1	10	0
Rep	101,628	15.9	12	0
Rep LP	14,678	2.3	1	0
Total	**638,316**	**100.0**	**39**	**12**
UNITED KINGDOM				
C	11,676,512	42.2	611	298
NL & C	326,130	1.2	19	6
(Total C)	(12,002,642)	(43.4)	(630)	(304)
L	3,099,283	11.2	365	9
Lab	12,205,808	44.1	628	317
Com	46,442	0.2	36	0
PC	69,507	0.2	23	0
Rep	101,628	0.4	12	0
Rep LP	14,678	0.1	1	0
SNP	64,044	0.2	15	0
Others	53,116	0.2	47[1]	0
Total	**27,657,148**	**100.0**	**1,757**	**630**

[1] Including 3 Loyalists, 2 INDEC, 2 Pat P, 2 SPGB, 1 BNP, 1 FP, 1 N Dem P.

Table 1.34 GENERAL ELECTION 1966

	Total Votes	%	Candidates	Elected
ENGLAND				
C	9,542,577	42.0	501	216
NL & C	149,779	0.7	9	3
(Total C)	(9,692,356)	(42.7)	(510)	(219)
L	2,036,793	9.0	273	6
Lab	10,886,408	48.0	511	286
Com	33,093	0.1	34	0
Others	44,045	0.2	35	0
Total	**22,692,695**	**100.0**	**1,363**	**511**
WALES				
C	396,795	27.9	36	3
L	89,108	6.2	11	1
Lab	863,692	60.7	36	32
Com	12,769	0.9	8	0
PC	61,071	4.3	20	0
Total	**1,423,435**	**100.0**	**111**	**36**
SCOTLAND				
C	960,675	37.7	71	20
L	172,447	6.8	24	5
Lab	1,273,916	49.9	71	46
Com	16,230	0.6	15	0
SNP	128,474	5.0	23	0
Others	638	0.0	2	0
Total	**2,552,380**	**100.0**	**206**	**71**
NORTHERN IRELAND				
C	368,629	61.8	12	11
L	29,109	4.9	3	0
Lab	72,613	12.2	4	0
N	22,167	3.7	1	0
Rep	62,782	10.5	5	0
Rep LP	26,292	4.4	1	1
Others	14,645	2.5	1	0
Total	**596,237**	**100.0**	**27**	**12**
UNITED KINGDOM				
C	11,268,676	41.3	620	250
NL & C	149,779	0.6	9	3
(Total C)	(11,418,455)	(41.9)	(629)	(253)
L	2,327,457	8.6	311	12
Lab	13,096,629	48.0	622	364
Com	62,092	0.2	57	0
N	22,167	0.1	1	0
PC	61,071	0.2	20	0
Rep	62,782	0.2	5	0
Rep LP	26,292	0.1	1	1
SNP	128,474	0.5	23	0
Others	59,328	0.2	38[1]	0
Total	**27,264,747**	**100.0**	**1,707**	**630**

[1] Including 4 UM, 3 BNP, 2 SPGB, 1 FP, 1 ILP, 1 N Dem P, 1 Pat P, 1 RA.

Table 1.35 GENERAL ELECTION 1970

	Total Votes	%	Candidates	Elected
ENGLAND				
C	11,282,524	48.3	510	292
L	1,853,616	7.9	282	2
Lab	10,131,555	43.4	511	217
Com	20,103	0.1	35	0
NF	10,467	0.0	9	0
Others	62,631	0.3	56	0
Total	23,360,896	100.0	1,403	511
WALES				
C	419,884	27.7	36	7
L	103,747	6.8	19	1
Lab	781,941	51.6	36	27
Com	6,459	0.4	8	0
NF	982	0.1	1	0
PC	175,016	11.5	36	0
Others	28,525	1.9	2	1
Total	1,516,554	100.0	138	36
SCOTLAND				
C	1,020,674	38.0	70	23
L	147,667	5.5	27	3
Lab	1,197,068	44.5	71	44
Com	11,408	0.4	15	0
SNP	306,802	11.4	65	1
Others	4,616	0.2	8	0
Total	2,688,235	100.0	256	71
NORTHERN IRELAND				
C	422,041	54.2	12	8
L	12,005	1.6	4	0
Lab	98,194	12.6	7	0
Nat DP	10,349	1.3	2	0
Prot U	35,303	4.5	2	1
Rep LP	30,649	3.9	1	1
Unity	140,930	18.1	5	2
Others	29,642	3.8	7	0
Total	779,113	100.0	40	12
UNITED KINGDOM				
C	13,145,123	46.4	628	330
L	2,117,035	7.5	332	6
Lab	12,208,758	43.1	625	288
Com	37,970	0.1	58	0
Nat DP	10,349	0.0	2	0
NF	11,449	0.0	10	0
PC	175,016	0.6	36	0
Prot U	35,303	0.1	2	1
Rep LP	30,649	0.1	1	1
SNP	306,802	1.1	65	1
Unity	140,930	0.5	5	2
Others	125,414	0.5	73[1]	1[2]
Total	28,344,798	100.0	1,837	630

[1] Including 5 DP, 4 N Dem P, 2 SPGB, 1 BM, 1 ILP, 1 MK, 1 VNP.
[2] Namely: S.O. Davies (Merthyr Tydfil—Ind Lab).

Table 1.36 GENERAL ELECTION 1974 (February)

	Total Votes	%	Candidates	Elected
ENGLAND				
C	10,508,977	40.2	516	268
L	5,574,934	21.3	452	9
Lab	9,842,468	37.6	516	237
Com	13,379	0.1	23	0
NF	76,865	0.3	54	0
Others	124,995	0.5	113	2
Total	**26,141,618**	**100.0**	**1,674**	**516**
WALES				
C	412,535	25.9	36	8
L	255,423	16.0	31	2
Lab	745,547	46.8	36	24
Com	4,293	0.3	6	0
PC	171,374	10.7	36	2
Others	4,671	0.3	3	0
Total	**1,593,843**	**100.0**	**148**	**36**
SCOTLAND				
C	950,668	32.9	71	21
L	229,162	8.0	34	3
Lab	1,057,601	36.6	71	40
Com	15,071	0.5	15	0
SNP	633,180	21.9	70	7
Others	1,393	0.1	4	0
Total	**2,887,075**	**100.0**	**265**	**71**
NORTHERN IRELAND				
DUP	58,656	8.2	2	1
UU (Anti-Assembly)	232,103	32.3	7	7
VUPP	75,944	10.6	3	3
(Total UUUC)	(366,703)	(51.1)	(12)	(11)
APNI	22,660	3.2	3	0
NI Lab	17,284	2.4	5	0
Rep C	15,152	2.1	4	0
SDLP	160,437	22.4	12	1
Unity	17,593	2.4	2	0
UU (Pro-Assembly)	94,301	13.1	7	0
Others	23,496	3.3	3	0
Total	**717,626**	**100.0**	**48**	**12**
UNITED KINGDOM				
C	11,872,180	37.9	623	297
L	6,059,519	19.3	517	14
Lab	11,645,616	37.2	623	301
Com	32,743	0.1	44	0
NF	76,865	0.2	54	0
PC	171,374	0.6	36	2
SNP	633,180	2.0	70	7
Others	848,685	2.7	168[1]	14[2]
Total	**31,340,162**	**100.0**	**2,135[3]**	**635**

[1] Including all candidates in Northern Ireland and 9 WRP, 6 CPE, 6 IDA, 6 People, 4 SD, 3 IMG, 1 BM, 1 CFMPB, 1 MK, 1 N Dem P, 1 NIP, 1 WR.

[2] The twelve members for Northern Ireland constituencies (7 UU, 3 VUPP, 1 SDLP, 1 UDUP) and E.J. Milne (Blyth—Ind Lab); D. Taverne (Lincoln—Dem Lab).

[3] The number of persons seeking election was 2,133 as one candidate contested three constituencies.

Table 1.37 GENERAL ELECTION 1974 (October)

	Total Votes	%	Candidates	Elected
ENGLAND				
C	9,414,008	38.9	515	253
L	4,878,792	20.2	515	8
Lab	9,695,051	40.1	516	255
Com	7,032	0.0	17	0
NF	113,757	0.5	89	0
Others	82,429	0.3	114	0
Total	24,191,069	100.0	1,766	516
WALES				
C	367,230	23.9	36	8
L	239,057	15.5	36	2
Lab	761,447	49.5	36	23
Com	2,941	0.2	3	0
PC	166,321	10.8	36	3
Others	844	0.1	3	0
Total	1,537,840	100.0	150	36
SCOTLAND				
C	681,327	24.7	71	16
L	228,855	8.3	68	3
Lab	1,000,581	36.3	71	41
Com	7,453	0.3	9	0
NF	86	0.0	1	0
SNP	839,617	30.4	71	11
Others	182	0.0	2	0
Total	2,758,101	100.0	293	71
NORTHERN IRELAND				
UDUP	59,451	8.5	2	1
UU	256,065	36.5	7	6
VUPP	92,262	13.1	3	3
(Total UUUC)	(407,778)	(58.1)	(12)	(10)
APNI	44,644	6.3	5	0
NI Lab	11,539	1.6	3	0
Rep C	21,633	3.1	5	0
SDLP	154,193	22.0	9	1
UPNI	20,454	2.9	2	0
Others	41,853	6.0	7	1
Total	702,094	100.0	43	12
UNITED KINGDOM				
C	10,462,565	35.8	622	277
L	5,346,704	18.3	619	13
Lab	11,457,079	39.2	623	319
Com	17,426	0.1	29	0
NF	113,843	0.4	90	0
PC	166,321	0.6	36	3
SNP	839,617	2.9	71	11
Others	785,549	2.7	162[1]	12[2]
Total	29,189,104	100.0	2,252[3]	635

[1] Including all candidates in Northern Ireland and 25 CFMPB, 13 UDP, 10 WRP, 8 CPE, 7 ICRA, 5 People, 1 MK, 1 SPGB.

[2] The twelve members for Northern Ireland constituencies (6 UU, 3 VUPP, 1 UDUP, 1 Ind Rep, 1 SDLP).

[3] The number of persons seeking election was 2,231 as one candidate contested twelve constituencies and another contested eleven constituencies.

Table 1.38 GENERAL ELECTION 1979

	Total Votes	%	Candidates	Elected
ENGLAND				
C	12,255,514	47.2	516	306
L	3,878,055	14.9	506	7
Lab	9,525,280	36.7	516	203
Com	6,622	0.0	18	0
EP	38,116	0.2	50	0
NF	189,150	0.7	297	0
WRP	11,708	0.0	53	0
Others	67,805	0.3	118	0
Total	**25,972,250**	**100.0**	**2,074**	**516**
WALES				
C	526,254	32.2	35	11
L	173,525	10.6	28	1
Lab	795,493	48.6	36	22
Com	4,310	0.3	8	0
EP	1,250	0.1	2	0
NF	2,465	0.1	5	0
PC	132,544	8.1	36	2
WRP	114	0.0	1	0
Others	633	0.0	3	0
Total	**1,636,588**	**100.0**	**154**	**36**
SCOTLAND				
C	916,155	31.4	71	22
L	262,224	9.0	43	3
Lab	1,211,445	41.6	71	44
Com	5,926	0.2	12	0
EP	552	0.0	1	0
NF	104	0.0	1	0
SNP	504,259	17.3	71	2
WRP	809	0.0	6	0
Others	15,163	0.5	8	0
Total	**2,916,637**	**100.0**	**284**	**71**
NORTHERN IRELAND				
UDUP	70,975	10.2	5	3
UPNI	8,021	1.2	3	0
UU	254,578	36.6	11	5
UUUP	39,856	5.7	2	1
Others	36,989	5.3	1	1
(Total 'Loyalist')	(410,419)	(59.0)	(22)	(10)
APNI	82,892	11.9	12	0
IIP	23,086	3.3	4	0
NI Lab	4,411	0.6	3	0
Rep C/TWP	12,098	1.7	7	0
SDLP	126,325	18.2	9	1
Others	36,656	5.3	7	1
Total	**695,887**	**100.0**	**64**	**12**

GENERAL ELECTION 1979 (Cont.)

	Total Votes	%	Candidates	Elected
UNITED KINGDOM				
C	13,697,923	43.9	622	339
L	4,313,804	13.8	577	11
Lab	11,532,218	36.9	623	269
Com	16,858	0.1	38	0
EP	39,918	0.1	53	0
NF	191,719	0.6	303	0
PC	132,544	0.4	36	2
SNP	504,259	1.6	71	2
WRP	12,631	0.1	60	0
Others	779,488	2.5	193[1]	12[2]
Total	**31,221,362**	**100.0**	**2,576**[3]	**635**

[1] Including all candidates in Northern Ireland and 10 SU, 7 WR, 6 CFMPB, 3 MK, 3 SCLP, 2 FP, 2 NBP, 2 UCP, 2 Wk P, 1 CNP, 1 ENP, 1 SPGB

[2] The twelve members for Northern Ireland constituencies (5 UU, 3 UDUP, 1 Ind Rep, 1 Ind UU, 1 SDLP, 1 UUUP).

[3] The number of persons seeking election was 2,569 as one candidate contested six constituencies and another contested three constituencies.

Table 1.39 GENERAL ELECTION 1983

	Total Votes	%	Candidates	Elected
ENGLAND				
C	11,711,519	46.0	523	362
L	3,658,903	14.4	267	10
SDP	3,056,054	12.0	256	3
(Total L/SDP)	(6,714,957)	(26.4)	(523)	(13)
Lab	6,862,422	26.9	523	148
BNP	14,364	0.1	52	0
Com	6,368	0.0	22	0
EP	46,484[1]	0.2	90[1]	0
NF	27,065	0.1	60	0
WRP	3,280	0.0	18	0
Others	86,187	0.3	189	0
Total	**25,472,646**	**100.0**	**2,000**	**523**
WALES				
C	499,310	31.1	38	14
L	194,988	12.1	19	2
SDP	178,370	11.1	19	0
(Total L/SDP)	(373,358)	(23.2)	(38)	(2)
Lab	603,858	37.5	38	20
BNP	154	0.0	1	0
Com	2,015	0.1	3	0
EP	3,510	0.2	7	0
PC	125,309	7.8	38	2
WRP	256	0.0	1	0
Others	1,216	0.1	5	0
Total	**1,608,986**	**100.0**	**169**	**38**
SCOTLAND				
C	801,487	28.4	72	21
L	356,224	12.6	36	5
SDP	336,410	11.9	36	3
(Total L/SDP)	(692,634)	(24.5)	(72)	(8)
Lab	990,654	35.1	72	41
BNP	103	0.0	1	0
Com	3,223	0.1	10	0
EP	3,854	0.1	11	0
SNP	331,975	11.8	72	2
WRP	262	0.0	2	0
Others	388	0.0	2	0
Total	**2,824,580**	**100.0**	**314**	**72**

GENERAL ELECTION 1983 (Cont.)

	Total Votes	%	Candidates	Elected
NORTHERN IRELAND				
UDUP	152,749	20.0	14	3
UPUP	22,861	3.0	1	1
UU	259,952	34.0	16	11
Others	1,134	0.1	1	0
(Total 'Loyalist')	(436,696)	(57.1)	(32)	(15)
APNI	61,275	8.0	12	0
EP	451	0.1	1	0
SDLP	137,012	17.9	17	1
SF	102,701	13.4	14	1
TWP	14,650	1.9	14	0
Others	12,140	1.6	5	0
Total	**764,925**	**100.0**	**95**	**17**
UNITED KINGDOM				
C	13,012,316	42.4	633	397
L	4,210,115	13.7	322	17
SDP	3,570,834	11.7	311	6
(Total L/SDP)	(7,780,949)	(25.4)	(633)	(23)
Lab	8,456,934	27.6	633	209
BNP	14,621	0.0	54	0
Com	11,606	0.0	35	0
EP	53,848[1]	0.2	108[1]	0
NF	27,065	0.1	60	0
PC	125,309	0.4	38	2
SNP	331,975	1.1	72	2
WRP	3,798	0.0	21	0
Others	852,716	2.8	291[2]	17[3]
Total	**30,671,137**	**100.0**	**2,578[4]**	**650**

[1] Including three joint EP/WFLOE candidates who polled 1,341 votes, but excluding one candidate in Northern Ireland who polled 451 votes.

[2] Including all candidates in Northern Ireland and 11 MRLP, 10 WR, 5 Nat Pty, 4 PAL, 4 Rev CP, 2 FTACMP, 2 MK, 2 NBP, 2 Wk P, 1 CNP, 1 FP, 1 N Lab P, 1 SPGB, 1 WFLOE.

[3] The seventeen members for Northern Ireland constituencies (11 UU, 3 UDUP, 1 SDLP, 1 SF 1 UPUP).

[4] The number of persons seeking election was 2,574 as one candidate contested five constituencies.

Table 1.40 GENERAL ELECTION 1987

	Total Votes	%	Candidates	Elected
ENGLAND				
C	12,546,186	46.2	523	358
L	3,684,813	13.6	271	7
SDP	2,782,537	10.3	252	3
(Total L/SDP)	(6,467,350)	(23.9)	(523)	(10)
Lab	8,006,466	29.5	523	155
Com	4,022	0.0	13	0
GP	82,787	0.3	117	0
Others	26,711	0.1	83	0
Total	**27,133,522**	**100.0**	**1,782**	**523**
WALES				
C	501,316	29.5	38	8
L	181,427	10.7	20	3
SDP	122,803	7.2	18	0
(Total L/SDP)	(304,230)	(17.9)	(38)	(3)
Lab	765,209	45.1	38	24
Com	869	0.1	1	0
GP	2,221	0.1	4	0
PC	123,599	7.3	38	3
Others	652	0.0	1	0
Total	**1,698,096**	**100.0**	**158**	**38**
SCOTLAND				
C	713,081	24.0	72	10
L	307,210	10.4	36	7
SDP	262,843	8.9	36	2
(Total L/SDP)	(570,053)	(19.3)	(72)	(9)
Lab	1,258,132	42.4	72	50
Com	1,187	0.0	5	0
GP	4,745	0.2	12	0
SNP	416,473	14.0	71	3
Others	4,137	0.1	4	0
Total	**2,967,808**	**100.0**	**308**	**72**
NORTHERN IRELAND				
UDUP	85,642	11.7	4	3
UPUP	18,420	2.5	1	1
UU	276,230	37.8	12	9
Others	20,138	2.8	2	0
(Total 'Loyalist')	(400,430)	(54.8)	(19)	(13)
APNI	72,671	10.0	16	0
NIEP	281	0.0	1	0
SDLP	154,087	21.1	13	3
SF	83,389	11.4	14	1
TWP	19,294	2.7	14	0
Total	**730,152**	**100.0**	**77**	**17**

GENERAL ELECTION 1987 (Cont.)

	Total Votes	%	Candidates	Elected
UNITED KINGDOM				
C	13,760,583	42.3	633	376
L	4,173,450	12.8	327	17
SDP	3,168,183	9.7	306	5
(Total L/SDP)	(7,341,633)	(22.5)	(633)	(22)
Lab	10,029,807	30.8	633	229
Com	6,078	0.0	19	0
GP	89,753	0.3	133	0
PC	123,599	0.4	38	3
SNP	416,473	1.3	71	3
Others	761,652	2.4	165[1]	17[2]
Total	**32,529,578**	**100.0**	**2,325**	**650**

[1] Including all candidates in Northern Ireland and 14 RF, 10 WRP, 5 MRLP, 4 HP, 2 BNP, 1 FP, 1 OSM, 1 SPGB.

[2] The seventeen members for Northern Ireland constituencies (9 UU, 3 UDUP, 1 UPUP, 3 SDLP, 1 SF).

Table 1.41 CANDIDATES AT GENERAL ELECTIONS 1832-1987

Election	C[1]	%	Lab	%	L[2]	%	Others	%	Total	Candidates per seat
1832	350	33.8	—	—	636	61.3	51	4.9	1,037	1.6
1835	407	43.1	—	—	538	56.9	0	—	945	1.4
1837	484	48.7	—	—	510	51.3	0	—	994	1.5
1841	498	54.4	—	—	388	42.3	30	3.3	916	1.4
1847	422	48.0	—	—	393	44.7	64	7.3	879	1.3
1852	461	48.4	—	—	488	51.2	4	0.4	953	1.5
1857	351	40.0	—	—	507	57.6	21	2.4	878	1.3
1859	394	45.8	—	—	465	54.1	1	0.1	860	1.3
1865	406	44.0	—	—	516	56.0	0	—	922	1.4
1868	436	42.0	—	—	600	57.7	3	0.3	1,039	1.6
1874	507	46.9	—	—	489	45.3	84	7.8	1,080	1.7
1880	521	47.2	—	—	499	45.3	83	7.5	1,103	1.7
1885	602	45.0	—	—	572	42.7	164	12.3	1,338	2.0
1886	563	50.5	—	—	449	40.3	103	9.2	1,115	1.7
1892	606	46.5	—	—	532	40.8	165	12.7	1,303	1.9
1895	588	49.8	—	—	447	37.9	145	12.3	1,180	1.8
1900	569	51.6	15	1.4	402	36.5	116	10.5	1,102	1.6
1906	556	43.7	50	3.9	536	42.1	131	10.3	1,273	1.9
1910(J)	594	45.2	78	5.9	511	38.9	132	10.0	1,315	2.0
1910(D)	548	46.0	56	4.7	467	39.2	120	10.1	1,191	1.8
1918	445	27.4	361	22.3	421	25.9	396	24.4	1,623	2.3
1922	482	33.4	414	28.7	485	33.7	60	4.2	1,441	2.3
1923	536	37.1	427	29.5	457	31.6	26	1.8	1,446	2.4
1924	534	37.4	514	36.0	339	23.7	41	2.9	1,428	2.3
1929	590	34.1	569	32.9	513	29.7	58	3.3	1,730	2.8
1931	583	45.1	516[3]	39.9	117[4]	9.1	76	5.9	1,292	2.1
1935	583	43.2	552	41.0	161	11.9	52	3.9	1,348	2.2
1945	618	36.7	603	35.8	306	18.2	156	9.3	1,683	2.6
1950	619	33.2	617	33.0	475	25.4	157	8.4	1,868	3.0
1951	617	44.8	617	44.8	109	8.0	33	2.4	1,376	2.2
1955	624	44.3	620	44.0	110	7.8	55	3.9	1,409	2.2
1959	625	40.7	621	40.4	216	14.1	74	4.8	1,536	2.4
1964	630	35.9	628	35.7	365	20.8	134	7.6	1,757	2.8
1966	629	36.9	622	36.4	311	18.2	145	8.5	1,707	2.7
1970	628	34.2	625	34.0	332	18.1	252	13.7	1,837	2.9
1974(F)	623	29.2	623	29.2	517	24.2	372	17.4	2,135	3.4
1974(O)	622	27.6	623	27.7	619	27.5	388	17.2	2,252	3.5
1979	622	24.1	623	24.2	577	22.4	754	29.3	2,576	4.1
1983	633	24.6	633	24.6	633	24.6	679	26.2	2,578	4.0
1987	633	27.2	633	27.2	633	27.2	426	18.4	2,325	3.6

[1] Including Liberal Conservatives, 1847-59; Liberal Unionists, 1886-1910(D); National, National Liberal and National Labour, 1931-45.
[2] Including both Liberal and National Liberal, 1922; Independent Liberal, 1931; SDP/Liberal Alliance, 1983-87.
[3] Including 25 unendorsed.
[4] Including Independent Liberals.

Table 1.42 MEMBERS ELECTED AT GENERAL ELECTIONS 1832-1987

Election	C[1]	%	Lab	%	L[2]	%	Others	%	Total	Overall majority[3]
1832	175*	26.6	—	—	441	67.0	42	6.4	658	L 225
1835	273*	41.5	—	—	385	58.5	0	—	658	L 113
1837	314	47.7	—	—	344*	52.3	0	—	658	L 29
1841	367	55.8	—	—	271*	41.2	20	3.0	658	C 77
1847	325	49.5	—	—	292*	44.5	39	6.0	656	None
1852	330	50.5	—	—	324*	49.5	0	—	654	C 7
1857	264	40.4	—	—	377	57.6	13	2.0	654	L 100
1859	298	45.6	—	—	356*	54.4	0	—	654	L 59
1865	289	43.9	—	—	369*	56.1	0	—	658	L 81
1868	271	41.2	—	—	387*	58.8	0	—	658	L 115
1874	350	53.7	—	—	242*	37.1	60	9.2	652	C 49
1880	237	36.3	—	—	352*	54.0	63	9.7	652	L 51
1885	249	37.2	—	—	319*	47.6	102	15.2	670	None
1886	393*	58.7	—	—	192	28.7	85	12.6	670	C 116
1892	313	46.7	—	—	272	40.6	85	12.7	670	None
1895	411	61.4	—	—	177*	26.4	82	12.2	670	C 153
1900	402	60.0	2	0.3	183*	27.3	83	12.4	670	C 135
1906	156*	23.3	29	4.3	399	59.6	86	12.8	670	L 129
1910(J)	272*	40.6	40	6.0	274	40.9	84	12.5	670	None
1910(D)	271*	40.4	42	6.3	272	40.6	85	12.7	670	None
1918	382*	54.0	57	8.1	163	23.1	105	14.8	707	Co 283[4]
1922	344	55.9	142	23.1	115*	18.7	14	2.3	615	C 74
1923	258	41.9	191	31.1	158*	25.7	8	1.3	615	None
1924	412	67.0	151	24.6	40*	6.5	12	1.9	615	C 210
1929	260*	42.3	287	46.7	59	9.6	9	1.4	615	None
1931	522*	84.9	52[5]	8.5	36[6]	5.8	5	0.8	615	Nat 492
1935	429*	69.8	154	25.0	21	3.4	11	1.8	615	Nat 242
1945	210*	32.8	393	61.4	12	1.9	25	3.9	640	Lab 147
1950	298*	47.7	315	50.4	9	1.4	3	0.5	625	Lab 6
1951	321	51.3	295	47.2	6	1.0	3	0.5	625	C 16
1955	345*	54.8	277	44.0	6	0.9	2	0.3	630	C 59
1959	365	57.9	258	41.0	6	0.9	1	0.2	630	C 99
1964	304*	48.3	317	50.3	9	1.4	0	—	630	Lab 5
1966	253	40.1	364*	57.8	12	1.9	1	0.2	630	Lab 97
1970	330	52.3	288*	45.7	6	1.0	6	1.0	630	C 31
1974(F)	297*	46.8	301	47.4	14	2.2	23	3.6	635	None
1974(O)	277*	43.6	319	50.2	13	2.1	26	4.1	635	Lab 4
1979	339	53.4	269*	42.4	11	1.7	16	2.5	635	C 44
1983	397	61.1	209	32.2	23	3.5	21	3.2	650	C 144
1987	376*	57.9	229	35.2	22	3.4	23	3.5	650	C 102

*Including the Speaker.

[1] Including Liberal Conservatives, 1847-59; Liberal Unionists, 1886-1910(D); National, National Liberal and National Labour, 1931-45.

[2] Including both Liberal and National Liberal, 1922; Independent Liberal, 1931; SDP/Liberal Alliance 1983-87.

[3] This figure represents the majority of the Government over all other parties combined. The Speaker has been excluded when calculating the majority.

[4] Theoretical majority. Seventy-three Sinn Fein members did not take their seats.

[5] Including 6 unendorsed.

[6] Of this total, four Liberals opposed the National Government and are counted with the Opposition in calculating the overall majority.

Table 1.43 **VOTES CAST AT GENERAL ELECTIONS 1832-1987**

Election	C[1]	%*	Lab	%*	L[2]	%*	Others	%*	Total
1832	241,284	29.4	–	–	554,719	66.7	31,773	3.9	827,776
1835	261,269	42.6	–	–	349,868	57.4	–	–	611,137
1837	379,694	48.3	–	–	418,331	51.7	–	–	798,025
1841	306,314	50.9	–	–	273,902	46.9	13,229	2.2	593,445
1847	205,481	42.2	–	–	259,310	53.9	17,637	3.9	482,429
1852	311,481	41.4	–	–	430,882	58.4	1,541	0.2	743,904
1857	239,712	33.1	–	–	464,127	65.1	12,713	1.8	716,552
1859	193,232	34.3	–	–	372,117	65.7	151	0.0	565,500
1865	346,035	39.8	–	–	508,821	60.2	–	–	854,856
1868	903,708	38.4	–	–	1,428,776	61.5	1,157	0.1	2,333,251
1874	1,091,622	43.9	–	–	1,281,159	52.7	93,170	3.4	2,466,037
1880	1,426,351	42.0	–	–	1,836,423	55.4	96,642	2.6	3,359,416
1885	2,020,927	43.5	–	–	2,199,998	47.4	417,310	9.1	4,638,235
1886	1,520,886	51.4	–	–	1,353,581	45.0	99,696	3.6	2,974,163
1892	2,159,150	47.0	–	–	2,088,019	45.1	351,150	7.9	4,598,319
1895	1,894,772	49.1	–	–	1,765,266	45.7	206,244	5.2	3,866,282
1900	1,767,958	50.3	62,698	1.3	1,572,323	45.0	120,503	3.4	3,523,482
1906	2,422,071	43.4	321,663	4.8	2,751,057	49.4	131,300	2.4	5,626,091
1910(J)	3,104,407	46.8	505,657	7.0	2,866,157	43.5	191,179	2.7	6,667,400
1910(D)	2,420,169	46.6	371,802	6.4	2,293,869	44.2	149,398	2.8	5,235,238
1918	4,144,192	38.7	2,245,777	20.8	2,785,374	25.6	1,611,475	14.9	10,786,818
1922	5,502,298	38.5	4,237,349	29.7	4,139,460	28.8	513,223	3.0	14,392,330
1923	5,514,541	38.0	4,439,780	30.7	4,301,481	29.7	291,893	1.6	14,547,695
1924	7,854,523	46.8	5,489,087	33.3	2,928,737	17.8	367,932	2.1	16,640,279
1929	8,656,225	38.1	8,370,417	37.1	5,308,738	23.5	312,995	1.3	22,648,375
1931	13,156,790	60.7	6,649,630[3]	30.9	1,476,123	7.0	373,830	1.4	21,656,373
1935	11,755,654	53.3	8,325,491	38.0	1,443,093	6.7	472,816	2.0	21,997,054
1945	9,972,010	39.6	11,967,746	48.0	2,252,430	9.0	903,009	3.4	25,095,195
1950	12,492,404	43.4	13,266,176	46.1	2,621,487	9.1	391,057	1.4	28,771,124
1951	13,718,199	48.0	13,948,883	48.8	730,546	2.6	198,966	0.6	28,596,594
1955	13,310,891	49.7	12,405,254	46.4	722,402	2.7	321,182	1.2	26,759,729
1959	13,750,875	49.4	12,216,172	43.8	1,640,760	5.9	254,845	0.9	27,862,652
1964	12,002,642	43.4	12,205,808	44.1	3,099,283	11.2	349,415	1.3	27,657,148
1966	11,418,455	41.9	13,096,629	48.0	2,327,457	8.6	422,206	1.5	27,264,747
1970	13,145,123	46.4	12,208,758	43.1	2,117,035	7.5	873,882	3.0	28,344,798
1974(F)	11,872,180	37.9	11,645,616	37.2	6,059,519	19.3	1,762,847	5.6	31,340,162
1974(O)	10,462,565	35.8	11,457,079	39.2	5,346,704	18.3	1,922,756	6.7	29,189,104
1979	13,697,923	43.9	11,532,218	36.9	4,313,804	13.8	1,677,417	5.4	31,221,362
1983	13,012,316	42.4	8,456,934	27.6	7,780,949	25.4	1,420,938	4.6	30,671,137
1987	13,760,583	42.3	10,029,807	30.8	7,341,633	22.5	1,397,555	4.4	32,529,578

*Adjusted to allow for the multi-member seats which existed prior to 1950. See Introductory Notes.

[1] Including Liberal Conservatives 1847-59; Liberal Unionists, 1886-1910(D); National, National Liberal and National Labour, 1931-45.

[2] Including Liberal and National Liberal 1922; Independent Liberal 1931; SDP/Liberal Alliance 1983-87.

[3] Including 324,893 (4.9%) votes cast for 25 unendorsed candidates (see Table 1.26, footnote[3]).

Table 1.44 PARTY VOTES AS PERCENTAGES OF ELECTORATE 1950-1987

Party	1950	1951	1955	1959	1964	1966	1970	1974(F)	1974(O)
Conservative	36.5	39.6	38.2	38.9	33.4	31.7	33.4	29.9	26.1
Labour	38.7	40.3	35.6	34.5	34.0	36.4	31.0	29.3	28.6
Liberal	7.6	2.1	2.1	4.6	8.6	6.5	5.4	15.2	13.3
Others	1.1	0.6	0.9	0.7	1.0	1.2	2.2	4.4	4.8
Non-voters	16.1[1]	17.4[1]	23.2	21.3	23.0	24.2	28.0	21.2	27.2

Party	1979	1983	1987
Conservative	33.3	30.8	31.9
Labour	28.1	20.0	23.2
Liberal[2]	10.5	18.5	17.0
Others	4.1	3.4	3.2
Non-voters	24.0	27.3	24.7

[1] Excluding electors in uncontested seats.   [2] SDP/Liberal Alliance 1983-87.

Table 1.45 CONSERVATIVE AND LABOUR VOTES AS PERCENTAGES OF TWO-PARTY VOTES 1950-1987

Party	1950	1951	1955	1959	1964	1966	1970	1974(F)	1974(O)
Conservative	48.5	49.6	51.8	53.0	49.6	46.6	51.8	50.5	47.7
Labour	51.5	50.4	48.2	47.0	50.4	53.4	48.2	49.5	52.3

Party	1979	1983	1987
Conservative	54.3	60.6	57.8
Labour	45.7	39.4	42.2

Table 1.46 CONSERVATIVE, LABOUR AND LIBERAL[1] VOTES AS PERCENTAGES OF THREE-PARTY VOTES 1950-1987

Party	1950	1951	1955	1959	1964	1966	1970	1974(F)	1974(O)
Conservative	44.0	48.3	50.4	49.8	44.0	42.5	47.9	40.1	38.4
Labour	46.8	49.1	46.9	44.3	44.7	48.8	44.4	39.4	42.0
Liberal	9.2	2.6	2.7	5.9	11.3	8.7	7.7	20.5	19.6

Party	1979	1983	1987
Conservative	46.4	44.5	44.2
Labour	39.0	28.9	32.2
Liberal[1]	14.6	26.6	23.6

[1] SDP/Liberal Alliance 1983-87.

Table 1.47 REPRESENTATION OF THE MAJOR TOWNS 1950-1987

The following table shows the party representation in the major towns after each General Election since 1950.

When using this table it should be noted that substantial boundary changes took place at the General Elections of 1955, February 1974 and 1983.

	1950	1951	1955	1959	1964	1966	1970	1974(F)	1974(O)	1979	1983	1987
ENGLAND												
BIRMINGHAM												
C	4	4	4	7	5	4	6	3	2	5	5	5
Lab	9	9	9	6	8	9	7	9	10	7	6	6
BOLTON												
C	0	1	1	1	0	0	2	1	0	0	2	2
Lab	2	0	0	0	2	2	0	1	2	2	1	1
L	0	1	1	1	0	0	0	0	0	0	0	0
BRADFORD												
C	1	1	2	2	1	0	1	0	0	0	1	0
Lab	3	3	2	2	3	4	3	3	3	3	2	3
BRISTOL												
C	2	2	1	3	3	1	3	2	1	2	3	3
Lab	4	4	5	3	3	5	3	3	4	3	1	1
COVENTRY												
C	0	0	0	1	0	0	0	0	0	1	1	1
Lab	3	3	3	2	3	3	3	4	4	3	3	3
KINGSTON UPON HULL												
C	2	2	1	1	0	0	0	0	0	0	0	0
Lab	2	2	2	2	3	3	3	3	3	3	3	3
LEEDS												
C	2	2	2	2	2	2	2	2	2	2	2	2
Lab	5	5	4	4	4	4	4	4	4	4	3	4
LEICESTER												
C	1	1	1	1	1	1	2	1	0	0	2	0
Lab	3	3	3	3	3	3	2	2	3	3	1	3
LIVERPOOL												
C	5	5	6	6	2	2	2	1	1	2	0	0
Lab	4	4	3	3	7	7	7	7	7	5	5	5
L[1]	0	0	0	0	0	0	0	0	0	1	1	1
LONDON[2]												
C	12	14	15	18	10	6	9	42	41	50	56	58
Lab	31	29	27	24	32	36	33	50	51	42	26	23
L[1]	0	0	0	0	0	0	0	0	0	0	2	3
MANCHESTER												
C	3	4	4	4	2	2	2	1	1	1	1	0
Lab	6	5	5	5	7	7	7	7	7	7	4	5
NEWCASTLE UPON TYNE												
C	1	1	1	2	1	1	1	1	1	1	1	0
Lab	3	3	3	3	3	3	3	3	3	3	2	3
NOTTINGHAM												
C	0	0	2	3	1	0	1	0	0	0	3	2
Lab	4	4	2	1	3	4	3	3	3	3	0	1

REPRESENTATION OF THE MAJOR TOWNS 1950-1987 (Cont.)

	1950	1951	1955	1959	1964	1966	1970	1974(F)	1974(O)	1979	1983	1987
PLYMOUTH												
C	0	1	2	2	2	1	1	2	2	2	2	2
Lab	2	1	0	0	0	1	1	1	1	1	0	0
L[1]	0	0	0	0	0	0	0	0	0	0	1	1
PORTSMOUTH												
C	3	3	3	3	3	2	2	1	1	2	2	2
Lab	0	0	0	0	0	1	1	1	1	0	0	0
SHEFFIELD												
C	2	2	2	2	2	1	2	1	1	1	1	1
Lab	5	5	4	4	4	5	4	5	5	5	5	5
STOKE-ON-TRENT												
Lab	3	3	3	3	3	3	3	3	3	3	3	3
TEESIDE[3]												
C	–	–	–	–	–	–	–	0	0	0	0	1
Lab	–	–	–	–	–	–	–	4	4	4	3	3
L[1]	–	–	–	–	–	–	–	0	0	0	1	0
WOLVERHAMPTON												
C	1	1	1	1	1	1	1	1	1	1	1	2
Lab	1	1	1	1	1	1	1	2	2	2	2	1
WALES												
CARDIFF												
C	1	1	1	1	1	0	1	2	2	2	3	2
Lab	2	2	2	2	2	3	2	2	2	2	1	2
SCOTLAND												
EDINBURGH												
C	4	4	4	4	4	4	4	4	4	4	4	2
Lab	3	3	3	3	3	3	3	3	3	3	2	4
GLASGOW												
C	7	7	7	5	2	2	2	2	2	1	0	0
Lab	8	8	8	10	13	13	13	11	11	12	10	11
L[1]	0	0	0	0	0	0	0	0	0	0	1	0
NORTHERN IRELAND												
BELFAST												
UDUP	–	–	–	–	–	–	–	0	0	2	1	1
UU	4	3	4	4	4	3	3	3	3	1	2	2
SDLP	–	–	–	–	–	–	–	1	1	1	0	0
Others	0	1	0	0	0	1	1	0	0	0	1	1

[1] SDP/Liberal Alliance 1983-87.
[2] Constituencies within the area covered by the London County Council and subsequently the Greater London Council, plus the City of London.
[3] An amalgamation of Middlesbrough, Redcar, Stockton-on-Tees and Thornaby-on-Tees.

Table 2.01 CONTESTED AND UNCONTESTED BY-ELECTIONS 1832-1987

From	Contested	%	Uncontested	%	Total[1]	% of total seats
1832-35	35	60.3	23	39.7	58	8.8
1835-37	47	52.8	42	47.2	89	13.5
1837-41	49	46.7	56	53.3	105	16.0
1841-47	62	26.8	169	73.2	231	35.1
1847-52	73	42.4	99	57.6	172	26.2
1852-57	98	45.0	120	55.0	218	33.3
1857-59	24	26.7	66	73.3	90	13.8
1859-65	102	46.2	119	53.8	221	33.8
1865-68	45	31.9	96	68.1	141	21.4
1868-74	104	59.1	72	40.9	176	26.7
1874-80	123	63.7	70	36.3	193	29.6
1880-85	99	51.3	94	48.7	193	29.6
1885-86	15	39.5	23	60.5	38	5.7
1886-92	102	57.0	77	43.0	179	26.7
1892-95	53	51.5	50	48.5	103	15.4
1895-1900	79	69.9	34	30.1	113	16.9
1900-06	81	71.1	33	28.9	114	17.0
1906-10(J)	68	68.0	32	32.0	100	14.9
1910(J)-10(D)	10	47.6	11	52.4	21	3.1
1910(D)-18	115	46.6	132	53.4	247[2]	36.9
1918-22	78	72.2	30	27.8	108	15.3
1922-23	16	100.0	0	—	16	2.6
1923-24	9	90.0	1	10.0	10	1.6
1924-29	61	96.8	2	3.2	63	10.2
1929-31	33	91.7	3	8.3	36	5.9
1931-35	50	80.6	12	19.4	62	10.1
1935-45	150	68.5	69	31.5	219[3]	35.6
1945-50	51	98.1	1	1.9	52	8.1
1950-51	15	93.8	1	6.2	16	2.6
1951-55	45	93.8	3	6.2	48	7.7
1955-59	52	100.0	0	—	52	8.3
1959-64	62	100.0	0	—	62	9.8
1964-66	13	100.0	0	—	13	2.1
1966-70	38	100.0	0	—	38	6.0
1970-74(F)	30	100.0	0	—	30	4.8
1974(F)-74(O)	1	100.0	0	—	1	0.2
1974(O)-79	30	100.0	0	—	30	4.7
1979-83	20	100.0	0	—	20	3.1
1983-87	31	100.0	0	—	31	4.8
TOTAL	2,169	58.5	1,540	41.5	3,709	14.7

[1] Prior to 1926, by-elections could occur through MPs seeking re-election after appointment to certain ministerial and other offices. This considerably increased the number of by-elections during the period. See Table 2.03, footnote[1].

[2] From the outbreak of the First World War on August 4, 1914 until the Dissolution in 1918 there were 29 contested and 89 uncontested by-elections. The three major parties observed a truce during the war by nominating candidates only for seats which they had previously held. Twenty members of the House of Commons were killed or died on active service.

[3] From the outbreak of the Second World War on September 3, 1939 until the Dissolution in 1945 there were 75 contested and 66 uncontested by-elections. The three major parties observed a truce during the war by nominating candidates only for seats which they had previously held. Twenty-three members of the House of Commons were killed or died on active service.

Table 2.02 CANDIDATES AT BY-ELECTIONS 1885-1987

From	C	Lab	L[1]	Com	ILP	N	NF	PC	SNP	Others	Total
1885-86	15	–	33	–	–	5	–	–	–	2	55
1886-92	151	–	98	–	–	29	–	–	–	11	289
1892-95	63	–	75	–	3	15	–	–	–	5	161
1895-1900	103	–	67	–	4	19	–	–	–	7	200
1900-06	93	7	70	–	0	19	–	–	–	12	201
1906-10(J)	72	13	66	–	0	22	–	–	–	17	190
1910(J)-10(D)	11	2	15	–	0	3	–	–	–	0	31
1910(D)-18	151	20	126	–	2	38	–	–	–	58	395
1918-22	76	56	69	1	0	0	–	–	–	21	223
1922-23	14	12	12	0	0	0	–	–	–	4	42
1923-24	10	8	7	0	0	0	–	–	–	1	26
1924-29	60	56	59	1	0	0	–	0	1	5	182
1929-31	32	31	14	7	1	1	–	0	3	7	96
1931-35	55	48	19	6	4	1	–	0	4	8	145
1935-45	176	98	20	4	11	0	–	3	7	112	431
1945-50	51	48	14	3	4	1	–	2	4	18	145
1950-51	16	14	1	1	2	0	–	0	0	2	36
1951-55	48	45	8	1	0	0	–	2	1	4	109
1955-59	50	50	19	1	3	1	–	3	0	11	138
1959-64	61	62	50	6	1	0	–	3	6	37	226
1964-66	13	13	12	0	0	0	–	1	0	10	49
1966-70	38	37	27	6	0	0	1	3	4	25	141
1970-74(F)	30	30	19	1	0	0	5	1	4	30	120
1974(F)-74(O)	1	1	1	0	0	0	1	0	0	1	5
1974(O)-79	30	30	29	1	0	0	18	0	3	65	176
1979-83	17	17	16	3	0	0	5	1	4	87	150
1983-87	16	16	16	1	0	0	2	2	0	106	159

[1] SDP/Liberal Alliance 1983-87

Table 2.03 REASONS FOR BY-ELECTIONS 1832-1987

Cause of by-election	Total	%
Death	1,190	32.1
Resignation (including resignations following appointment as Lord Chancellor and elevation to the Peerage)	1,054	28.4
Ministerial (appointments to Ministerial office which required re-election)	678	18.3
Succession to the Peerage	228	6.1
Elevation to the Peerage (including Life Peerages and those summoned to the House of Lords in one of their fathers' Peerages)	220	5.9
Elections declared void following petitions	192	5.2
Members seeking re-election (for various reasons) in their constituency[1]	51	1.4
Acceptance of an appointment which did not disqualify but necessitated re-election	36	1.0
Members elected for more than one constituency declining the seats they did not wish to represent[1]	26	0.7
Members disqualified from sitting in the House of Commons[1]	16	0.4
Expulsion from the House of Commons[1]	8	0.2
Bankruptcy[1]	3	0.1
Creation of additional seats in the House of Commons during a Parliament	2	0.1
Unseated for voting in the House of Commons before taking the Oath[1]	2	0.1
Lunacy[1]	1	0.0
TOTAL	**3,707**	**100.0**

[1] For a detailed list see *Chronology of British Parliamentary By-Elections 1833-1987* by F.W.S. Craig (Chichester, 1987).

Table 3.01 CANDIDATES' EXPENSES 1857-1880

Election	Total (£)	Average per candidate[1] (£)
1857	433,006	493
1859	403,852[2]	470
1865	705,429	765
1868	1,287,122	1,239
1874	1,023,566	948
1880	1,623,537	1,472

Until 1885 (see Table 3.02) there was no limit on the amount a candidate could spend during an election campaign but from 1857 candidates were required to lodge details of their expenses with specially appointed Election Auditors. From 1865 the Returning Officers became responsible for obtaining the expenses returns.

The figures above calculated from official returns should be regarded as only approximately correct. A substantial number of candidates, especially in Ireland, failed to make returns of their expenses and there must have been a good deal of corrupt election expenditure which was not recorded.

Prior to 1918, candidates also paid the expenses of the Returning Officers (see Table 3.03) and except in 1859, these charges have not been included in the above totals.

[1] Average expenditure per candidate to nearest £. This figure is distorted for some elections due to the high proportion of uncontested seats.

[2] Including Returning Officers charges.

Sources: 1857-59; House of Commons Papers, 1860 (236), lv, 1
           1865; House of Commons Papers, 1866 (160-160vii), lvi, 25
           1868-80; Returns of Election Expenses (Home Office)

Table 3.02 CANDIDATES' EXPENSES 1885-1987

Election	Agents[1]	Clerks[2]	Printing[3]	Meetings[4]	Rooms[5]	Miscellaneous[6]	Personal Expenses[7]	Total[8]	Average[9]
	£	£	£	£	£	£	£	£	£
1885	220,150	103,119	284,190	28,080	35,517	62,729	56,502	790,287	610
1886	123,523	64,635	201,077	13,630	18,794	35,276	28,213	485,148	544
1892	192,874	98,999	310,379	19,627	29,709	60,033	49,437	761,058	614
1895	151,177	82,500	259,248	13,786	24,090	47,194	40,001	617,996	624
1900	148,245	78,605	274,061	15,831	24,265	44,683	41,422	627,112	730
1906	196,656	130,051	418,596	30,456	46,137	71,670	65,355	958,921	827
1910(J)	195,177	146,100	469,949	43,946	54,232	93,020	65,801	1,068,225	861
1910(D)	156,611	104,915	335,160	33,446	39,627	71,272	49,929	790,960	769
1918*	-	-	-	-	-	-	-	-	-
1922	131,783	171,604	465,182	50,113	52,000	81,773	65,620	1,018,075	707
1923	124,631	167,296	436,411	58,529	52,647	82,334	60,492	982,340	679
1924	111,407	148,746	415,684	60,657	50,614	78,736	55,321	921,165	645
1929	138,148	188,043	577,344	68,221	66,852	106,715	68,184	1,213,507	701
1931	76,729	101,993	298,544	40,373	36,823	61,922	37,721	654,105	506
1935	83,699	107,020	340,493	41,628	40,484	68,047	40,722	722,093	536
1945	98,064	82,417	623,774	51,804	42,525	110,672	63,960	1,073,216	638
1950	90,536	65,321	714,870	67,415	53,893	114,057	64,032	1,170,124	626
1951	74,877	52,297	589,979	52,095	45,581	80,039	51,150	946,018	688
1955	78,808	51,923	557,055	37,333	42,096	85,205	52,257	904,677	642
1959	80,722	55,910	669,688	36,672	46,729	100,490	61,008	1,051,219	684
1964	85,616	51,683	824,085	40,950	51,578	104,665	70,626	1,229,203	700
1966	82,856	46,449	762,706	33,046	49,461	96,228	66,136	1,136,882	666
1970	86,061	50,480	1,046,373	30,296	50,759	128,827	73,184	1,465,980	798
1974(F)	102,996	49,926	1,591,994	37,517	64,043	162,184	87,747	2,096,407	982
1974(O)	103,010	46,528	1,748,728	41,585	67,164	161,499	92,714	2,261,228	1,004
1979	175,874	65,799	2,873,765	58,796	93,682	289,525	131,817	3,689,258	1,432
1983	285,916	101,756	4,887,627	100,230	185,753	584,037	169,469	6,314,788	2,449
1987	326,927	107,974	6,612,952	88,652	260,756	641,913	266,547	8,305,721	3,572

CANDIDATES' EXPENSES 1885-1987 (Cont.)

*No figures available.

A limit on the amout a candidate could spend on an election campaign was first introduced by the Corrupt and Illegal Practices Prevention Act, 1883. It fixed the legal maximum in a borough constituency at £350 where the number of electors on the register did not exceed 2,000. In boroughs with an electorate of over 2,000 the limit was £380 plus an additional £30 for each complete 1,000 electors above 2,000. In counties, the limit was £650 where the electorate did not exceed 2,000 and £710 in constituencies with over 2,000 electors plus an additional £60 for every complete 1,000 electors above 2,000.

The following is a summary of subsequent changes:

1918   Borough constituencies — 5d per elector; county constituencies — 7d (reduced to 6d in 1929). Personal expenses and the fee, if any, paid to an election agent up to a maximum of £50 in a borough and £75 in a county were excluded from the limit.

1949   Borough constituencies — £450 plus 1½d per elector; county constituencies — £450 plus 2d per elector. Personal expenses excluded from the limit.

     [In Northern Ireland until 1957 expenditure was limited to 2d per elector with personal expenses and election agent's fee (up to a maximum of £50 in a borough and £75 in a county) excluded from the limit.]

1969   Borough constituencies — £750 plus one shilling (5p) for every eight electors; county constituencies — £750 plus one shilling (5p) for every six electors. Personal expenses excluded from the limit.

1974   Borough constituencies — £1,075 plus 6p for every eight electors; county constituencies — £1,075 plus 6p for every six electors. Personal expenses excluded from the limit.

1978   Borough constituencies — £1,750 plus 1½p per elector; county constituencies — £1,750 plus 2p per elector. Personal expenses excluded from the limit.

1982   Borough constituencies — £2,700 plus 2.3p per elector; county constituencies — £2,700 plus 3.1p per elector. Personal expenses excluded from the limit.

1986   Borough constituencies — £3,240 plus 2.8p per elector; county constituencies — £3,240 plus 3.7p per elector. Personal expenses excluded from the limit.

1987   Borough constituencies — £3,370 plus 2.9p per elector; county constituencies — £3,370 plus 3.8p per elector. Personal expenses excluded from the limit.

Prior to 1918, candidates also paid the expenses of the Returning Officers (see Table 3.03) and these charges have not been included in the above totals.

[1] Fees paid to election agents, sub-agents and polling agents.

[2] Payments for clerks and messengers.

[3] The expenses of printing, of advertising, of publishing, issuing and distributing addresses and notices, and of stationery, postage, telegrams.

[4] Expenses of holding public meetings, including payments to speakers.

[5] Cost of hire of committee rooms.

[6] All expenses in respect of miscellaneous matters not included in the previous columns.

[7] The personal expenses of the candidate.

[8] This figure has not always been complete owing to the fact that at most elections a small number of candidates have failed to lodge a return of their expenses. The total expenditure at the General Elections of 1886, 1895, 1900, 1910(D), 1922, 1923, 1924, 1931 and 1935 were substantially reduced due to the high proportion of uncontested seats. The expenses of unopposed candidates were either nil or very small.

[9] Average expenditure per candidate to nearest £. This figure is distorted for some elections due to the number of uncontested seats. See footnote [8] above.

Sources: Returns of Election Expenses (Home Office).

Table 3.03 RETURNING OFFICERS' EXPENSES 1832-1987

This table shows the costs incurred by Returning Officers in the conduct of General Elections. The figures from 1918 onwards are probably a slight overestimate of the actual expenses of each election as the cost of by-elections falling within the same financial year (April 1 to March 31) are included in the totals, separate figures not being published by the Treasury. This distortion may however be offset by the fact that disputes sometimes arise between Returning Officers and the Treasury as to expenses and as a result some payments to Returning Officers are delayed and would not be included in the figures for the financial year which included the General Election.

Returning Officers' expenses include the administrative costs of the election, printing, etc. Prior to 1918 these charges were paid by the candidates (the total charges in each constituency being divided equally among the candidates) in addition to their own election expenses (see Tables 3.01 and 3.02).

The total cost to the taxpayer of a General Election is however considerably greater than figures given below would suggest. It is not possible to estimate the cost of diverting civil servants, local government staff, police officers, etc. from their normal duties to election work. A proportion of the annual cost (which since 1958 has been borne by ratepayers but partly recovered from government grants) of compiling the electoral register should also be allowed for in any attempt to estimate the cost of an election. The cost of compiling the 1986-87 register was £28.9m. A further expenditure is the free delivery of the election address of each candidate, poll-cards and postal ballot papers. Since 1964, the Post Office has been able to recover this cost from the Treasury and figures supplied by the Treasury give their costs as: 1964—£990,275; 1966—£1,118,193; 1970—£1,648,854; 1974(F)—£2,895,853; 1974(O)- £3,331,459; 1979—£6,668,614; 1983—£11,281,228; 1987—£12,152,497.

Election	Returning Officers' expenses	Average per constituency[1]	Election	Returning Officers' expenses	Average per constituency[1]
	£	£		£	£
1832	56,441	141	1918	490,716	694[3]
1835	Not available	—	1922	280,138	456
1837	Not available	—	1923	324,566	528
1841	31,621[2]	111	1924	339,028	551
1847	Not available	—	1929	422,244	687
1852	48,978	123	1931	305,945	497
1857	35,566	89	1935	314,500	511
1859	Not available	—	1945	667,999	1,044
1865	47,320	118	1950	806,974	1,291
1868	95,130	226	1951	850,657	1,361
1874	140,976	339	1955	996,560	1,582
1880	130,813	314	1959	1,147,856	1,822
1885	235,907	352	1964	1,698,286	2,696
1886	138,938	207	1966	1,551,496	2,463
1892	197,542	295	1970	2,078,165	3,299
1895	156,742	234	1974(F)		
1900	150,279	224	1974(O)	6,349,362	4,999[4]
1906	206,335	308	1979	7,115,539	11,206
1910(J)	227,557	340	1983	12,139,634	18,676
1910(D)	187,753	280	1987	14,741,334	22,679

[1] This figure is distorted for several elections prior to 1955 due to the number of uncontested constituencies in which expenses would be low.

[2] England and Wales only.

[3] The high expenditure at this election was probably due to the considerable increase in the number of polling stations which must have necessitated the purchase of new ballot-boxes and other equipment.

RETURNING OFFICERS' EXPENSES 1832-1987 (Cont.)

[4] As the February election was at the end of the 1973-74 financial year, many of the accounts from Returning Officers were not paid by the Treasury until after April 1 and were therefore included in the expenditure figures for the year 1974-75. It is therefore not possible to provide separate figures for the two 1974 elections and the figure represents the total expenses in the financial years of 1973-74 and 1974-75.

Sources: 1832; House of Commons Papers, 1834 (591) ix, 263
1841; House of Commons Papers, 1842 (113), xxxiii, 623
House of Commons Papers, 1843 (67), xliv, 117
1852; House of Commons Papers, 1852-53 (311), lxxxiii, 289
1857; House of Commons Papers, 1857 (Session 2), xxxiv, 131
1865; House of Commons Papers, 1866 (160), lvi, 25
1868-1910; Returns of Election Expenses (Home Office)
1918; House of Commons Debates (1921), 142, c. 1893
1922-66; Finance Accounts of the United Kingdom
1970 onwards: Consolidated Fund and National Loans Fund Accounts (Supplementary Statements)

Table 3.04   RETURNS OF ELECTION EXPENSES 1868-1987

Since 1868 (with the exception of 1918) the Home Office have published after each election a Return of Election Expenses giving details not only of election expenses but of the number of votes cast for candidates, the full names of the candidates and a great deal of other statistical information relating to the election.
The following list gives a reference to the House of Commons Bound Sets of Sessional Papers. From the 1979/80 Session the allocation of a volume and page number was discontinued and Papers were bound in numerical order.

Election	Session	Paper No.	Volume No.	Page No.
1868	1868-69	424	I	3
1874	1874	358	liii	1
1880	1880	382	lvii	1
	1882	368	lii	373
1885	1886	199	lii	401
1886	1886	45	lii	485
1892	1893-4	423	lxx	719
1895	1896	145	lxvii	321
1900	1901	352	lix	145
1906	1906	302	xcvi	19
1910 (Jan)	1910	299	lxxiii	705
1910 (Dec.)	1911	272	lxii	701
1922	1924	2	xviii	681
1923	1924	151	xviii	775
1924	1926	1	xxii	523
1929	1929-30	114	xxiv	755
1931	1931-32	109	xx	1
1935	1935-36	150	xx	217
1945	1945-46	128	xix	539
1950	1950	146	xviii	311
1951	1951-52	210	xxi	841
1955	1955-56	141	xxxii	913
	1956-57	28	xxiii	577
1959	1959-60	173	xxi	1031
1964	1964-65	220	xxv	587
1966	1966-67	162	liv	1
1970	1970-71	305	xxii	417
1974 (Feb.)	1974-75	69	xii	31
1974 (Oct.)	1974-75	478	xii	147
1979	1979-80	374	—	—
1983	1983-84	130	—	—
1987	1987-88	426	—	—

Table 4.01 ELECTORATE AND TURNOUT 1832-1987

	Total Electorate	Electorate in uncontested seats	% of total	Age of Register[1] (months)	Turnout %[2]
1832					
ENGLAND	609,772	132,859	21.8	–	68.1
WALES	41,763	30,385	72.8	–	76.2
SCOTLAND	64,447	14,047	21.8	–	85.0
IRELAND	90,068	25,314	28.1	–	73.9
UNIVERSITIES	6,888	4,815	69.9	–	82.2
UNITED KINGDOM	**812,938**	**207,420**	**25.5**	**4**	**70.4**
1835					
ENGLAND	625,255	263,517	42.1	–	65.1
WALES	42,426	29,427	69.4	–	75.1
SCOTLAND	72,778	23,744	32.6	–	70.9
IRELAND	98,402	42,494	43.2	–	57.1
UNIVERSITIES	6,915	6,915	100.0	–	–
UNITED KINGDOM	**845,776**	**366,097**	**43.3**	**5**	**65.0**
1837					
ENGLAND	741,374	234,711	31.7	–	64.0
WALES	49,706	27,800	55.9	–	71.7
SCOTLAND	84,302	31,704	37.6	–	68.0
IRELAND	122,073	57,822	47.4	–	55.0
UNIVERSITIES	7,209	5,109	70.9	–	44.7
UNITED KINGDOM	**1,004,664**	**357,146**	**35.6**	**12**	**63.6**
1841					
ENGLAND	777,560	394,005	50.7	–	64.1
WALES	54,653	43,429	79.5	–	68.7
SCOTLAND	83,632	47,611	56.9	–	62.2
IRELAND	94,065	49,632	52.8	–	57.0
UNIVERSITIES	7,469	7,469	100.0	–	–
UNITED KINGDOM	**1,017,379**	**542,146**	**53.3**	**11**	**63.4**
1847					
ENGLAND	828,819	489,058	59.0	–	57.3
WALES	55,251	45,044	81.5	–	65.1
SCOTLAND	88,792	56,520	63.7	–	51.1
IRELAND	124,825	66,113	53.0	–	29.2
UNIVERSITIES	8,827	–	–	–	59.1
UNITED KINGDOM	**1,106,514**	**656,735**	**59.4**	**12**	**53.4**
1852					
ENGLAND	858,081	375,324	43.8	–	57.7
WALES	54,858	41,669	76.0	–	74.5
SCOTLAND	98,967	54,232	54.8	–	45.5
IRELAND	163,546	54,880	33.6	–	62.3
UNIVERSITIES	9,237	5,763	62.4	–	46.5
UNITED KINGDOM	**1,184,689**	**531,868**	**44.9**	**11**	**57.9**
1857					
ENGLAND	878,803	432,596	49.2	–	57.3
WALES	55,686	44,889	80.6	–	68.1
SCOTLAND	100,206	60,049	59.9	–	66.3
IRELAND	191,045	72,977	38.2	–	61.8
UNIVERSITIES	9,790	8,090	82.6	–	59.1
UNITED KINGDOM	**1,235,530**	**618,601**	**50.1**	**8**	**58.9**

ELECTORATE AND TURNOUT 1832-1987 (Cont.)

	Total Electorate	Electorate in uncontested seats	% of total	Age of Register[1] (months)	Turnout %[2]
1859					
ENGLAND	900,128	512,747	57.0	—	61.9
WALES	56,033	50,078	89.4	—	73.1
SCOTLAND	105,608	93,737	88.8	—	65.6
IRELAND	200,242	134,147	67.0	—	73.2
UNIVERSITIES	9,889	9,889	100.0	—	—
UNITED KINGDOM	**1,271,900**	**800,598**	**62.9**	**9**	**63.7**
1865					
ENGLAND	970,096	413,250	42.6	—	62.0
WALES	61,656	53,542	86.8	—	76.0
SCOTLAND	105,069	63,484	60.4	—	70.7
IRELAND	202,683	119,709	59.1	—	59.2
UNIVERSITIES	10,900	5,184	48.7	—	84.5
UNITED KINGDOM	**1,350,404**	**655,169**	**48.5**	**12**	**62.5**
1868					
ENGLAND	1,880,368	313,183	16.7	—	67.6
WALES	127,385	53,303	41.8	—	74.8
SCOTLAND	231,376	87,798	37.9	—	74.1
IRELAND	223,400	149,095	66.7	—	67.2
UNIVERSITIES	22,184	10,785	48.6	—	88.4
UNITED KINGDOM	**2,484,713**	**614,164**	**24.7**	**4**	**68.5**
1874					
ENGLAND	2,097,206	495,141	23.6	—	65.8
WALES	137,143	41,805	30.5	—	71.3
SCOTLAND	271,240	62,512	23.0	—	70.9
IRELAND	222,622	40,117	18.0	—	64.0
UNIVERSITIES	24,931	24,931	100.0	—	—
UNITED KINGDOM	**2,753,142**	**664,506**	**24.1**	**6**	**66.4**
1880					
ENGLAND	2,338,809	291,245	12.5	—	71.3
WALES	149,841	48,668	32.5	—	78.3
SCOTLAND	293,581	53,675	18.3	—	80.0
IRELAND	229,204	34,953	15.2	—	67.3
UNIVERSITIES	28,615	14,733	51.5	—	80.5
UNITED KINGDOM	**3,040,050**	**443,274**	**14.6**	**8**	**72.2**
1885					
ENGLAND	4,094,674	42,595	1.0	—	81.9
WALES	282,242	33,095	11.7	—	82.2
SCOTLAND	560,580	30,462	0.1	—	82.0
IRELAND	737,965	146,461	19.9	—	75.0
UNIVERSITIES	32,569	25,709	78.9	—	77.2
UNITED KINGDOM	**5,708,030**	**278,322**	**4.9**	**4**	**81.2**
1886					
ENGLAND	4,094,674	1,265,691	30.9	—	74.1
WALES	282,242	107,350	38.0	—	74.5
SCOTLAND	560,580	80,772	14.4	—	72.3
IRELAND	737,965	493,550	66.9	—	79.8
UNIVERSITIES	32,569	25,835	79.3	—	55.8
UNITED KINGDOM	**5,708,030**	**1,973,198**	**34.6**	**11½**	**74.2**

ELECTORATE AND TURNOUT 1832-1987 (Cont.)

	Total Electorate	Electorate in uncontested seats	% of total	Age of Register[1] (months)	Turnout %[2]
1892					
ENGLAND	4,478,524	301,868	6.7	—	78.7
WALES	314,647	40,010	12.7	—	75.6
SCOTLAND	589,520	—	—	—	78.3
IRELAND	740,536	171,499	23.2	—	67.7
UNIVERSITIES	37,314	32,962	88.3	—	56.2
UNITED KINGDOM	**6,160,541**	**546,339**	**8.9**	**11½**	**77.4**
1895					
ENGLAND	4,620,320	1,195,625	25.9	—	79.2
WALES	322,784	19,296	6.0	—	79.3
SCOTLAND	616,178	35,714	5.8	—	76.3
IRELAND	732,046	442,807	60.5	—	72.7
UNIVERSITIES	39,191	39,191	100.0	—	—
UNITED KINGDOM	**6,330,519**	**1,732,633**	**27.4**	**12**	**78.4**
1900					
ENGLAND	4,929,485	1,647,537	33.4	—	76.0
WALES	340,290	114,552	33.7	—	76.4
SCOTLAND	661,748	33,260	5.0	—	75.3
IRELAND	757,849	524,739	69.2	—	**60.9**
UNIVERSITIES	41,563	41,563	100.0	—	—
UNITED KINGDOM	**6,730,935**	**2,361,651**	**35.1**	**14½**	**75.1**
1906					
ENGLAND	5,416,537	227,095	4.2	—	83.6
WALES	387,535	148,487	38.3	—	82.6
SCOTLAND	728,725	7,464	1.0	—	80.9
IRELAND	686,661	522,612	76.1	—	82.1
UNIVERSITIES	45,150	11,290	25.0	—	67.0
UNITED KINGDOM	**7,264,608**	**916,948**	**12.6**	**6**	**83.2**
1910(J)					
ENGLAND	5,774,892	54,348	0.9	—	87.7
WALES	425,744	—	—	—	84.9
SCOTLAND	762,184	—	—	—	84.7
IRELAND	683,767	420,304	61.5	—	80.3
UNIVERSITIES	48,154	19,060	39.6	—	71.3
UNITED KINGDOM	**7,694,741**	**493,712**	**6.4**	**6**	**86.8**
1910(D)					
ENGLAND	5,774,892	1,025,512	17.8	—	82.1
WALES	425,744	123,423	29.0	—	78.3
SCOTLAND	779,012	90,057	11.6	—	81.8
IRELAND	683,767	419,489	61.4	—	74.8
UNIVERSITIES	46,566	40,496	87.9	—	73.1
UNITED KINGDOM	**7,709,981**	**1,698,977**	**22.0**	**16½[3]**	**81.6**
1918[4]					
ENGLAND	16,021,600	2,023,222	12.6	—	55.7
WALES	1,170,974	367,641	31.4	—	65.9
SCOTLAND	2,205,383	216,015	9.8	—	55.1
IRELAND	1,926,274	474,778	24.6	—	69.5
UNIVERSITIES	68,091	—	—	—	60.2
UNITED KINGDOM	**21,392,322**	**3,081,656**	**14.4**	**5**	**57.2**

ELECTORATE AND TURNOUT 1832-1987 (Cont.)

	Total Electorate	Electorate in uncontested seats	% of total	Age of Register[1] (months)	Turnout %[2]
1922					
ENGLAND	16,726,739	1,272,920	7.6	—	72.8
WALES	1,235,579	111,898	9.1	—	79.4
SCOTLAND	2,231,532	82,053	3.7	—	70.4
N. IRELAND	608,877	447,468	73.5	—	77.2
UNIVERSITIES	71,729	32,355	45.1	—	65.9
UNITED KINGDOM	**20,874,456**	**1,946,694**	9.3	5	73.0
1923					
ENGLAND	17,079,822	951,223	5.6	—	71.1
WALES	1,258,973	166,044	13.2	—	77.3
SCOTLAND	2,250,826	105,500	4.7	—	67.9
N. IRELAND	615,320	404,818	65.8	—	76.5
UNIVERSITIES	78,120	34,109	43.6	—	72.6
UNITED KINGDOM	**21,283,061**	**1,661,694**	7.8	6	71.1
1924					
ENGLAND	17,471,109	611,975	3.5	—	77.4
WALES	1,287,543	301,355	23.4	—	80.0
SCOTLAND	2,279,893	72,258	3.2	—	75.1
N. IRELAND	610,064	87,744	14.4	—	66.7
UNIVERSITIES	82,379	3,104	3.8	—	66.9
UNITED KINGDOM	**21,730,988**	**1,076,436**	5.0	4½	77.0
1929[5]					
ENGLAND	23,424,580	129,401	0.6	—	76.6
WALES	1,598,509	—	—	—	82.4
SCOTLAND	2,940,456	—	—	—	73.5
N. IRELAND	771,946	199,989	25.9	—	63.8
UNIVERSITIES	119,257	3,361	2.8	—	65.8
UNITED KINGDOM	**28,854,748**	**332,751**	1.2	6	76.3
1931					
ENGLAND	24,423,766	1,660,748	6.8	—	76.1
WALES	1,625,118	251,865	15.5	—	79.3
SCOTLAND	2,992,433	291,440	9.7	—	77.4
N. IRELAND	773,302	521,178	67.4	—	74.5
UNIVERSITIES	137,742	97,011	70.4	—	69.8
UNITED KINGDOM	**29,952,361**	**2,822,242**	9.4	5	76.4
1935					
ENGLAND	25,618,571	811,794	3.2	—	70.7
WALES	1,669,793	529,638	31.7	—	76.4
SCOTLAND	3,115,917	42,079	1.4	—	72.6
N. IRELAND	805,220	403,947	50.2	—	72.0
UNIVERSITIES	164,948	30,663	18.6	—	57.9
UNITED KINGDOM	**31,374,449**	**1,818,121**	5.8	5½	71.1
1945					
ENGLAND	27,045,729	21,325	0.1	—	73.4
WALES	1,798,199	39,652	2.2	—	75.7
SCOTLAND	3,343,120	—	—	—	69.0
N. IRELAND	835,980	68,752	8.2	—	67.4
UNIVERSITIES	217,363	—	—	—	53.3
UNITED KINGDOM	**33,240,391**	**129,729**	0.4	5	72.8

ELECTORATE AND TURNOUT 1832-1987 (Cont.)

	Total Electorate	Electorate in uncontested seats	% of total	Age of Register[1] (months)	Turnout %[2]
1950					
ENGLAND	28,374,288	—	—	—	84.4
WALES	1,802,356	—	—	—	84.8
SCOTLAND	3,370,190	—	—	—	80.9
N. IRELAND	865,421	140,501	16.2	—	77.4
UNITED KINGDOM	**34,412,255**	**140,501**	**0.4**	**8½**	**83.9**
1951					
ENGLAND	28,813,343	—	—	—	82.7
WALES	1,812,664	—	—	—	84.4
SCOTLAND	3,421,419	—	—	—	81.2
N. IRELAND	871,905	292,271	33.5	—	79.9
UNITED KINGDOM	**34,919,331**	**292,271**	**0.8**	**11**	**82.6**
1955					
ENGLAND	28,790,285	—	—	—	76.9
WALES	1,801,217	—	—	—	79.6
SCOTLAND	3,387,536	—	—	—	75.1
N. IRELAND	873,141	—	—	—	74.1
UNITED KINGDOM	**34,852,179**	**—**	**—**	**7½**	**76.8**
1959					
ENGLAND	29,303,126	—	—	—	78.9
WALES	1,805,686	—	—	—	82.6
SCOTLAND	3,413,732	—	—	—	78.1
N. IRELAND	874,760	—	—	—	65.9
UNITED KINGDOM	**35,397,304**	**—**	**—**	**12**	**78.7**
1964					
ENGLAND	29,804,627	—	—	—	77.0
WALES	1,805,454	—	—	—	80.1
SCOTLAND	3,393,421	—	—	—	77.6
N. IRELAND	890,552	—	—	—	71.7
UNITED KINGDOM	**35,894,054**	**—**	**—**	**12**	**77.1**
1966					
ENGLAND	29,894,141	—	—	—	75.9
WALES	1,800,925	—	—	—	79.0
SCOTLAND	3,359,891	—	—	—	76.0
N. IRELAND	902,288	—	—	—	66.1
UNITED KINGDOM	**35,957,245**	**—**	**—**	**5½**	**75.8**
1970[6]					
ENGLAND	32,737,025	—	—	—	71.4
WALES	1,958,778	—	—	—	77.4
SCOTLAND	3,629,017	—	—	—	74.1
N. IRELAND	1,017,193	—	—	—	76.6
UNITED KINGDOM	**39,342,013**	**—**	**—**	**8**	**72.0**
1974(F)[7]					
ENGLAND	33,077,571	—	—	—	79.0
WALES	1,993,516	—	—	—	80.0
SCOTLAND	3,655,621	—	—	—	79.0
N. IRELAND	1,027,155	—	—	—	69.9
UNITED KINGDOM	**39,753,863**	**—**	**—**	**4½**	**78.8**

ELECTORATE AND TURNOUT 1832-1987 (Cont.)

	Total Electorate	Electorate in uncontested seats	% of total	Age of Register[1] (months)	Turnout %[2]
1974(O)[7]					
ENGLAND	33,341,371	—	—	—	72.6
WALES	2,008,284	—	—	—	76.6
SCOTLAND	3,686,792	—	—	—	74.8
N. IRELAND	1,036,523	—	—	—	67.7
UNITED KINGDOM	**40,072,970**	—	—	12	**72.8**
1979[7]					
ENGLAND	34,211,471	—	—	—	75.9
WALES	2,061,109	—	—	—	79.4
SCOTLAND	3,795,865	—	—	—	76.8
N. IRELAND	1,027,204	—	—	—	67.7
UNITED KINGDOM	**41,095,649**	--	—	7	**76.0**
1983[7]					
ENGLAND	35,143,479	—	—	—	72.5
WALES	2,113,855	—	—	—	76.1
SCOTLAND	3,886,899	—	—	—	72.7
N. IRELAND	1,048,766	—	—	—	72.9
UNITED KINGDOM	**42,192,999**	—	—	8	**72.7**
1987[7]					
ENGLAND	35,987,776	—	—	—	75.4
WALES	2,151,352	—	—	—	78.9
SCOTLAND	3,952,465	—	—	—	75.1
N. IRELAND	1,089,160	--	—	—	67.0
UNITED KINGDOM	**43,180,753**	—	—	8	**75.3**

[1] This figure is based on the qualifying date in England and Wales. The qualifying date in the other parts of the United Kingdom sometimes varied by a few weeks from that in England and Wales.

[2] This figure makes allowance, prior to 1950, for the multi-member seats. See Introductory Notes.

[3] In Scotland the election was contested on the November 1910 Register which had a qualifying date of July 31.

[4] Those who had served in the war were enfranchised at 19 years of age. Women were enfranchised at 30 years of age.

[5] Extension of the franchise to women at 21 years of age.

[6] Extension of the franchise to persons at 18 years of age.

[7] Estimated figure, see Introductory Notes. The formula used was number of "dated names" multiplied by $\frac{12}{364}$ February 1974; $\frac{236}{364}$ October 1974; $\frac{76}{364}$ 1979; $\frac{113}{364}$ 1983; $\frac{115}{364}$ 1987.

Table 4.02 THE ELECTORATE 1945-1987

Year	Total Electorate	Service voters qualification	Business premises qualification	Full age attainers[1]
ENGLAND				
1945[2]	27,544,167	2,602,934	53,916	—
1946	28,865,697	955,918	50,653	—
1947	29,376,680	451,951	53,148	—
1948	29,715,892	268,138	48,856	—
1949	28,371,842	121,724	—	—
1950	28,408,683	157,261	—	—
1951	28,813,384	215,403	—	220,882
1952	28,896,772	269,101	—	225,306
1953	28,904,032	271,175	—	213,443
1954	28,923,119	276,609	—	200,483
1955	29,018,827	289,542	—	229,113
1956	29,117,160	292,370	—	234,764
1957	29,173,270	300,946	—	230,576
1958	29,237,876	293,711	—	236,924
1959	29,303,126	282,814	—	244,756
1960	29,415,941	289,451	—	231,749
1961	29,469,255	269,531	—	237,341
1962	29,589,260	223,226	—	227,295
1963	29,684,814	194,386	—	256,941
1964	29,804,374	192,211	—	283,200
1965	30,025,849	195,915	—	293,310
1966	30,185,780	196,583	—	293,698
1967	30,290,803	194,008	—	304,896
1968	30,570,603	190,401	—	399,448
1969	30,819,095	177,872	—	359,693
1970[3]	32,960,554	122,349	—	379,169
1971	33,186,051	79,385	—	432,397
1972	33,316,464	90,956	—	431,396
1973	33,412,961	87,435	—	428,833
1974	33,492,353	86,064	—	428,656
1975	33,755,747	104,057	—	424,285
1976	33,928,554	99,511	—	456,757
1977	34,084,807	95,255	—	461,341
1978	34,279,940	164,766	—	479,897
1979	34,611,408	208,255	—	504,984
1980	34,831,958	206,111	—	507,794
1981	35,068,122	205,743	—	585,568
1982	35,363,733	212,321	—	629,028
1983	35,569,726	234,301	—	617,759
1984	35,800,362	237,609	—	605,954
1985	35,937,374	237,428	—	570,649
1986	36,158,417	235,466	—	575,955
1987	36,393,203	236,549	—	593,024

THE ELECTORATE 1945-1987 (Cont.)

Year	Total Electorate	Service voters qualification	Business premises qualification	Full age attainers[1]
WALES				
1945[2]	1,824,517	146,597	1,248	—
1946	1,871,665	59,341	992	—
1947	1,893,824	26,134	1,014	—
1948	1,913,969	15,866	719	—
1949	1,802,124	5,610	—	—
1950	1,797,984	7,482	—	—
1951	1,812,676	10,927	—	12,719
1952	1,813,666	13,895	—	12,844
1953	1,813,088	14,616	—	11,986
1954	1,814,300	14,548	—	11,746
1955	1,815,011	15,412	—	13,794
1956	1,810,769	15,504	—	13,656
1957	1,807,892	16,731	—	13,217
1958	1,808,422	16,379	—	13,540
1959	1,805,686	15,943	—	13,932
1960	1,803,777	15,920	—	13,715
1961	1,801,781	15,035	—	13,216
1962	1,804,483	11,699	—	13,341
1963	1,805,495	9,734	—	14,722
1964	1,805,495	9,846	—	15,516
1965	1,813,203	10,230	—	15,438
1966	1,816,565	10,217	—	15,635
1967	1,817,616	10,390	—	16,081
1968	1,827,670	10,285	—	20,331
1969	1,842,335	9,863	—	19,587
1970[3]	1,971,629	5,764	—	22,180
1971	1,990,094	3,738	—	25,230
1972	1,997,400	4,298	—	24,304
1973	2,005,749	4,089	—	23,647
1974	2,016,741	3,901	—	23,999
1975	2,032,966	4,705	—	24,271
1976	2,046,444	4,767	—	26,153
1977	2,055,172	4,860	—	26,176
1978	2,065,019	7,222	—	27,585
1979	2,083,772	9,290	—	28,629
1980	2,098,552	9,129	—	28,363
1981	2,115,093	9,204	—	34,789
1982	2,127,935	9,961	—	36,719
1983	2,138,385	10,856	—	35,546
1984	2,148,484	11,264	—	34,931
1985	2,142,609	11,379	—	32,320
1986	2,160,147	11,569	—	34,694
1987	2,175,168	12,101	—	34,814

THE ELECTORATE 1945-1987 (Cont.)

Year	Total Electorate	Service voters qualification	Business premises qualification	Full age attainers[1]
SCOTLAND				
1945[2]	3,451,935	323,230	9,663	—
1946	3,584,289	115,431	9,776	—
1947	3,614,201	54,583	9,492	—
1948	3,642,497	31,006	7,495	—
1949	3,370,320	10,831	—	—
1950	3,404,101	15,052	—	—
1951	3,421,433	22,388	—	26,903
1952	3,413,792	28,151	—	24,079
1953	3,408,777	28,928	—	23,457
1954	3,407,253	30,079	—	21,804
1955	3,414,592	31,861	—	27,054
1956	3,410,718	32,408	—	26,951
1957	3,410,152	34,315	—	24,827
1958	3,407,801	33,303	—	25,033
1959	3,413,732	32,128	—	25,414
1960	3,414,572	31,488	—	24,414
1961	3,402,449	30,364	—	24,681
1962	3,404,172	25,474	—	23,992
1963	3,397,839	21,064	—	24,983
1964	3,393,391	21,432	—	27,583
1965	3,389,908	21,795	—	25,348
1966	3,385,710	21,503	—	25,833
1967	3,374,151	21,209	—	26,396
1968	3,387,905	20,782	—	35,691
1969	3,398,392	19,650	—	31,406
1970[3]	3,659,107	12,347	—	47,231
1971	3,685,283	7,585	—	49,234
1972	3,691,007	8,955	—	49,479
1973	3,688,186	8,907	—	49,029
1974	3,704,631	8,327	—	50,641
1975	3,733,232	10,053	—	49,488
1976	3,764,194	9,867	—	53,654
1977	3,786,051	9,289	—	49,709
1978	3,809,091	15,240	—	52,672
1979	3,837,019	19,828	—	51,973
1980	3,860,551	19,572	—	58,285
1981	3,885,462	19,910	—	64,720
1982	3,913,385	20,829	—	70,260
1983	3,934,220	23,175	—	68,572
1984	3,957,276	23,890	—	68,636
1985	3,967,943	24,696	—	65,940
1986	3,986,654	24,762	—	63,739
1987	3,994,893	25,300	—	61,965

THE ELECTORATE 1945-1987 (Cont.)

Year	Total Electorate	Service voters qualification	Business premises qualification	Full age attainers[1]
NORTHERN IRELAND				
1945[2]	851,417	25,821	3,613	---
1946	864,709	10,879	4,042	—
1947	865,558	6,484	3,703	—
1948	874,342	5,095	3,330	—
1949	865,421	1,388	—	—
1950	865,364	2,768	—	—
1951	871,905	4,008	—	4,107
1952	873,596	6,609	—	4,017
1953	874,958	5,096	—	3,834
1954	874,701	4,348	—	3,858
1955	877,051	5,887	—	3,876
1956	875,384	5,178	—	4,031
1957	873,987	4,415	—	4,074
1958	872,647	5,573	—	4,080
1959	874,739	4,633	—	4,223
1960	880,202	5,382	—	4,392
1961	880,149	6,184	—	3,702
1962	883,693	5,354	—	3,556
1963	888,490	4,916	—	3,877
1964	891,043	5,532	—	4,258
1965	899,427	5,186	—	4,462
1966	906,634	4,942	—	4,333
1967	909,841	—[4]	—	—[4]
1968	916,866	3,810	—	4,607
1969	926,549	3,516	—	4,404
1970[3]	1,025,215	1,728	—	15,529
1971	1,033,801	1,433	—	12,922
1972	1,033,608	1,282	—	12,606
1973	1,032,034	1,211	—	12,096
1974	1,041,886	1,227	—	15,227
1975	1,041,117	1,497	—	15,978
1976	1,033,240	1,123	—	15,511
1977	1,032,914	885	—	15,968
1978	1,033,702	1,507	—	16,152
1979	1,040,506	1,861	—	16,804
1980	1,049,466	1,783	—	15,739
1981	1,053,332	1,776	—	16,472
1982	1,057,263	2,268	—	18,197
1983	1,061,185	2,797	—	17,997
1984	1,077,605	3,157	—	20,135
1985	1,082,609	3,196	—	18,543
1986	1,087,399	3,397	—	17,780
1987	1,103,111	3,344	—	20,384

THE ELECTORATE 1945-1987 (Cont.)

Year	Total Electorate	Service voters qualification	Business premises qualification	Full age attainers[1]
UNITED KINGDOM				
1945[2]	33,672,036	3,098,582	68,440	–
1946	35,186,360	1,141,569	65,463	–
1947	35,750,263	539,152	67,357	–
1948	36,146,700	320,105	60,400	–
1949	34,409,707	139,553	–	–
1950	34,476,132	182,563	–	–
1951	34,919,398	252,726	–	264,611
1952	34,997,826	317,756	–	266,246
1953	35,000,855	319,815	–	252,720
1954	35,019,373	325,584	–	237,891
1955	35,125,481	342,702	–	273,837
1956	35,214,031	345,460	–	279,402
1957	35,265,301	356,407	–	272,694
1958	35,326,746	348,966	–	279,577
1959	35,397,283	335,518	–	288,325
1960	35,514,492	342,241	–	274,270
1961	35,553,634	321,114	–	278,940
1962	35,681,608	265,753	–	268,184
1963	35,774,575	230,100	–	300,523
1964	35,894,303	229,021	–	330,557
1965	36,128,387	232,882	–	338,558
1966	36,294,689	233,245	–	339,499
1967	36,392,411	225,607[5]	–	347,373[5]
1968	36,703,044	225,278	–	460,077
1969	36,986,371	210,901	–	415,090
1970[3]	39,616,505	142,188	–	464,109
1971	39,895,229	92,141	–	519,783
1972	40,038,479	105,491	–	517,785
1973	40,138,930	101,642	–	513,605
1974	40,255,611	99,519	–	518,523
1975	40,563,062	120,312	–	514,022
1976	40,772,432	115,268	–	552,075
1977	40,958,944	110,289	–	553,194
1978	41,187,752	188,735	–	576,306
1979	41,572,705	239,234	–	602,390
1980	41,840,527	236,595	–	610,181
1981	42,122,009	236,633	–	701,549
1982	42,462,316	245,379	–	754,204
1983	42,703,516	271,129	–	739,874
1984	42,983,727	275,920	–	729,656
1985	43,130,535	276,699	–	687,452
1986	43,392,617	275,194	–	694,168
1987	43,666,375	277,294	–	710,187

THE ELECTORATE 1945-1987 (Cont.)

[1] From 1951 until 1969 this figure relates to the number of persons attaining full age (21) after the qualifying date for the Register and before June 16 (April 14 in Northern Ireland) who were able to vote at elections where polling took place after October 1. From 1970 those attaining full age during the currency of the Register had their date of birth given in the Register and they could vote from that date.

[2] The Register published on October 15.

[3] Extension of the franchise to persons at 18 years of age.

[4] Figures not available.

[5] Excluding figures for Northern Ireland which are not available.

Sources: England and Wales; *Registrar-General's Statistical Reviews of England and Wales, Part 2. Tables.* 1945-1973.
Electoral Statistics (Office of Population Censuses and Surveys), 1974 onwards.
Scotland; *Registrar-General for Scotland, Annual Report, Part 2, Population and Vital Statistics.*
Northern Ireland; Ministry of Home Affairs, 1945-1972; Chief Electoral Officer for Northern Ireland 1973 onwards.

Table 4.03 BUSINESS ELECTORATE 1918-1945

Election	Total	% of Total Electorate	Election	Total	% of Total Electorate
1918	159,013	0.9	1929[1]	371,594	1.5
1922	199,904	1.1	1931	365,090	1.4
1923	208,694	1.1	1935	367,797	1.3
1924	211,257	1.1	1945[2]	48,974	0.2

This table shows the number of persons on the Business Premises Register in England and Wales until the Business Vote was abolished in 1949. Figures for Scotland (except in 1945) and Northern Ireland were not published.

[1] The Representation of the People (Equal Franchise) Act, 1928 increased the number of those eligible to be included in the Business Premises Register.

[2] The total for Scotland was 8,479 (0.3%).

Sources: 1918; House of Commons Papers, 1918 (138) xix, 925.
            1922-45; *Registrar-General's Statistical Reviews of England and Wales, Part 2, Tables.*
            Registrar-General for Scotland, Annual Report, 1945.

Table 4.04 MALE AND FEMALE ELECTORATE 1918-1935

Election	Males	%	Females	%	Total
1918	12,913,166	60.4	8,479,156	39.6	21,392,322
1922	10,681,899	57.4	7,931,157	42.6	18,613,056[1]
1923	12,101,039	57.3	9,002,499	42.7	21,286,195[2]
1924	12,431,253	57.2	9,297,924	42.8	21,731,672[3]
1929[4]	13,657,434	47.3	15,193,925	52.7	28,851,359
1931	14,098,181	47.1	15,854,630	52.9	29,952,811
1935	14,801,402	47.2	16,571,821	52.8	31,373,223

This table shows the number of men and women electors at each General Election until 1935. The compilation of statistics relating to the sex of electors ceased in 1938.

These statistics were compiled by the Registrar-General and are reproduced from the *Statistical Abstract of the United Kingdom, No. 83, 1924-38.* In some instances, the figure of total electorate is slightly different from that given (supplied by Returning Officers) in Home Office Returns of Election Expenses on which other tables in this book have been based. The discrepancies are however of no statistical significance.

[1] Excluding Scotland where, except for the City of Glasgow, statistics of male and female voters were not compiled.

[2] Including 182,657 electors in constituencies where statistics of male and female electors were not compiled.

[3] Including 2,495 electors in constituencies where statistics of male and female electors were not compiled.

[4] Extension of the franchise to women at 21 years of age.

Source: House of Commons Papers, 1939-40 (Cmd. 6232) x, 431.

Table 4.05 OVERSEAS ELECTORS 1987

The Representation of the People Act 1985 made provision for British citizens who are resident outside the U.K. to qualify as 'overseas electors' in the constituency for which they were last registered for a period of 5 years after they leave. The Government have announced that in due course it is their intention to extend the 5 years limit but estimates that up to half a million British citizens living abroad could claim to be registered have not been borne out by the number registering in the first year.

Year	England	Wales	Scotland	N. Ireland	Total
1987	9,980	250	800	70	11,100

Table 4.06 VOLUNTARY PATIENTS IN MENTAL HOSPITALS 1984-198'

The Representation of the People Act 1983 made provision for voluntary patients in mental hospitals to register for an address other than that of the hospital.
The new provisions have given those voluntary patients who previously could not vote the right to be included on the electoral register for an address at which they would reside if they were not in hospital.

Year	England	Wales	Scotland	N. Ireland	Total
1984	N/A	N/A	807	N/A	N/A
1985	3,057	325	235	295	3,912
1986	2,412	272	201	N/A	N/A
1987	1,966	221	458	225	2,870

N/A — Figures not available.

Table 4.07 ELECTORATE CALCULATOR

This calendar shows the number of days the Electoral Register has been in force from its publication on February 16 in each year. For Leap Years, (1976 and every fourth year thereafter), February 29 becomes Day 13 and all following consecutive numbers should be increased by one.

February	March	April	May	June	July	August	September	October	November	December	January	February
16— 0	1–13	1–44	1–74	1–105	1–135	1–166	1–197	1–227	1–258	1–288	1–319	1–350
17— 1	2–14	2–45	2–75	2–106	2–136	2–167	2–198	2–228	2–259	2–289	2–320	2–351
18— 2	3–15	3–46	3–76	3–107	3–137	3–168	3–199	3–229	3–260	3–290	3–321	3–352
19— 3	4–16	4–47	4–77	4–108	4–138	4–169	4–200	4–230	4–261	4–291	4–322	4–353
20— 4	5–17	5–48	5–78	5–109	5–139	5–170	5–201	5–231	5–262	5–292	5–323	5–354
21— 5	6–18	6–49	6–79	6–110	6–140	6–171	6–202	6–232	6–263	6–293	6–324	6–355
22— 6	7–19	7–50	7–80	7–111	7–141	7–172	7–203	7–233	7–264	7–294	7–325	7–356
23— 7	8–20	8–51	8–81	8–112	8–142	8–173	8–204	8–234	8–265	8–295	8–326	8–357
24— 8	9–21	9–52	9–82	9–113	9–143	9–174	9–205	9–235	9–266	9–296	9–327	9–358
25— 9	10–22	10–53	10–83	10–114	10–144	10–175	10–206	10–236	10–267	10–297	10–328	10–359
26—10	11–23	11–54	11–84	11–115	11–145	11–176	11–207	11–237	11–268	11–298	11–329	11–360
27—11	12–24	12–55	12–85	12–116	12–146	12–177	12–208	12–238	12–269	12–299	12–330	12–361
28—12	13–25	13–56	13–86	13–117	13–147	13–178	13–209	13–239	13–270	13–300	13–331	13–362
	14–26	14–57	14–87	14–118	14–148	14–179	14–210	14–240	14–271	14–301	14–332	14–363
	15–27	15–58	15–88	15–119	15–149	15–180	15–211	15–241	15–272	15–302	15–333	15–364
	16–28	16–59	16–89	16–120	16–150	16–181	16–212	16–242	16–273	16–303	16–334	
	17–29	17–60	17–90	17–121	17–151	17–182	17–213	17–243	17–274	17–304	17–335	
	18–30	18–61	18–91	18–122	18–152	18–183	18–214	18–244	18–275	18–305	18–336	
	19–31	19–62	19–92	19–123	19–153	19–184	19–215	19–245	19–276	19–306	19–337	
	20–32	20–63	20–93	20–124	20–154	20–185	20–216	20–246	20–277	20–307	20–338	
	21–33	21–64	21–94	21–125	21–155	21–186	21–217	21–247	21–278	21–308	21–339	
	22–34	22–65	22–95	22–126	22–156	22–187	22–218	22–248	22–279	22–309	22–340	
	23–35	23–66	23–96	23–127	23–157	23–188	23–219	23–249	23–280	23–310	23–341	
	24–36	24–67	24–97	24–128	24–158	24–189	24–220	24–250	24–281	24–311	24–342	
	25–37	25–68	25–98	25–129	25–159	25–190	25–221	25–251	25–282	25–312	25–343	
	26–38	26–69	26–99	26–130	26–160	26–191	26–222	26–252	26–283	26–313	26–344	
	27–39	27–70	27–100	27–131	27–161	27–192	27–223	27–253	27–284	27–314	27–345	
	28–40	28–71	28–101	28–132	28–162	28–193	28–224	28–254	28–285	28–315	28–346	
	29–41	29–72	29–102	29–133	29–163	29–194	29–225	29–255	29–286	29–316	29–347	
	30–42	30–73	30–103	30–134	30–164	30–195	30–226	30–256	30–287	30–317	30–348	
	31–43		31–104		31–165	31–196		31–257		31–318	31–349	

For an explanation of the use of this calendar see the entry under 'Electorate' in the Introductory Notes.

Table 4.08 DATES ON WHICH ELECTORAL REGISTERS CAME INTO FORCE 1832-1987

ENGLAND and WALES

Year	Date
1832-1842	November 1
1843-1866	December 1
1868	January 1
1868	November 1
1870-1884	January 1
1885	November 19
1887-1915	January 1
1918	October 15
1919-1926	April 15[1] and October 15
1927-1928	October 15
1929	May 1
1930-1938	October 15
1939	November 15
1945	May 7 and October 15
1946	March 1[2] and October 15
1947-1949	October 15
1950-1954	March 16
1955-	February 16

SCOTLAND

Year	Date
1832	October 12 (Burghs)
	October 15 (Counties)
1833-1855	September 15 (Burghs)
1833-1861	September 15 (Counties)
1856-1918	November 1 (Burghs)
1862-1918	November 1 (Counties)
1918-	As England and Wales q.v.

IRELAND (Northern Ireland from 1922)

Year	Date
1832-1850	February 1
1851	March 15
1852-1867	December 1
1869-1884	January 1
1885	November 18
1887-1915	As England and Wales q.v.
1918-1921	October 15[3]
1922-1928	December 15
1929	As England and Wales q.v.
1930-1939	December 15
1945-1949	As England and Wales q.v.
1950-1954	April 2
1955-	As England and Wales q.v.

[1] In 1919 and 1920 publication of the April register was advanced to May 15 by Orders in Council.
[2] A supplementary register of service voters and those who had ceased to be members of H.M. Forces.
[3] In 1921 publication of the register was advanced to February 15 1922 by an Order in Council.

Table 5.01 FORFEITED DEPOSITS—GENERAL ELECTIONS 1918-1987

Election	C	Lab	L[1]	Com	NF	PC	SNP	Others	Total[1]	% of total opposed candidates
1918	3	6	44	—	—	—	—	108	161	10.6
1922	1	7	32	1	—	—	—	11	52	3.8
1923	0	17	8	0	—	—	—	2	27	1.9
1924	1	28	30	1	—	—	—	8	68	4.9
1929	18	35	25	21	—	1	2	11	113	6.6
1931	5	21[2]	6	21	—	1	2	29	85	6.9
1935	1	16	40	0	—	1	5	18	81	6.2
1945	6	2	76	12	—	6	6	74	182	10.8
1950	5	0	319	97	—	6	3	31	461	24.7
1951	3	1	66	10	—	4	1	11	96	7.0
1955	3	1	60	15	—	7	1	13	100	7.1
1959	2	1	55	17	—	14	3	24	116	7.6
1964	5	8	52	36	—	21	12	52	186	10.6
1966	9	3	104	57	—	18	10	36	237	13.9
1970	10	6	184	58	10	25	43	72	408	22.2
1974(F)	8	25	23	43	54	26	7	135	321	15.0
1974(O)	28	13	125	29	90	26	0	131	442	19.6
1979	3	22	303	38	303	29	29	274	1,001	38.9
1983	5	119	11	35	60	32	53	424	739	28.7
1987	0	0	1	19	—	25	1	243	289	12.4

From the General Election of 1918 until October 1, 1985, a candidate forfeited the deposit of £150 if he failed to poll more than one-eighth of the total votes cast, exclusive of spoilt papers. In the case of the two-member constituencies which existed until 1950, the number of votes was deemed to be the number of good ballot papers counted. The money from forfeited deposits goes to the Treasury but in the case of the University constituencies (where a candidate had to poll more than one-eighth of the first preference votes) the deposit was forfeited to the University. In the Combined Scottish Universities, the only three-member constituency, the requirement was that a candidate must poll more than one-eighth of the first preference votes divided by three.

On October 1, 1985, the deposit was raised to £500 but the threshold was raised to one-twentieth of the total votes cast, exclusive of spoilt papers.

Where a candidate is nominated at a General Election in more than one constituency not more than one of the deposits can be returned irrespective of the number of votes polled. Eight deposits were forfeited in Ireland in 1918 owing to this rule.

Until 1950, the deposit was not returned to a successful candidate until he had taken the Oath as a Member of Parliament and, especially in 1918, Sinn Fein MPs must have forfeited their deposits through refusing to take their seats in the House of Commons.

Throughout this table, forfeited deposits due to multiple candidatures or failure to take the Oath have been ignored.

[1] SDP/Liberal Alliance 1983-87.

Table 5.02 FORFEITED DEPOSITS—BY-ELECTIONS 1918-1987

From	C	Lab	L[1]	Com	NF	PC	SNP	Others	Total[1]	% of total opposed candidates
1918-22	1	0	2	1	—	—	—	8	12	6.2
1922-23	0	1	1	0	—	—	—	2	4	9.5
1923-24	0	0	2	0	—	—	—	0	2	8.0
1924-29	0	5	10	0	—	0	1	4	20	11.1
1929-31	0	0	2	6	—	0	1	2	11	11.8
1931-35	0	0	3	5	—	0	2	6	16	12.0
1935-45	0	1	2	3	—	0	2	43	51	14.1
1945-50	3	1	9	2	—	0	4	16	35	24.3
1950-51	0	0	1	1	—	0	0	3	5	14.3
1951-55	0	0	7	1	—	1	1	4	14	13.2
1955-59	0	0	1	1	—	3	0	12	17	12.3
1959-64	2	1	8	6	—	3	4	37	61	27.0
1964-66	0	1	4	0	—	1	0	10	16	32.7
1966-70	4	2	12	6	1	0	0	23	48	34.0
1970-74	4	2	9	1	4	0	0	29	49	40.8
1974(F)-1974(O)	1	0	0	0	1	0	0	1	3	60.0
1974(O)-1979	1	0	20	1	18	0	1	65	106	60.2
1979-83	6	2	2	3	5	1	2	80	101	67.3
1983-87	1	3	0	1	2	2	0	72	81	50.9

[1] SDP/Liberal Alliance 1983-87.

Table 6.01 SEATS WHICH CHANGED HANDS AT GENERAL ELECTIONS 1950-1987

	1950	1951	1955	1959	1964	1966	1970	1974(F)	1974(O)	1979	1983	1987
C from												
L[1]	0	2	0	1	0	0	5	2	2	3	2	6
Lab	10	21	11	28	5	0	68	1	0	51	6	6
DP	0	0	0	0	0	0	1	0	0	0	0	0
Irish LP	1	0	1	0	0	0	0	0	0	0	0	0
Ind	2	0	0	0	0	0	0	0	0	0	0	0
Ind C	0	0	0	0	0	0	1	0	0	0	0	0
Ind L	1	0	0	0	0	0	0	0	0	0	0	0
SNP	0	0	0	0	0	0	0	0	0	7	0	0
Lab from												
C	1	0	1	5	58	47	6	11	17	6	0	22
L[1]	0	2	0	0	2	2	2	0	1	0	1	2
PC	0	0	0	0	0	0	1	0	0	1	0	0
SNP	0	0	0	0	0	0	1	0	0	2	0	2
Ind	0	1	0	0	0	0	0	0	0	0	0	1
Ind C	0	0	0	0	1	0	0	0	0	0	0	0
Ind Lab	1	0	0	0	0	0	0	0	2	0	0	0
SCLP	0	0	0	0	0	0	0	0	0	2	0	0
L[1] from												
C	2	0	0	1	3	3	0	2	1	0	1	3
Lab	0	1	0	0	0	1	0	2	0	0	0	0
Ind C	0	0	0	0	1	0	0	0	0	0	0	0
UDUP from												
UU	0	0	0	0	0	0	0	0	0	2	0	0
Irish LP from												
C	0	1	0	0	0	0	0	0	0	0	0	0
PC from												
C	0	0	0	0	0	0	0	0	0	0	0	1
Lab	0	0	0	0	0	0	0	2	1	0	0	0
Prot U from												
C	0	0	0	0	0	0	1	0	0	0	0	0
Rep LP from												
C	0	0	0	0	0	1	0	0	0	0	0	0
SF from												
N	0	0	2	0	0	0	0	0	0	0	0	0
SDLP from												
UU	0	0	0	0	0	0	0	0	0	0	0	1
SNP from												
C	0	0	0	0	0	0	0	4	4	0	0	3
Lab	0	0	0	0	0	0	1	2	0	0	0	0
Unity from												
C	0	0	0	0	0	0	1	0	0	0	0	0
UU from												
Unity	0	0	0	0	0	0	0	1	0	0	0	0
Ind Soc	0	0	0	0	0	0	0	1	0	0	0	0
Ind Lab from												
Lab	0	0	0	0	0	0	1	1	0	0	0	0
Ind Rep from												
UUUC	0	0	0	0	0	0	0	0	1	0	0	0
TOTAL	18	28	15	35	70	54	89	29	29	74	10	47

[1] SDP/Liberal Alliance 1983-87

Table 6.02   **SEATS WHICH CHANGED HANDS
AT BY-ELECTIONS 1950-1987**

	1950-1951	1951-1955	1955-1959	1959-1964	1964-1966	1966-1970	1970-1974(F)	1974(F)-1974(O)	1974(O)-1979	1979-1983	1983-1987
C from											
Lab	0	1	0	1	1	12	0	0	5	0	0
Ind C	0	0	2	0	0	0	0	0	0	0	0
ENP	0	0	0	0	0	0	0	0	1	0	0
Ind SDP	0	0	0	0	0	0	0	0	0	1	0
Lab from											
C	0	0	3	6	0	0	1	0	0	1	1
L	0	0	1	0	0	0	0	0	0	0	0
Ind Lab	0	0	0	0	0	0	2	0	0	0	0
L[1] from											
C	0	0	1	1	1	0	4	0	0	3	3
Lab	0	0	0	0	0	1	1	0	1	0	0
Ind Lab	0	0	0	0	0	0	0	0	0	1	1
PC from											
Lab	0	0	0	0	0	1	0	0	0	0	0
SNP from											
Lab	0	0	0	0	0	1	1	0	0	0	0
Unity from											
C	0	0	0	0	0	1	0	0	0	0	0
Ind C from											
SF	0	0	1	0	0	0	0	0	0	0	0
Ind Lab from											
Lab	0	0	0	0	0	0	1	0	0	0	0
TOTAL	0	1	8	8	2	16	10	0	7	6	5

[1] SDP/Liberal Alliance 1983-87

Table 6.03 GAINS AND LOSSES AT GENERAL ELECTIONS 1885-1987

Election	C^1 net ±	Lab net ±	L^2 net ±	Others net ±
1885[3]				
1886	+ 44		− 44	●
1892	− 49		+ 51	− 2
1895	+ 90		− 89	− 1
1900	+ 3	+ 2	− 4	− 1
1906	−211	+ 25	+185	+ 1
1910(J)	+103	− 4	− 98	− 1
1910(D)	●	+ 2	− 4	+ 2
1918[3]				
1922	− 18	+ 67	− 39	−10
1923	− 88	+ 47	+ 42	− 1
1924	+155	− 42	−114	+ 1
1929	−140	+126	+ 14	●
1931	+217	−215	+ 6	− 8
1935	− 84	+ 94	− 12	+ 2
1945[4]	−187	+199	− 8	− 4
1950[5]	+ 11	− 8	+ 2	− 5
1951	+ 22	− 19	− 3	●
1955[6]	+ 11	− 10	●	− 1
1959	+ 23	− 23	●	●
1964	− 56	+ 56	+ 2	− 2
1966	− 51	+ 48	+ 2	+ 1
1970	+ 67	− 60	− 7	●
1974(F)[7]	− 14	+ 3	+ 2	+ 9
1974(O)	− 20	+ 19	− 2	+ 3
1979	+ 55	− 40	− 3	−12
1983	+ 7	− 5	− 2	●
1987[8]	− 17	+ 21	− 5	+ 1

● No overall gain or loss.

[1] Including Liberal Unionists 1886-1910(D); National, National Liberal and National Labour, 1931-45.

[2] Including both Liberal and National Liberals in 1922; Independent Liberals in 1931; SDP/Liberal Alliance 1983-87.

[3] Boundary changes. Calculation of gains and losses not applicable.

[4] Boundary changes. Calculations are based on the 593 constituencies with either unchanged boundaries or minor changes only.

[5] Boundary changes. Calculations are based on the 88 constituencies with either unchanged boundaries or minor changes only.

[6] Boundary changes. Calculations are based on the 454 constituencies with either unchanged boundaries or minor changes only.

[7] Boundary changes. Calculations are based on the 322 constituencies with either unchanged boundaries or minor changes only.

[8] Boundary changes. Calculations are based on the 109 constituencies with either unchanged boundaries or minor changes only.

Table 6.04 GAINS AND LOSSES AT BY-ELECTIONS 1885-1987

From	C[1] net ±	Lab net ±	L[2] net ±	Others net ±
1885-86	+ 2		− 1	− 1
1886-92	−20		+19	+ 1
1892-95	+ 4		− 4	●
1895-1900	−11		+10	+ 1
1900-06	−25	+ 3	+17	+ 5
1906-10(J)	+11	+ 3	−16	+ 2
1910(J)-10(D)	●	●	●	●
1910(D)-18	+13	− 5	−10	+ 2
1918-22	−10	+13	− 6	+ 3
1922-23	− 3	+ 2	+ 2	− 1
1923-24	+ 1	●	− 1	●
1924-29	−16	+12	+ 4	●
1929-31	+ 3	− 2	− 1	●
1931-35	− 9	+10	− 1	●
1935-45	−28	+12	●	+16
1945-50	+ 4	− 1	●	− 3
1950-51	●	●	●	●
1951-55	+ 1	− 1	●	●
1955-59	− 2	+ 4	●	− 2
1959-64	− 5	+ 4	+ 1	●
1964-66	●	− 1	+ 1	●
1966-70	+11	−15	+ 1	+ 3
1970-74(F)	− 5	●	+ 5	●
1974(F)-74(O)	●	●	●	●
1974(O)-79	+ 6	− 6	+ 1	− 1
1979-83	− 3	+ 1	+ 4	− 2
1983-87	− 4	●	+ 4	●

●No overall gain or loss

[1] Including Liberal Unionists 1886-1910(D); National, National Liberal and National Labour 1931-45.

[2] Including both Liberal and National Liberal in 1922; Independent Liberal in 1931; SDP/Liberal Alliance 1983-87.

Table 6.05 GAINS AND LOSSES AT GENERAL ELECTIONS BY PETITIONS 1832-1987

At a number of General Elections (and a few by-elections) seats have changed hands subsequent to a General Election as the result of petitions claiming the seats. See Appendix 13 for details.

A seat can be claimed on the grounds that the successful candidate was disqualified from being elected (and that the electors had been informed of this before they voted) or that he or she did not have a majority of the lawful votes cast.

If a seat is successfully claimed the MP is unseated and the candidate with the next highest votes elected *without* a by-election being held.

Election	C net ±	L net ±	Others net ±
1832	●	+ 3	− 3
1835	+ 3	− 3	●
1837	− 2	+ 2	●
1841	+ 1	●	− 1
1847	●	+ 1	− 1
1852	− 1	+ 1	●
1857	+ 1	− 1	●
1865	+ 1	− 1	●
1868	− 1	+ 1	●
1874	●	●	●
1886	●	− 1	+ 1
1892	+ 1	− 1	●
1910(D)	+ 1	− 1	●
1955	+ 1	●	− 1

●No overall gain or loss

Table 7.01 THE CONSERVATIVE VOTE 1832-1987

Election	Candidates	Unopposed Returns	MPs Elected	Forfeited Deposits	Total votes	% of UK total
1832	350	66	175	—	241,284	29.4
1835	407	121	273	—	261,269	42.6
1837	484	121	314	—	379,694	48.3
1841	498	212	367	—	306,314	50.9
1847	422	213	325	—	205,481	42.2
1852	461	160	330	—	316,718	41.4
1857	351	148	264	—	239,712	33.1
1859	394	196	298	—	193,232	34.3
1865	406	142	289	—	346,035	39.8
1868	436	91	271	—	903,318	38.4
1874	507	125	350	—	1,091,708	43.9
1880	521	58	237	—	1,426,351	42.0
1885	602	10	249	—	2,020,927	43.5
1886	563	118	393	—	1,520,886	51.4
1892	606	40	313	—	2,159,150	47.0
1895	588	132	411	—	1,894,772	49.1
1900	569	163	402	—	1,767,958	50.3
1906	556	13	156	—	2,422,071	43.4
1910(J)	594	19	272	—	3,104,407	46.8
1910(D)	548	72	271	—	2,420,169	46.6
1918	445	41	382	3	4,144,192	38.7
1922	482	42	344	1	5,502,298	38.5
1923	536	35	258	0	5,514,541	38.0
1924	534	16	412	1	7,854,523	46.8
1929	590	4	260	18	8,656,225	38.1
1931	583	61	522	5	13,156,790	60.7
1935	583	26	429	1	11,755,654	53.3
1945	618	1	210	6	9,972,010	39.6
1950	619	2	298	5	12,492,404	43.4
1951	617	4	321	3	13,718,199	48.0
1955	624	0	345	3	13,310,891	49.7
1959	625	0	365	2	13,750,875	49.4
1964	630	0	304	5	12,002,642	43.4
1966	629	0	253	9	11,418,455	41.9
1970	628	0	330	10	13,145,123	46.4
1974(F)	623	0	297	8	11,872,180	37.9
1974(O)	622	0	277	28	10,462,565	35.8
1979	622	0	339	3	13,697,923	43.9
1983	633	0	397	5	13,012,316	42.4
1987	633	0	376	0	13,760,583	42.3

Including Liberal Conservative 1847-59; Liberal Unionist 1886-1910(D); National, National Liberal and National Labour 1931-45.

Table 7.02 THE LABOUR VOTE 1900-1987

Election	Candidates	Unopposed Returns	MPs Elected	Forfeited Deposits	Total votes	% of UK total
1900	15[1]	0	2	–	62,698	1.3
1906	50	0	29	–	321,663	4.8
1910(J)	78	0	40	–	505,657	7.0
1910(D)	56	3	42	–	371,802	6.4
1918	361	11	57	6	2,245,777	20.8
1922	414	4	142	7	4,237,349	29.7
1923	427	3	191	17	4,439,780	30.7
1924	514	9	151	28	5,489,087	33.3
1929	569	0	287	35	8,370,417	37.1
1931[2]	516	6	52	21	6,649,630	30.9
1935	552	13	154	16	8,325,491	38.0
1945	603	2	393	2	11,967,746	48.0
1950	617	0	315	0	13,266,176	46.1
1951	617	0	295	1	13,948,883	48.8
1955	620	0	277	1	12,405,254	46.4
1959	621	0	258	1	12,216,172	43.8
1964	628	0	317	8	12,205,808	44.1
1966	622	0	364	3	13,096,629	48.0
1970	625	0	288	6	12,208,758	43.1
1974(F)	623	0	301	25	11,645,616	37.2
1974(O)	623	0	319	13	11,457,079	39.2
1979	623	0	269	22	11,532,218	36.9
1983	633	0	209	119	8,456,934	27.6
1987	633	0	229	0	10,029,807	30.8

[1] J. Keir Hardie is counted twice in this total. He contested both Preston and Merthyr Tydfil and was elected for the latter.
[2] Including twenty-five unendorsed candidates (see Table 1.26, footnote[3]) of whom six (including one unopposed) were elected, one deposit was forfeited and the total votes polled were 324,893 (4.9%).

Table 7.03 SPONSORSHIP OF LABOUR CANDIDATES 1900-1987

	CLPs[1]	%	ILP	%	Co-op Party	%	Trade Unions[2]	%	Others[3]	%	Total
1900	–	–	9	60.0	–	–	3	20.0	3	20.0	15
1906	3	6.0	10	20.0	–	–	35	70.0	2	4.0	50
*1910(J)	?	–	14	17.9	–	–	?	–	2	2.6	78
*1910(D)	?	–	12	21.4	–	–	?	–	2	3.8	56
1918	144	39.9	50	13.8	–	–	163	45.2	4	1.1	361
*1922	?	–	55	13.3	11	2.7	?	–	0	–	414
*1923	?	–	89	20.8	10	2.3	?	–	0	–	427
*1924	?	–	87	16.9	10	1.9	?	–	0	–	514
1929	363	63.8	55	9.7	12	2.1	139	24.4	0	–	569
1931	341	69.4	–	–	18	3.7	132	26.9	0	–	491
1935	400	72.5	–	–	20	3.6	128	23.2	4	0.7	552
1945	443	73.5	–	–	34	5.6	126	20.9	0	–	603
1950	441	71.5	–	–	33	5.3	140	22.7	3	0.5	617
1951	441	71.5	–	–	38	6.1	137	22.2	1	0.2	617
1955	452	72.9	–	–	38	6.1	129	20.8	1	0.2	620
1959	461	74.2	–	–	30	4.8	129	20.8	1	0.2	621
1964	463	73.7	–	–	27	4.3	138	22.0	0	–	628
1966	460	73.9	–	–	24	3.9	138	22.2	0	–	622
1970	460	73.6	–	–	28	4.5	137	21.9	0	–	625
1974(F)	443	71.1	–	–	25	4.0	155	24.9	0	–	623
1974(O)	458	73.5	–	–	24	3.9	141	22.6	0	–	623
1979	432	69.3	–	–	25	4.0	165	26.5	1	0.2	623
1983	463	73.1	–	–	17	2.7	153	24.2	0	–	633
1987	465	73.5	–	–	19	3.0	149	23.5	0	–	633

*No complete figures are available.

Including (prior to February 1974) candidates of the Northern Ireland Labour Party if they received Labour Party endorsement.

These figures are based on the Annual Conference Reports of the Labour Party but Martin Harrison in his book *Trade Unions and the Labour Party since 1945* (London, 1960) produces slightly modified figures as the result of an examination of union accounts.

1900: Two sponsored by the Social Democratic Federation and one by a local trades council.
1906: Sponsored by local trades councils.
1910(J): Sponsored by the Fabian Society.
1910(D): Sponsored by the Fabian Society.
1918: Sponsored by the British Socialist Party.
1935: Sponsored by the Scottish Socialist Party.
1950-59: Sponsored by the Royal Arsenal Co-operative Society.
1979: Sponsored by the Royal Arsenal Co-operative Society.

Sources: Annual Conference Reports of the Labour Party, the Co-operative Party, the ILP and the Social Democratic Federation.
Labour and Politics, 1900-1906 by Frank Bealey and Henry Pelling (London, 1958).
The History of the Fabian Society by Edward R. Pease (London, 1916).

Table 7.04 SPONSORSHIP OF LABOUR MEMBERS 1900-1987

	CLPs	%	ILP	%	Co-op Party	%	Trade Unions[1]	%	Others[2]	%	Total
1900	—	—	1	50.0	—	—	1	50.0	0	—	2
1906	1	3.5	7	24.1	—	—	21	72.4	0	—	29
*1910(J)	?	—	6	15.0	—	—	?	—	0	—	40
*1910(D)	?	—	8	19.0	—	—	?	—	1	2.4	42
1918	5	8.8	3	5.2	—	—	49	86.0	0	—	57
1922	18	12.7	32	22.5	4	2.8	86	60.6	2	1.4	142
1923	32	16.8	45	23.6	6	3.1	102	53.4	6	3.1	191
1924	27	17.9	27	17.9	5	3.3	88	58.3	4	2.6	151
1929	126	43.9	37	12.9	9	3.1	115	40.1	0	—	287
1931	13	28.2	—	—	1	2.2	32	69.6	0	—	46
1935	66	42.9	—	—	9	5.8	79	51.3	0	—	154
1945	249	63.4	—	—	23	5.8	121	30.8	0	—	393
1950	186	59.1	—	—	18	5.7	110	34.9	1	0.3	315
1951	174	59.0	—	—	16	5.4	104	35.3	1	0.3	295
1955	161	58.1	—	—	19	6.9	96	34.6	1	0.4	277
1959	148	57.4	—	—	16	6.2	93	36.0	1	0.4	258
1964	178	56.1	—	—	19	6.0	120	37.9	0	—	317
1966	214	58.8	—	—	18	4.9	132	36.3	0	—	364
1970	159	55.2	—	—	15	5.2	114	39.6	0	—	288
1974(F)	158	52.5	—	—	16	5.3	127	42.2	0	—	301
1974(O)	176	55.2	—	—	16	5.0	127	39.8	0	—	319
1979	119	44.2	—	—	17	6.3	133	49.5	0	—	269
1983	87	41.6	—	—	8	3.8	114	54.6	0	—	209
1987	86	37.6	—	...	9	3.9	134	58.5	0	—	229

*No complete figures are available.

[1] These figures are based on the Annual Conference Reports of the Labour Party but Martin Harrison in his book *Trade Unions and the Labour Party since 1945* (London, 1960) produces slightly modified figures as the result of an examination of union accounts.

[2] 1910(D): Sponsored by the Fabian Society.
1922: One sponsored by the Fabian Society and one by the Social Democratic Federation.
1923: Two sponsored by the Fabian Society and four by the Social Democratic Federation.
1924: One sponsored by the Fabian Society and three by the Social Democratic Federation.
1950-59: Sponsored by the Royal Arsenal Co-operative Society.

Sources: Annual Conference Reports of the Labour Party, the Co-operative Party, the ILP and the Social Democratic Federation.
Labour and Politics, 1900-1906 by Frank Bealey and Henry Pelling (London, 1958).
The History of the Fabian Society by Edward R. Pease (London, 1916).

Table 7.05 THE LIBERAL VOTE 1832-1987

Election	Candidates	Unopposed Returns	MPs Elected	Forfeited Deposits	Total votes	% of UK total
1832	636	109	441	—	554,719	66.7
1835	538	154	385	—	349,868	57.4
1837	510	115	344	—	418,331	51.7
1841	388	113	271	—	273,902	46.9
1847	393	136	292	—	259,311	53.9
1852	488	95	324	—	430,882	58.4
1857	507	176	377	—	464,127	65.1
1859	465	183	356	—	372,117	65.7
1865	516	161	369	—	508,821	60.2
1868	600	121	387	—	1,428,776	61.5
1874	489	52	242	—	1,281,159	52.7
1880	499	41	352	—	1,836,423	55.4
1885	572	14	319	—	2,199,998	47.4
1886	449	40	192	—	1,353,581	45.0
1892	532	13	272	—	2,088,019	45.1
1895	447	11	177	—	1,765,266	45.7
1900	402	22	183	—	1,572,323	45.0
1906	536	27	399	—	2,751,057	49.4
1910(J)	511	1	274	—	2,866,157	43.5
1910(D)	467	35	272	—	2,293,869	44.2
1918	421	27	163	44	2,785,374	25.6
1922	485	10	115	32	4,139,460	28.8
1923	457	11	158	8	4,301,481	29.7
1924	339	6	40	30	2,928,737	17.8
1929	513	0	59	25	5,308,738	23.5
1931	117	5	36	6	1,476,123	7.0
1935	161	0	21	40	1,443,093	6.7
1945	306	0	12	76	2,252,430	9.0
1950	475	0	9	319	2,621,487	9.1
1951	109	0	6	66	730,546	2.6
1955	110	0	6	60	722,402	2.7
1959	216	0	6	55	1,640,760	5.9
1964	365	0	9	52	3,099,283	11.2
1966	311	0	12	104	2,327,457	8.6
1970	332	0	6	184	2,117,035	7.5
1974(F)	517	0	14	23	6,059,519	19.3
1974(O)	619	0	13	125	5,346,704	18.3
1979	577	0	11	303	4,313,804	13.8
1983	633	0	23	11	7,780,949	25.4
1987	633	0	27	1	7,341,633	22.5

Including both Liberal and National Liberal 1922; Independent Liberal 1931 SDP/Liberal Alliance 1983-87.

Table 7.06 THE NATIONAL LIBERAL VOTE 1931-1966

Election	Candidates	Unopposed Returns	MPs Elected	Forfeited Deposits	Total votes	% of UK total
1931	41	7	35	0	809,302	3.7
1935	44	3	33	0	866,354	3.7
1945	49	0	11	0	737,732	2.9
1950	55	0	16[1]	0	985,343	3.4
1951	55	0	19[1]	0	1,058,138	3.7
1955	45	0	21[1]	0	842,113	3.1
1959	39	0	20[1]	0	765,794	2.8
1964	19	0	6[2]	0	326,130	1.2
1966	9	0	3	0	149,779	0.6

From 1950, only those candidates who actually *used* the National Liberal and Conservative (or one of the numerous variations) label have been included in this table. Between 1955 and 1966 the official lists of candidates issued by the National Liberal Organization included a number of candidates who did not use the joint label, preferring to run as straight Conservatives.
The National Liberal Organization was disbanded in May 1968.

[1] Excluding G.R.H. Nugent (Surrey, Guildford) who although elected as a Conservative joined the Liberal-Unionist Group as an associate member.
[2] Excluding J.H. Osborn (Sheffield, Hallam) and Sir P.G. Roberts, Bt. (Sheffield, Heeley) who although elected as Conservatives joined the Liberal-Unionist Group as associate members.

Table 7.07 THE COMMUNIST VOTE 1922-1987

Election	Candidates	MPs Elected	Forfeited Deposits	Total votes	% of UK total
1922	5	1	1	33,637	0.2
1923	4	0	0	39,448	0.2
1924	8	1	1	55,346	0.3
1929	25	0	21	50,634	0.2
1931	26	0	21	74,824	0.3
1935	2	1	0	27,117	0.1
1945	21	2	12	102,780	0.4
1950	100	0	97	91,765	0.3
1951	10	0	10	21,640	0.1
1955	17	0	15	33,144	0.1
1959	18	0	17	30,896	0.1
1964	36	0	36	46,442	0.2
1966	57	0	57	62,092	0.2
1970	58	0	58	37,970	0.1
1974(F)	44	0	43	32,743	0.1
1974(O)	29	0	29	17,426	0.1
1979	38	0	38	16,858	0.1
1983	35	0	35	11,606	0.0
1987	19	0	19	6,078	0.0

Until 1924 it was possible for members of the Communist Party to secure adoption and endorsement as official Labour Party candidates. The following is a summary of these candidates who are not included in the above table: 1922: S. Saklatvala (Battersea, North), polled 11,311 votes and was elected; M.P. Price (Gloucester), polled 7,871 votes and was defeated. It appears that Price was not an actual member of the Communist Party at this election but *The Communist* of November 25, 1922 described him as 'sympathetic'.
1923: The following candidates were defeated — W. Paul (Manchester, Rusholme) 5,366 votes; M.P. Price (Gloucester) 8,127 votes; S. Saklatvala (Battersea, North) 12,341 votes; J.J. Vaughan (Bethnal Green, South-West) 5,251 votes; Miss E.C. Wilkinson (Ashton-under-Lyne) 6,208 votes.

Table 7.08   THE PLAID CYMRU VOTE 1929-1987

Election	Candidates	MPs Elected[1]	Forfeited Deposits	Total votes	% of Welsh total
1929	1	0	1	609	0.0
1931	2	0	1	2,050	0.2
1935	1	0	1	2,534	0.3
1945	7	0	6	16,017	1.2
1950	7	0	6	17,580	1.2
1951	4	0	4	10,920	0.7
1955	11	0	7	45,119	3.1
1959	20	0	14	77,571	5.2
1964	23	0	21	69,507	4.8
1966	20	0	18	61,071	4.3
1970	36	0	25	175,016	11.5
1974(F)	36	2	26	171,374	10.7
1974(O)	36	3	26	166,321	10.8
1979	36	2	29	132,544	8.1
1983	38	2	32	125,309	7.8
1987	38	3	25	123,599	7.3

Table 7.09   THE SCOTTISH NATIONAL PARTY VOTE 1929-1987

Election	Candidates	MPs Elected[1]	Forfeited Deposits	Total votes	% of Scottish total
1929	2	0	2	3,313	0.2
1931	5	0	2	20,954	1.0
1935	8	0	5	29,517	1.3
1945	8	0	6	30,595	1.2
1950	3	0	3	9,708	0.4
1951	2	0	1	7,299	0.3
1955	2	0	1	12,112	0.5
1959	5	0	3	21,738	0.8
1964	15	0	12	64,044	2.4
1966	23	0	10	128,474	5.0
1970	65	1	43	306,802	11.4
1974(F)	70	7	7	633,180	21.9
1974(O)	71	11	0	839,617	30.4
1979	71	2	29	504,259	17.3
1983	72	2	53	331,975	11.8
1987	71	3	1	416,473	14.0

Table 7.10 THE NATIONAL FRONT VOTE 1970-1987

Election	Candidates	MPs Elected	Forfeited Deposits	Total votes	% of UK total
1970	10	0	10	11,449	0.0
1974(F)	54	0	54	76,865	0.2
1974(O)	90	0	90	113,843	0.4
1979	303	0	303	191,719	0.6
1983	60	0	60	27,065	0.1
1987	0	0	0	—	—

Table 7.11 THE SOCIAL DEMOCRATIC PARTY VOTE 1983-1987

Election	Candidates	MPs Elected	Forfeited Deposits	Total votes	% of UK total
1983	311	6	6	3,570,834	11.7
1987	306	5	0	3,168,183	9.7

Table 7.12 THE GREEN PARTY VOTE 1979-1987

Election	Candidates	MPs Elected	Forfeited Deposits	Total votes	% of UK total
1979	53	0	53	39,918	0.1
1983	108	0	108	53,848	0.2
1987	133	0	133	89,753	0.3

The Ecology Party formed in February 1974 changed its name to the Green Party in September 1985.

Table 8.01 ABSENT VOTERS 1924-1945

	1924	1929	1931	1935	1945
ENGLAND	160,141	169,338	166,511	158,282	1,044,761
WALES	6,701	7,907	8,542	8,326	55,487
SCOTLAND	15,082	18,796	18,426	17,444	168,574
N. IRELAND	2,277	1,965	2,135	1,924	12,298
UNITED KINGDOM	**184,201**	**198,006**	**195,614**	**185,976**	**1,281,120**

Statistics of absent voters were not compiled until the General Election of 1924. The above figures give the number of electors on the absent voters list at each election. This list contained the names of civilian and service voters eligible to vote by post plus a small number of proxy voters. There are no statistics available of the number of absent voters who actually voted.

Source: Returns of Election Expenses (Home Office).

Table 8.02 POSTAL BALLOT PAPERS 1945-1987

	No. of postal ballot papers issued	No. of covering envelopes returned before close of poll	No. rejected[1]	No. of postal ballot papers included at the start of the count
1945[2]				
ENGLAND	1,037,298	882,762	11,911	870,851
WALES	54,434	45,763	726	45,037
SCOTLAND	121,336	99,797	1,688	98,109
N. IRELAND	6,451	4,366	34	4,332
UNITED KINGDOM	**1,219,519**	**1,032,688**	**14,359**	**1,018,329**
1950				
ENGLAND	410,126	386,884	7,879	379,005
WALES	23,916	22,500	815	21,685
SCOTLAND	49,444	46,150	2,084	44,066
N. IRELAND	24,231	22,504	913	21,591
UNITED KINGDOM	**507,717**	**478,038**	**11,691**	**466,347**
1951				
ENGLAND	688,427	627,415	10,618	616,797
WALES	38,819	34,986	862	34,124
SCOTLAND	79,294	71,367	2,029	69,338
N. IRELAND	25,337	23,199	884	22,315
UNITED KINGDOM	**831,877**	**756,967**	**14,393**	**742,574**
1955				
ENGLAND	489,248	435,097	8,506	426,591
WALES	30,412	26,596	711	25,885
SCOTLAND	53,341	45,854	1,485	44,369
N. IRELAND	21,999	19,357	609	18,748
UNITED KINGDOM	**595,000**	**526,904**	**11,311**	**515,593**

POSTAL BALLOT PAPERS 1945-1987 (Cont.)

	No. of postal ballot papers issued	No. of covering envelopes returned before close of poll	No. rejected[1]	No. of postal ballot papers included at the start of the count
1959				
ENGLAND	585,776	520,551	10,922	509,629
WALES	34,054	29,532	848	28,684
SCOTLAND	55,739	48,204	1,481	46,723
N. IRELAND	17,258	13,944	421	13,523
UNITED KINGDOM	**692,827**	**612,231**	**13,672**	**598,559**
1964				
ENGLAND	692,674	614,344	12,818	601,526
WALES	39,286	34,343	1,094	33,249
SCOTLAND	68,184	59,376	1,841	57,535
N. IRELAND	18,757	15,864	538	15,326
UNITED KINGDOM	**818,901**	**723,927**	**16,291**	**707,636**
1966				
ENGLAND	505,637	433,708	11,338	422,370
WALES	33,966	28,677	1,129	27,548
SCOTLAND	55,486	46,711	1,695	45,016
N. IRELAND	22,392	18,910	803	18,107
UNITED KINGDOM	**617,481**	**528,006**	**14,965**	**513,041**
1970				
ENGLAND	599,638	525,842	10,820	515,022
WALES	41,088	35,919	1,017	34,902
SCOTLAND	62,656	53,603	1,550	52,053
N. IRELAND	27,867	24,310	932	23,378
UNITED KINGDOM	**731,249**	**639,674**	**14,319**	**625,355**
1974(F)[3]				
ENGLAND	606,468	530,583	13,098	517,485
WALES	45,004	35,152	1,377	33,775
SCOTLAND	62,261	54,278	1,391	52,887
N. IRELAND	29,708	25,067	307	24,760
UNITED KINGDOM	**743,441**	**645,080**	**16,173**	**628,907**
1974(O)[4]				
ENGLAND	882,433	718,240	20,516	697,724
WALES	59,970	48,714	2,014	46,700
SCOTLAND	90,136	73,190	1,875	71,315
N. IRELAND	42,592	35,180	814	34,366
UNITED KINGDOM	**1,075,131**	**875,324**	**25,219**	**850,105**
1979				
ENGLAND	680,930	572,835	17,953	554,882
WALES	56,647	48,095	2,105	45,990
SCOTLAND	76,917	65,082	1,965	63,117
N. IRELAND	32,841	28,880	900	27,980
UNITED KINGDOM	**847,335**	**714,892**	**22,923**	**691,969**

POSTAL BALLOT PAPERS 1945-1987 (Cont.)

	No. of postal ballot papers issued	No. of covering envelopes returned before close of poll	No. rejected[1]	No. of postal ballot papers included at the start of the count
1983				
ENGLAND	622,013	529,243	16,017	513,226
WALES	46,862	40,001	1,892	38,109
SCOTLAND	54,017	43,593	1,461	42,132
N. IRELAND	34,712	30,797	710	30,087
UNITED KINGDOM	**757,604**	**643,634**	**20,080**	**623,554**
1987				
ENGLAND	792,412	683,399	20,270	663,129
WALES	56,093	48,221	2,193	46,028
SCOTLAND	64,077	54,354	1,857	52,497
N. IRELAND	35,366	32,375	967	31,408
UNITED KINGDOM	**947,948**	**818,349**	**25,287**	**793,062**

Statistics of postal voting were not compiled until the General Election of 1945. Prior to 1945, the only General Election in which there must have been a substantial number of postal votes was that of 1918. Between the wars only members of His Majesty's Forces serving in the United Kingdom and a few civilians could vote by post. The Representation of the People Act, 1949, considerably increased the categories of those eligible to vote by post.

The Representation of the People Act 1985 extended postal voting to anyone who could not reasonably be expected to vote in person and this allowed people going on holiday to apply for a postal or proxy vote.

[1] Number of cases in which the covering envelope or its contents were marked "empty", "rejected", "declaration rejected" or "vote rejected".

[2] These figures relate only to Service voters. In addition, a total of 1,381 civilian postal voters had their ballot papers included in constituency counts.

[3] Columns 2, 3 and 4 are exclusive of the figures for Ashford, Bassetlaw, Bath, Abertillery, Bedwellty, Ebbw Vale, Monmouth and Pontypool. The Returning Officers failed to make the statutory return to the Home Office.

[4] Columns 2, 3 and 4 are exclusive of the figures for Devizes and Northwich. The Returning Officers failed to make the statutory return to the Home Office.

Sources: 1945: House of Commons Papers, 1945-46 (22) xx, 609.
                1950 onwards: Returns compiled by the Home Office and the Scottish Home and Health Department.

Table 8.03 POSTAL BALLOT PAPERS (Summary) 1945-1987

Election	Issued Postal Ballot Papers as % of total electorate	No. returned as % of No. issued	No. of covering envelopes rejected as % of No. returned	No. of Postal Ballot Papers included at the start of the count as % of total poll
1945[1]	3.7	84.7	1.4	4.2
1950	1.5	94.2	2.4	1.6
1951	2.4	91.0	1.9	2.6
1955	1.7	88.6	2.1	1.9
1959	2.0	88.4	2.2	2.1
1964	2.3	88.4	2.3	2.6
1966	1.7	85.5	2.8	1.9
1970	1.9	87.5	2.2	2.2
1974(F)	1.9	87.8	2.5	2.0
1974(O)	2.7	81.7	2.9	2.9
1979	2.1	84.4	3.2	2.2
1983	1.8	85.0	3.1	2.0
1987	2.2	86.3	3.1	2.4

[1] These figures relate only to Service voters.

Table 9.01 PUBLIC OPINION POLLS —
VOTING INTENTION (GALLUP POLL) 1945-1987

Date[†]	C%	Lab%	L%	Others%	*Don't Know%	C Lead %
1945						
February	27½	47½	12½	12½	(12)	−20
April	28	47	14	11	(15)	−19
June	32	45	15	8	(?)	−13
1946						
January	32	52½	11	4½	(7)	−20½
May	40	43½	13	3½	(8)	− 3½
1947						
January	41	44½	12	2½	(8)	− 3½
March	43½	43½	10½	2½	(13)	nil
June	42½	42½	12½	2½	(11)	nil
July	42½	42½	12½	2½	(11)	nil
August	44½	41	11	3½	(17)	3½
September	44½	39½	11½	4½	(12)	5
November	50½	38	9	2½	(13)	12½
1948						
January	44½	43½	10½	1½	(15)	1
February	46	42	8½	3½	(17)	4
March	46	43	8½	2½	(17)	3
April	42½	41	10½	6	(15)	1½
May	45	41½	11	2½	(18)	3½
July	48	39½	9	3½	(12)	8½
August	48	41	8½	2½	(17)	7
September	47½	41	10	1½	(20)	6½
October	46½	41½	9½	2½	(18)	5
November	46	43	8½	2½	(17)	3
1949						
January	44	40½	13	2½	(14)	3½
February	44½	43½	9½	2½	(15)	1
March	41½	43	13	2½	(14)	− 1½
April	42	43½	13	1½	(15)	− 1½
May	46	40	11	3	(15)	6
June	46	41½	10	2½	(18)	4½
July	44½	40½	12½	2½	(13)	4
August	46½	40½	11½	1½	(14)	6
September	46	40	12	2	(15)	6
October	45½	39½	12½	2½	(19)	6
November	43½	40	14	2½	(13)	3½
December	45	41	12½	1½	(13)	4
1950						
January	44	41½	12½	2	(7½)	2½
February	43	44½	12	½	(11½)	− 1½
March	43½	45½	8½	2½	(8)	− 2
April	45½	47	7	½	(9)	− 1½
May	43½	46½	9½	½	(9)	− 3
June	43½	46	9	1½	(9)	− 2½
July	42	43½	11	3½	(10)	− 1½
August	44½	46	8½	1	(9)	− 1½
September	43	45½	10	1½	(12)	− 2½
October	42½	45	10	2½	(11)	− 2½
December	43	44	11½	1½	(12)	− 1

PUBLIC OPINION POLLS — VOTING INTENTION (GALLUP POLL) 1945-1987 (Cont.)

Date [†]	C%	Lab%	L%	Others%	*Don't Know%	C Lead %
1951						
January	51	38	10	1	(13)	13
February	51½	37½	9½	1½	(13)	14
March	51	36½	10½	2	(14)	14½
April	50½	38½	9	2	(13)	12
May	49	40	9½	1½	(13½)	9
June	48	41	10	1	(12)	7
July	49	39	10½	1½	(13)	10
August	50½	38	10½	1	(11½)	12½
September	52	41	6½	½	(11)	11
October	50½	44	4½	1	(11½)	6½
December	47	45	6½	1½	(9)	2
1952						
January	44½	48	6	1½	(10½)	− 3½
February	41	47	10½	1½	(14)	− 6
March	41½	48	9½	1	(9)	− 6½
May	43½	49	7	½	(9)	− 5½
June	40½	49	9½	1	(6½)	− 8½
July	40	50	8½	1½	(9)	−10
September	41	48½	9	1½	(9½)	− 7½
October	41½	48	9	1½	(11)	− 6½
November	43½	46½	9	1	(12½)	− 3
December	44	45½	9½	1	(11½)	− 1½
1953						
January	42½	46	10	1½	(11)	− 3½
February	42½	46	10	1½	(11)	− 3½
March	46½	44½	8	1	(11½)	2
April	47	45	7½	½	(13)	2
May	47	45	7½	½	(12½)	2
June	46	46	7	1	(11½)	nil
August	45	46	8	1	(13)	− 1
September	44½	47½	7	1	(12)	− 3
October	45	47½	7	½	(11½)	− 2½
December	45	47	7	1	(12½)	− 2
1954						
January	45½	46½	7	1	(14)	− 1
February	45½	47	7	½	(13)	− 1½
March	46½	45½	7	1	(12)	1
April	46½	46	7	½	(13)	½
May	45½	47½	6½	½	(12)	− 2
June	45	47½	7	½	(12½)	− 2½
August	42½	48½	8	1	(11)	− 6
September	43	48	8	1	(11)	− 5
October	45	45½	8	1½	(16)	− ½
November	46	47	6	1	(15)	− 1
December	48	49½	2½	—	(13)	− 1½
1955						
January	46½	45½	7	1	(14)	1
February	46½	44½	8	1	(13)	2
March	46½	44½	8	1	(13)	2
April	48	44	7	1	(14)	4
May	51	47	2	—	(12½)	4
July	47	43	9	1	(11)	4
August	44½	47½	7	1	(14)	− 3
September	48	44	7	1	(10)	4
October	46½	44½	8	1	(13)	2
November	44½	45½	9	1	(12½)	− 1
December	45½	46½	7½	½	(12)	− 1

PUBLIC OPINION POLLS – VOTING INTENTION (GALLUP POLL) 1945-1987 (Cont.)

Date[†]	C%	Lab%	L%	Others%	*Don't Know%	C Lead %
1956						
January	45½	46½	7½	½	(12)	− 1
February	44	46	9	1	(12½)	− 2
March	44½	47½	7	1	(19)	− 3
April	43	48	8	1	(17½)	− 5
May	43	47	9	1	(15)	− 4
July	42	49	8	1	(14½)	− 7
August	43½	49½	6	1	(16)	− 6
September	43	46½	10	½	(15)	− 3½
October	42½	47	9½	1	(15)	− 4½
November	45	46	8½	½	(17)	− 1
December	45	46	8	1	(15)	− 1
1957						
January	43½	48½	7	1	(10½)	− 5
February	42	48	8½	1½	(19)	− 6
March	40	51½	7½	1	(21½)	−11½
April	41	51	7	1	(14½)	−10
May	41½	50	7½	1	(16½)	− 8½
July	41½	49½	8	1	(16)	− 8
August	40½	48½	10	1	(17)	− 8
September	33½	52	14	½	(25)	−18½
October	37	49	13	1	(16½)	−12
November	38½	49	12	½	(19½)	−10½
December	41½	47½	9½	1½	(16)	− 6
1958						
January	40	47½	12	½	(17)	− 7½
February	36	44½	18½	1	(19)	− 8½
April	38	46½	15	½	(18½)	− 8½
May	34	47	19	−	(18½)	−13
June	39½	43	17	½	(13)	− 3½
August	42½	42	15	½	(14)	½
September	44	43	13	−	(17)	1
October	45½	41½	12	1	(15½)	4
November	46½	42½	10	1	(15)	4
December	47	42½	9½	1	(15)	4½
1959						
January	45½	45	8½	1	(19)	½
February	43	47	8½	1½	(22½)	− 4
March	45½	47	6½	1	(22)	− 1½
April	44½	44	10	1½	(14)	½
May	45	44	10	1	(14½)	1
June	45	43½	11	½	(14½)	2½
July	45½	41½	12½	½	(15½)	4
August	47½	41½	10	1	(13½)	6
September	50½	43½	5½	½	(17½)	7
October	48	46	5	1	(16)	2
November	48	44	7	1	(11)	4
December	47½	44	7½	1	(15)	3½
1960						
January	47	43½	8½	1	(16)	3½
February	47	43½	9	½	(16)	3½
March	47	42	10	1	(17)	5
April	45	42½	11½	1	(17)	2½
May	45½	42½	11	1	(15½)	3
June	45½	43	10½	1	(14½)	2½
July	47	43	9	1	(17)	4
August	47½	42	10	½	(16½)	5½
September	47½	40½	11	1	(16)	7
October	50	37	12½	½	(19)	13
November	46	40½	13½	−	(14)	5½
December	47½	37½	14	1	(15)	10

PUBLIC OPINION POLLS — VOTING INTENTION (GALLUP POLL) 1945-1987 (Cont.)

Date †	C%	Lab%	L%	Others%	*Don't Know%	C Lead %
1961						
January	45	41½	12½	1	(19)	3½
February	44	42	13	1	(18½)	2
March	44	40	15	1	(12)	4
April	43½	40½	15	1	(18)	3
May	44½	40½	14	1	(18)	4
June	43½	40	15	1½	(16½)	3½
July	44	41½	14	½	(18)	2½
August	38	43	17	2	(17)	− 5
September	40	45½	13½	1	(18)	− 5½
October	43½	43½	12	1	(14½)	nil
November	41½	43	14½	1	(17)	− 1½
December	38½	43	17½	1	(20)	− 4½
1962						
January	42	42	15	1	(18½)	nil
February	40	42½	17	½	(18)	− 2½
March	39½	44	16	½	(18)	− 4½
April	33	41	25	1	(12½)	− 8
May	34½	39½	25½	½	(17)	− 5
June	35½	39	25	½	(14)	− 3½
July	35½	41½	22	1	(14½)	− 6
August	34	43	22	1	(13½)	− 9
September	34	45	20	1	(15)	−11
October	34½	43½	20	2	(17½)	− 9
November	39	47	13	1	(16)	− 8
December	37	46	16	1	(17½)	− 9
1963						
January	35	48	16½	½	(8½)	−13
February	32½	48	18½	1	(8)	−15½
March	33½	50	15½	1	(9½)	−16½
April	34	49½	16	½	(10)	−15½
May	36	47	16	1	(10½)	−11
June	31	51½	16½	1	(8)	−20½
July	33½	51½	14	1	(12½)	−18
August	34	50	15	1	(11)	−16
September	33½	49	16½	1	(10½)	−15½
October	36½	48	14½	1	(11)	−11½
November	37½	49½	12	1	(10½)	−12
December	39	47½	13	½	(11½)	− 8½
1964						
January	39	47½	13	½	(10½)	− 8½
February	39	48	12	1	(9½)	− 9
March	39	48½	12	½	(9)	− 9½
April	38½	50½	10½	½	(8)	−12
May	39	50½	10	½	(7½)	−11½
June	41	50½	8	½	(7½)	− 9½
July	40½	49½	9½	½	(6½)	− 9
August	43	49¼	7½	¼	(8½)	− 6¼
September	44½	47	8	½	(7)	− 2½
October	44½	46½	8½	½	(3½)	− 2
November	38½	50	11	½	(7)	−11½
December	40	50½	9	—	(6½)	−10½

PUBLIC OPINION POLLS – VOTING INTENTION (GALLUP POLL) 1945-1987 (Cont.)

Date[†]	C%	Lab%	L%	Others%	*Don't Know%	C Lead %
1965						
January	42½	46½	10½	½	(8)	− 4
February	45½	45	9	½	(6)	½
March	43½	46	9½	1	(8)	− 2½
April	39½	47½	12½	½	(9½)	− 8
May	44	43	12½	½	(9½)	1
June	47	42½	9½	1	(9½)	4½
July	46½	45	8	½	(10½)	1½
August	49	41½	8½	1	(10)	7½
September	42	48½	8½	1	(6½)	− 6½
October	41½	49	9	½	(7½)	− 7½
November	42	48½	8½	1	(8½)	− 6½
December	40½	48½	10	1	(7½)	− 8
1966						
January	42	47½	9½	1	(8)	− 5½
February	42½	50	7	½	(10½)	− 7½
March	40	51	8	1	(7)	−11
May	35½	53½	10	1	(6)	−18
June	39½	52	7½	1	(7)	−12½
July	41	48½	8½	2	(9)	− 7½
August	44½	44	10½	1	(9½)	½
September	42½	45	11½	1	(8½)	− 2½
October	43	44½	11½	1	(7)	− 1½
November	44	42	12½	1½	(9)	2
December	42	46	10½	1½	(6½)	− 4
1967						
January	42½	45½	10½	1½	(7½)	− 3
February	37	48½	13	1½	(5½)	−11½
March	42½	42½	12½	2½	(9½)	nil
April	45½	41½	11	2	(9)	4
May	46½	40	12	1½	(8½)	6½
June	48	41	9½	1½	(11)	7
July	43½	41	13	2½	(9½)	2½
August	43	42	13	2	(11½)	1
September	45	41½	10½	3	(9)	3½
October	45	38	14	3	(7)	7
November	46½	36	11½	6	(9)	10½
December	49½	32	12	6½	(9½)	17½
1968						
January	45	39½	11	4½	(10)	5½
February	52½	30	12½	5	(12)	22½
March	50	31	15	4	(13½)	19
April	54½	30	12½	3	(12½)	24½
May	56	28	11	5	(13)	28
June	51½	28	14	6½	(12)	23½
July	50	30	13	7	(10)	20
August	49½	34½	11½	4½	(11)	15
September	47	37	11½	4½	(8)	10
October	47	39	9½	4½	(9)	8
November	50½	32	14	3½	(9½)	18½
December	55	29½	11	4½	(11½)	25½

PUBLIC OPINION POLLS — VOTING INTENTION (GALLUP POLL) 1945-1987 (Cont.)

Date†	C%	Lab%	L%	Others%	*Don't Know%	C Lead %
1969						
January	53	31	11½	4½	(11½)	22
February	54½	32	11	2½	(13½)	22½
March	52½	34	10	3½	(11½)	18½
April	51	30½	13	5½	(12½)	20½
May	52	30½	13½	4	(13)	21½
June	51	35	12	2	(12)	16
July	55	31½	11	2½	(12½)	23½
August	47	34½	15½	3	(12)	12½
September	46½	37	13	3½	(9½)	9½
October	46½	44½	7	2	(10½)	2
November	45	41½	10	3½	(9½)	3½
December	50	39½	9	1½	(12)	10½
1970						
January	48½	41	7	3½	(10½)	7½
February	48	41	9	2	(10)	7
March	46½	41	9½	3	(10½)	5½
April	47	42½	7½	3	(9)	4½
May	42	49½	7	1½	(8)	− 7½
June	42	49	7½	1½	(8)	− 7
August	47	43½	7½	2	(9½)	3½
September	46½	44	8	1½	(10½)	2½
October	46½	46½	6½	½	(13½)	nil
November	43½	48	6½	2	(12)	− 4½
December	46	44½	6	3½	(12)	1½
1971						
January	42½	47	8½	2	(10½)	− 4½
February	41½	49	8	1½	(10)	− 7½
March	38½	50½	8	3	(11)	−12
April	44½	48	6	1½	(10)	− 3½
May	38	50	9½	2½	(8)	−12
June	36	54	8	2	(11)	−18
July	33½	55	8½	3	(8)	−21½
August	42	48½	7	2½	(10½)	− 6½
September	35	54	8½	2½	(10½)	−19
October	40	50	8	2	(8½)	−10
November	42½	48½	7	2	(12½)	− 6
December	42	48	7½	2½	(13)	− 6
1972						
January	40½	48	9	2½	(11)	− 7½
February	40½	49	8½	2	(11)	− 8½
March	39½	48½	9½	2½	(9½)	− 9
April	43½	44½	10	2	(10)	− 1
May	40½	46½	11	2	(8½)	− 6
June	41	47	10	2	(9½)	− 6
July	39	49	9½	2½	(8½)	−10
August	40	49	7½	3½	(11½)	− 9
September	38½	49½	9½	2½	(9½)	−11
October	40	48	8½	3½	(10½)	− 8
November	37½	45½	15	2	(10)	− 8
December	38	46½	12½	3	(11½)	− 8½

PUBLIC OPINION POLLS — VOTING INTENTION (GALLUP POLL) 1945-1987 (Cont.)

Date[†]	C%	Lab%	L%	Others%	*Don't Know%	C Lead %
1973						
January	38½	44	15½	2	(11)	− 5½
February	38	47	12½	2½	(10½)	− 9
March	39	43	16	2	(9)	− 4
April	38	41	17½	3½	(11)	− 3
May	38	43½	14½	4	(7½)	− 5½
June	41	42	14½	2½	(10)	− 1
July	35½	45	17½	2	(10)	− 9½
August	31½	38	28	2½	(8½)	− 6½
September	33½	43	22	1½	(9½)	− 9½
October	33	39½	25½	2	(11)	− 6½
November	36½	38½	22½	2½	(9)	− 2
December	36	42½	18½	3	(10½)	− 6½
1974						
January	40	38	19	3	(10½)	2
February	39½	37½	20½	2½	(3½)	2
March	35	43	19	3	(7½)	− 8
April	33	49	15½	2½	(7)	−16
May	33	46½	17	3½	(7½)	−13½
June	35½	44	17	3½	(9)	− 8½
July	35	38	21	6	(10½)	− 3
August	35½	39½	21	4	(10)	− 4
September	37½	40½	18	4	(10½)	− 3
October	36	41½	19	3½	(5)	− 5½
November	35	46½	14½	4	(9)	−11½
December	33	47	16½	3½	(10½)	−14
1975						
January	34	48½	13	4½	(11)	−14½
February	45	41	11	3	(11)	4
March	42	44	11	3	(7)	− 2
April	43	45	10	2	(10)	− 2
May	45½	39½	11	4	(11)	6
June	44	40½	13	2½	(11)	3½
July	43	40½	12½	4	(8)	2½
August	40½	42	14	3½	(8)	− 1½
September	38½	41½	16½	3½	(10½)	− 3
October	42½	40½	13½	3½	(6)	2
November	39	44½	12½	4	(11)	− 5½
December	40½	41	14	4½	(10½)	− ½
1976						
January	40½	42	14	3½	(11)	− 1½
February	45½	40½	10½	3½	(11½)	5
March	44	41½	9½	5	(9)	2½
April	41	46½	9	3½	(8½)	− 5½
May	44	41	10½	4½	(11½)	3
June	44	40½	11	4½	(11½)	3½
July	41	41	13	5	(11)	nil
August	44	41	10	5	(12)	3
September	42½	42	11	4½	(10)	½
October	48	36½	11½	4	(13)	11½
November	55	30	11½	3½	(9)	25
December	49½	34	11½	5	(11½)	15½

PUBLIC OPINION POLLS — VOTING INTENTION (GALLUP POLL) 1945-1987 (Cont.)

Date†	C%	Lab%	L%	Others%	*Don't Know%	C Lead %
1977						
January	47	34	14½	4½	(10½)	13
February	46	33½	14	6½	(13)	12½
March	49½	33	13	4½	(10)	16½
April	49	33½	11½	6	(11½)	15½
May	53½	33	8½	5	(10)	19½
June	47½	37	10½	5	(10½)	10½
July	49	34½	10½	6	(11)	14½
August	48½	37½	9	5	(11½)	11
September	45½	41	8½	5	(8)	4½
October	45	45	8	2	(8½)	nil
November	45½	42	8½	4	(10)	3½
December	44	44½	8	3½	(9½)	— ½
1978						
January	43½	43½	8½	4½	(10)	nil
February	48	39	9	4	(8)	9
March	48	41	8	3	(9)	7
April	45½	43½	7½	3½	(10)	2
May	43½	43½	8½	4½	(9)	nil
June	45½	45½	6	3	(9)	nil
July	45	43	8½	3½	(9½)	2
August	43½	47½	6	3	(11)	— 4
September	49½	42½	6	2	(10½)	7
October	42	47½	7½	3	(8)	— 5½
November	43	48	6½	2½	(11)	— 5
December	48	42½	6	3½	(10½)	5½
1979						
January	49	41½	6	3½	(11)	7½
February	53	33	11	3	(11)	20
March	51½	37	8½	3	(11½)	14½
April	50	40	8	2	(5)	10
May	43	41	13½	2½	(5)	2
June	42	43½	12	2½	(6)	— 1½
July	41	46	11½	1½	(8)	— 5
August	41½	44	12½	2	(6½)	— 2½
September	40½	45	12	2½	(9)	— 4½
October	40½	45	12½	2	(9½)	— 4½
November	39	43½	15½	2	(8½)	— 4½
December	38	42	18	2	(7)	— 4
1980						
January	36	45	16	3	(7½)	— 9
February	37½	42	18	2½	(10)	— 4½
March	37	49½	11½	2	(6½)	—12½
April	36½	45	15	3½	(7½)	— 8½
May	39	43½	15½	2	(7½)	— 4½
June	40½	45	11½	3	(6½)	— 4½
July	40	43½	14	2½	(8)	— 3½
August	38½	44	14½	3	(11)	— 5½
September	35½	45	16½	3	(6½)	— 9½
October	40	43	14	3	(8)	— 3
November	36½	47	15	1½	(9)	—10½
December	35	47½	14½	3	(9)	—12½

PUBLIC OPINION POLLS — VOTING INTENTION (GALLUP POLL) 1945-1987 (Cont.)

Date[†]	C%	Lab%	L%[1]	Others%	*Don't Know%	C Lead %
1981						
January	33	46½	18½	2	(10)	−13½
February	36	35½	20	8½	(11½)	½
March	30	34	32	4	(11½)	− 4
April	30	34½	33	2½	(10)	− 4½
May	32	35½	29	3½	(9½)	− 3½
June	29½	37½	30½	2½	(10)	− 8
July	30	40½	26½	3	(10½)	−10½
August	28	38½	32	1	(11½)	−10½
September	32	36½	29	2½	(8½)	− 4
October	29½	28	40	2½	(9½)	1½
November	26½	29	32	2½	(9)	− 2½
December	23	23½	50½	3	(11½)	− ½
1982						
January	27½	29½	39½	3½	(9½)	− 2
February	27½	34	36	2½	(10)	− 6½
March	31½	33	31	2½	(10)	− 1½
April	31½	29	33	2½	(11)	2½
May	41½	28	29	1½	(8)	13½
June	45	25	28½	1½	(9½)	20
July	46½	27½	24	2	(7)	19
August	44½	26½	27½	1½	(10½)	18
September	44	30½	23	2½	(8½)	13½
October	40½	29	27	3½	(8½)	11½
November	42	34½	21½	2	(9½)	7½
December	41	34½	22	2½	(10)	6½
1983						
January	44	31½	22½	2	(9)	12½
February	43½	32½	22	2	(8)	11
March	39½	28½	29	3	(8)	11
April	40½	35	22½	2	(9)	5½
May	49	31½	17½	2	(5)	17½
June	45½	26½	26	2	(2)	19
July	44	28½	26	1½	(6)	15½
August	44½	25	29	1½	(6½)	19½
September	45½	24½	29	1	(6)	21
October	42	35½	20½	2	(6½)	6½
November	43½	36	19½	1	(7)	7½
December	42½	36	19½	2	(6½)	6½
1984						
January	41½	38	19½	1	(7)	3½
February	43	33½	21½	2	(6)	9½
March	41	38½	19½	1	(8)	2½
April	41	36½	20½	2	(6½)	4½
May	38½	36½	23	2	(6)	2
June	37½	38	23	1½	(8½)	− ½
July	37½	38½	22	2	(7)	− 1
August	36	39	22½	2½	(8)	− 3
September	37	36	25½	1½	(9)	1
October	44½	32	21½	2	(9)	12½
November	44½	30½	23½	1½	(8)	14
December	39½	31	27½	2	(8)	8½

PUBLIC OPINION POLLS — VOTING INTENTION (GALLUP POLL) 1945-1987 (Cont.)

Date[†]	C%	Lab%	L%[1]	Others%	*Don't Know%	C Lead %
1985						
January	39	33	25½	2½	(8)	6
February	35	32	31½	1½	(9)	− 3
March	33	39½	25½	2	(8)	− 6½
April	34	37½	26½	2	(8½)	− 3½
May	30½	34	33½	2	(8½)	− 3½
June	34½	34½	30	1	(7)	nil
July	27½	38	32½	2	(6)	−10½
August	24	40	34	2	(8)	−16
September	29	29½	39	2½	(9)	− ½
October	32	38	28	2	(9)	− 6
November	35	34	29½	1½	(7½)	1
December	33	32½	32½	2	(10½)	½
1986						
January	29½	34	35	1½	(9)	− 4½
February	29½	35½	33½	1½	(9½)	− 6
March	29½	34	34½	2	(7)	− 4½
April	28	38½	31½	2	(10½)	−10½
May	27½	37	32½	3	(7)	− 9½
June	34	39	24½	2½	(9)	− 5
July	33	38	27	2	(8½)	− 5
August	30	36½	30	3½	(8½)	− 6½
September	32½	38	27½	2	(8½)	− 5½
October	37½	37½	22	3	(6½)	nil
November	36	39½	22	2½	(9½)	− 3½
December	41	32½	23½	3	(8½)	8.5
1987						
January	34½	39½	23½	2½	(9½)	− 5
February	36	34½	27½	2	(8½)	1½
March	37½	29½	31½	1½	(8½)	8
April	40½	28	29	2½	(8)	12½
May	39	28	30	3	(6½)	11
June	41	34	23½	1½	(5½)	7
July	44½	33	20½	2	(4½)	11½
August	45½	35½	17½	1½	(7)	10
September	44	33	20	3	(6)	11
October	52	31½	13½	3	(6½)	20½
November	46½	33	17	3½	(6½)	13½
December	46½	34½	16	3	(5½)	12

[†] If there was more than one poll in a month the figures given are those of the poll published nearest to the 15th of the month.

*The voting intention figures in this table reflect the answers to the question: "If there was a General Election tomorrow, which party would you support?", *including* the answers of the "don't knows" to an additional question: "Which would you be most inclined to vote for?", but *excluding* those who remain "don't knows", even after the incliner question. The column headed "Don't Know" shows the percentage of the total sample answering "Don't Know" to the incliner question, *excluded* in computing the figures in the four previous columns.

[1] SDP/Liberal Alliance from March 1981.

Source: Social Surveys (Gallup Poll) Ltd.

Table 9.02 PUBLIC OPINION POLLS – VOTING INTENTION (GENERAL ELECTIONS) 1945-1987

This table shows the errors in the final predictions of the major public opinion polls forecasting the results of General Elections since 1945. As surveys are not normally carried out in Northern Ireland (Marplan in 1970 did cover Northern Ireland but their forecast has been adjusted to provide only Great Britain figures for the sake of uniformity) the figures relate only to Great Britain.

Polls carried out by Business Decisions in 1974 (both elections), Research Services in 1951, 1964, 1966 and 1979 and the *Daily Express* from 1950-64 have been omitted for reasons of space but details appeared in the previous (4th edition) of this book, pp. 117-119.

Telephone polls carried out for the *Sun* in 1983 and 1987 by Audience Selection Limited have not been included.

The final opinion poll findings were published in the following newspapers:

Gallup: *News Chronicle* (1945-59); *Daily Telegraph* (1964-)
Harris: *Daily Express* (1970-74); *The Observer* (1983). The 1987 poll was carried out for TV-am.
Marplan: *The Times* (1970); *Birmingham Evening Mail* (February 1974); *The Sun* (October 1974 and 1979); *Guardian* (1983-).
MORI: *Evening Standard* (1979-83); *The Times* (1987).
NOP: *Daily Mail* (1959-79); Northcliffe Newspapers Group, 1983; *The Independent* (1987).
ORC: *Evening Standard.*

+ indicates an overestimate   − indicates an underestimate

Election	%	Gallup	Harris	MORI	Marplan	NOP	ORC
1945							
C	39.3	+1.7					
Lab	48.8	−1.8	NO	NO	NO	NO	NO
L	9.2	+1.3	POLL	POLL	POLL	POLL	POLL
Others	2.7	−1.2					
1950							
C	43.0	+0.5					
Lab	46.8	−1.8	NO	NO	NO	NO	NO
L	9.3	+1.2	POLL	POLL	POLL	POLL	POLL
Others	0.9	+0.1					
1951							
C	47.8	+1.7					
Lab	49.3	−2.3	NO	NO	NO	NO	NO
L	2.6	+0.2	POLL	POLL	POLL	POLL	POLL
Others	0.3						
1955							
C	49.3	+1.7					
Lab	47.3	+0.2	NO	NO	NO	NO	NO
L	2.8	−1.3	POLL	POLL	POLL	POLL	POLL
Others	0.6	−					
1959							
C	48.8	−0.3				−0.8	
Lab	44.6	+1.9	NO	NO	NO	−0.5	NO
L	6.0	−1.5	POLL	POLL	POLL	+1.3[1]	POLL
Others	0.6	−0.1				−	
1964							
C	42.9	+1.6				+1.4	
Lab	44.8	+1.7	NO	NO	NO	+2.6	NO
L	11.4	−2.9	POLL	POLL	POLL	−3.5	POLL
Others	0.9	−0.4				−0.5	

PUBLIC OPINION POLLS—VOTING INTENTION (GENERAL ELECTIONS) 1945-1987 (Cont.)

Election	%	Gallup	Harris	MORI	Marplan	NOP	ORC
1966							
C	41.5	−1.5				+0.1	
Lab	48.8	+2.2	NO	NO	NO	+1.8	NO
L	8.6	−0.6	POLL	POLL	POLL	−1.2	POLL
Others	1.1	−0.1				−0.7	
1970							
C	46.2	−4.2	−0.2		−5.2	−2.1	+0.3
Lab	43.9	+5.1	+4.1	NO	+6.7	+4.3	+1.6
L	7.6	−0.1	−2.6	POLL	−0.5	−1.2	−1.1
Others	2.3	−0.8	−1.3		−1.0	−1.0	−0.8
1974(F)							
C	38.8	+0.7	+1.4	NO	−2.3	+0.7	+0.9
Lab	38.0	−0.5	−2.8	NO	−3.5	−2.5	−1.3
L	19.8	+0.7	+2.2	POLL	+5.2	+2.2	+1.4
Others	3.4	−0.9	−0.8		+0.6	−0.4	−1.0
1974(O)							
C	36.7	−0.7	−2.1		−3.4	−5.7	−2.3
Lab	40.2	+1.3	+2.8	NO	+2.8	+5.3	+1.6
L	18.8	+0.2	+0.5	POLL	+0.7	+0.7	+0.6
Others	4.3	−0.8	−1.2		−0.1	−0.3	+0.1
1979							
C	44.9	−1.9		+0.1	+0.1	+1.1	
Lab	37.8	+3.2	NO	−0.8	+0.7	+1.2	NOW
L	14.1	−0.6	POLL	+0.9	−0.6	−1.6	HARRIS
Others	3.2	−0.7		−0.2	−0.2	−0.7	
1983							
C	43.5	+2.0	+3.5	+0.5	+2.5	+3.5	
Lab	28.3	−1.8	−3.3	−0.3	−2.3	−3.3	NOW
L[2]	26.0	0.0	0.0	0.0	0.0	0.0	HARRIS
Others	2.2	−0.2	−0.2	−0.2	−0.2	−0.2	
1987							
C	43.3	−2.3	−1.3	+0.7	−1.3	−1.3	
Lab	31.5	+2.5	+3.5	+0.5	+3.5	+3.5	NOW
L[2]	23.1	+0.4	−2.1	−1.1	−2.1	−2.1	HARRIS
Others	2.1	−0.6	−0.1	−0.1	−0.1	−0.1	

[1] These polls published a combined forecast of the Liberal and Others vote. This figure is therefore the error in prediction of the Liberal and Others vote combined.
[2] SDP/Liberal Alliance.

Table 9.03 PUBLIC OPINION POLLS — WINNER AND LEAD (GENERAL ELECTIONS) 1945-1987

Election	Party and Lead %		Gallup	Harris	MORI	Marplan	NOP	ORC	Average error
1945	Lab	9.5	−3.5						3.5
1950	Lab	3.8	−2.3						2.3
1951	Lab	1.5[1]	−4.0						4.0
1955	C	2.0	+1.5						1.5
1959	C	4.2	−2.2				− 0.3		1.3
1964	Lab	1.9	−0.1				+ 1.2		0.7
1966	Lab	7.3	+3.7				+ 1.7		2.7
1970	C	2.3	−9.3	−4.3		−11.9	− 6.4	−1.3	6.6
1974(F)	C	0.8[2]	+1.2	+4.4		+ 1.2	+ 3.2	+2.2	2.4
1974(O)	Lab	3.5	+2.0	+4.9		+ 6.2	−11.0	+3.9	5.6
1979	C	7.1	−5.1		+0.9	− 0.6	− 0.1		1.7
1983	C	15.2	+3.8	+6.8	+0.8	+ 4.8	+ 6.8		4.6
1987	C	11.8	−4.8	−4.8	+0.2	− 4.8	− 4.8		3.9
Average error on lead			**3.3**	**5.0**	**0.6**	**4.9**	**3.9**	**2.5**	

[1] Labour won 1.5% more votes in Great Britain than the Conservatives but the latter obtained a majority in the House of Commons.
[2] Conservatives won 0.8% more votes in Great Britain than Labour but the latter formed a minority Government.

Table 9.04 PUBLIC OPINION POLLS — OVERALL RECORD (GENERAL ELECTIONS) 1945-1987

Poll	No. of elections covered	Minimum % error[1]	Maximum % error[1]	Average % error[2]
Gallup Poll	13	0.2	5.1	1.3
National Opinion Polls	9	0.1	5.7	1.7
Marplan	6	0.1	6.7	1.9
Louis Harris	5	0.2	4.1	1.8
Market and Opinion Research International	3	0.1	0.9	0.5
Opinion Research Centre	3	0.3	2.3	1.1

[1] These figures are based on the forecasts for Conservatives and Labour only.
[2] These figures are based on the forecasts for Conservative, Labour, Liberal (SDP/Liberal Alliance 1983-87) and Others.

Table 10.01 WOMEN CANDIDATES—GENERAL ELECTIONS 1918-1987

Election	C	Lab	L[1]	Com	NF	PC	SNP	Others	Total	% of total candidates
1918	1	4	4	—	—	—	—	8	17	1.0
1922	5	10	16	0	—	—	—	2	33	2.3
1923	7	14	12	0	—	—	—	1	34	2.4
1924	12	22	6	0	—	—	—	1	41	2.9
1929	10	30	25	3	—	0	0	1	69	4.0
1931	16	36[2]	5	2	—	0	1	2	62	4.8
1935	19	33	11	0	—	0	0	4	67	5.0
1945	14	41	20	2	—	1	0	9	87	5.2
1950	29[3]	42	45	9	—	0	0	2	127[3]	6.8
1951	25	41	11	0	—	0	0	0	77	5.6
1955	33	43	14	1	—	1	0	0	92	6.5
1959	28	36	16	1	—	0	0	0	81	5.3
1964	24	33	24	4	—	1	0	4	90	5.1
1966	21	30	20	6	—	0	0	4	81	4.7
1970	26	29	23	6	1	0	10	4	99	5.4
1974(F)	33	40	40	3	3	2	8	14	143	6.7
1974(O)	30	50	49	2	5	1	8	16	161	7.1
1979	31	52	52	4	36	1	6	34	216	8.4
1983	40	78	75	5	6	6	9	61	280	10.9
1987	46	92	106	4	0	9	6	66	329	14.2

[1] SDP/Liberal Alliance 1983-87.

[2] Including 6 unendorsed.

[3] Miss Florence Horsbrugh (C) is counted twice in this total. She was defeated at Midlothian and Peeblesshire but subsequently elected for Manchester, Moss Side where polling had been postponed due to the death of the Conservative candidate.

Table 10.02 WOMEN ELECTED—GENERAL ELECTIONS 1918-1987

Election	C	Lab	L[1]	Com	NF	PC	SNP	Others	Total	% of total MPs
1918	0	0	0	—	—	—	—	1[2]	1	0.1
1922	1	0	1	0	—	—	—	0	2	0.3
1923	3	3	2	0	—	—	—	0	8	1.3
1924	3	1	0	0	—	—	—	0	4	0.7
1929	3	9	1	0	—	0	0	1	14	2.3
1931	13	0	1	0	—	0	0	1	15	2.4
1935	6	1	1	0	—	0	0	1	9	1.5
1945	1	21	1	0	—	0	0	1	24	3.8
1950	6	14	1	0	—	0	0	0	21	3.4
1951	6	11	0	0	—	0	0	0	17	2.7
1955	10	14	0	0	—	0	0	0	24	3.8
1959	12	13	0	0	—	0	0	0	25	4.0
1964	11	18	0	0	—	0	0	0	29	4.6
1966	7	19	0	0	—	0	0	0	26	4.1
1970	15	10	0	0	0	0	0	1[3]	26	4.1
1974(F)	9	13	0	0	0	0	1	0	23	3.6
1974(O)	7	18	0	0	0	0	2	0	27	4.3
1979	8	11	0	0	0	0	0	0	19	3.0
1983	13	10	0	0	0	0	0	0	23	3.5
1987	17	21	2	0	0	0	1	0	41	6.3

[1] SDP/Liberal Alliance 1983-87.
[2] Countess Markievicz (SF) who was elected for Dublin, St. Patrick's. She did not take her seat in the House of Commons.
[3] Miss B.J. Devlin (Mid-Ulster—Unity).

Table 10.03 WOMEN CANDIDATES—BY-ELECTIONS 1918-1987

From	C	Lab	L[1]	Com	NF	PC	SNP	Others	Total	% of total candidates
1918-22	1	2	1	0	—	—	—	0	4	1.8
1922-23	1	0	0	0	—	—	—	0	1	2.4
1923-24	0	0	0	0	—	—	—	0	0	—
1924-29	3	7	2	0	—	0	0	0	12	6.6
1929-31	1	3	2	1	—	0	1	1	9	9.4
1931-35	0	4	0	0	—	0	0	1	5	3.4
1935-45	5	4	2	1	—	0	0	13	25	5.8
1945-50	1	1	0	0	—	0	1	3	6	4.1
1950-51	0	0	1	0	—	0	0	0	1	2.8
1951-55	3	5	0	0	—	0	0	0	8	7.3
1955-59	4	3	2	0	—	1	0	1	11	8.0
1959-64	4	1	0	0	—	0	0	1	6	2.7
1964-66	0	0	2	0	—	0	0	0	2	4.1
1966-70	1	3	3	1	0	0	1	1	10	7.1
1970-74(F)	0	3	0	0	0	0	1	3	7	5.8
1974(F)- 1974(O)	0	0	0	0	0	0	0	0	0	—
1974(O)-79	1	2	3	0	3	0	2	6	17	9.7
1979-83	2	3	1	0	0	0	0	6	12	8.0
1983-87	2	6	3	1	0	1	0	8	21	13.2

[1] SDP/Liberal Alliance 1983-87.

Table 10.04 WOMEN ELECTED—BY-ELECTIONS 1918-1987

From	C	Lab	L[1]	Com	NF	PC	SNP	Others	Total	% of MPs elected
1918-22	1[2]	0	1[3]	0	—	—	—	0	2	1.9
1922-23	1	0	0	0	—	—	—	0	1	6.3
1923-24	0	0	0	0	—	—	—	0	0	—
1924-29	1	4	1	0	—	0	0	0	6	9.5
1929-31	0	2	0	0	—	0	0	0	2	5.6
1931-35	0	0	0	0	—	0	0	0	0	—
1935-45	3	3	0	0	—	0	0	0	6	2.7
1945-50	1	1	0	0	—	0	0	0	2	3.8
1950-51	0	0	0	0	—	0	0	0	0	—
1951-55	2	2	0	0	—	0	0	0	4	8.3
1955-59	2	2	0	0	—	0	0	0	4	7.7
1959-64	1	0	0	0	—	0	0	0	1	1.6
1964-66	0	0	0	0	—	0	0	0	0	—
1966-70	0	0	0	0	0	0	1	1[4]	2	5.3
1970-74(F)	0	1	0	0	0	0	1	0	2	6.7
1974(F)-1974(O)	0	0	0	0	0	0	0	0	0	—
1974(O)-79	0	1	0	0	0	0	0	0	1	3.3
1979-83	1	2	1	0	0	0	0	0	4	20.0
1983-87	1	2	2	0	0	0	0	0	5	16.1

[1] SDP/Liberal Alliance 1983-87.

[2] Viscountess Astor, the first woman to sit in the House of Commons. She was returned for Plymouth, Sutton at a by-election on November 15, 1919. The by-election was caused by the succession of her husband to the Peerage.

[3] Mrs. Margaret Wintringham, the first Liberal woman to be elected. She was returned for Lincolnshire, Louth at a by-election on September 22, 1921. The by-election was caused by the death of her husband.

[4] Miss B.J. Devlin (Mid-Ulster—Unity).

Table 10.05 **WOMEN MEMBERS OF PARLIAMENT 1918-1987**

The following is a complete list of women elected to the House of Commons since 1918 showing their party and period of service. An asterisk * denotes a member of the present Parliament.

*Abbott, Miss D.J. (Lab), 1987-
Adamson, Mrs. J.L. (Lab), 1938-46
Apsley, Lady (C), 1943-45
*Armstrong, Miss H.J. (Lab), 1987-
Astor, Viscountess[1] (C), 1919-45
Atholl, Duchess of (C), 1923-38

Bacon, Miss A.M. (Lab), 1945-70
Bain, Mrs. M.A., see Ewing, Mrs. M.A.
*Barnes, Mrs. R.S. (SDP), 1987-
*Beckett, Mrs. M.M. (Lab), 1974(O)-79 and 1983-
Bentham, Dr. Ethel (Lab), 1929-31
Bondfield, Miss M.G. (Lab), 1923-24 and 1926-31
*Boothroyd, Miss B. (Lab), 1973-
*Bottomley, Mrs. V.H.B.M. (C), 1984-
Braddock, Mrs. E.M. (Lab), 1945-70
Burton, Miss E.F. (Lab), 1950-59
Butler, Mrs. J.S. (Lab), 1955-79

Castle, Mrs. B.A. (Lab), 1945-79
Cazalet, Miss T., see Cazalet-Keir, Mrs. T.
Cazalet-Keir, Mrs. T. (C), 1931-45
*Chalker, Mrs. L. (C), 1974(F)-
*Clwyd, Miss A. (Lab), 1984-
Colman, Miss G.M. (Lab), 1945-50
Colquhoun, Mrs. M.M. (Lab), 1974(F)-79
Copeland, Mrs. I. (C), 1931-35
Corbet, Mrs. F.K. (Lab), 1945-74(F)
Cullen, Mrs. A. (Lab), 1948-69
*Currie, Mrs. E. (C), 1983-

Dalton, Mrs. F.R. (Lab), February-May 1929
Davidson, Viscountess (C), 1937-59
Devlin, Miss B.J. see McAliskey, Mrs. B.J.
*Dunwoody, Hon. Mrs. G.P. (Lab), 1966-70 and 1974(F)-

Emmet, Hon. Mrs. E.V.E. (C), 1955-65
*Ewing, Mrs. M.A. (SNP), 1974(O)-79 and 1987-
Ewing, Mrs. W.M. (SNP), 1967-70 and 1974(F)-79

Faith, Mrs. I.S. (C), 1979-83
*Fenner, Mrs. P.E. (C), 1970-74(O) and 1979-
Fisher, Mrs. D.M.G. (Lab), 1970-74(F)
*Fookes, Miss J.E. (C), 1970-
Ford, Mrs. P. (C), 1953-55
*Fyfe, Mrs. C.M. (Lab), 1987-

Gammans, Lady (C), 1957-66
Ganley, Mrs. C.S. (Lab), 1945-51
*Golding, Mrs. L. (Lab), 1986-
*Gordon, Mrs. M. (Lab), 1987-
*Gorman, Mrs. T.E. (C), 1987-
Gould, Mrs. B.A. (Lab), 1945-50
Grant, Lady, see Tweedsmuir, Lady
Graves, Miss F.M. (C), 1931-35

Hall, Miss J.V. (C), 1970-74(F)
Hamilton, Mrs. M.A. (Lab), 1929-31

Hardie, Mrs. A. (Lab), 1937-45
*Harman, Miss H.R. (Lab), 1982-
Hart, Mrs. J.C.M. (Lab), 1959-87
Havie Anderson, Miss M.B. (C), 1959-79
Hayman, Mrs. H.V. (Lab), 1974(O)-79
Herbison, Miss M.M. (Lab), 1945-70
*Hicks, Mrs. M.P. (C), 1987-
Hill, Mrs. E. (C), 1950-64
Holt, Miss M. (C), 1970-74(F)
Hornsby-Smith, Dame Patricia (C), 1950-66 and 1970-74(F)
Horsbrugh, Dame Florence (C), 1931-45 and 1950-59

Iveagh, Countess of (C), 1927-35

Jackson, Miss M.M., see Beckett, Mrs. M.M.
Jeger, Mrs. L.M. (Lab), 1953-59 and 1964-79
Jewson, Miss D. (Lab), 1923-24

Kellett, Mrs. M.E., see Kellett-Bowman, Mrs. M.E.
*Kellett-Bowman, Mrs. M.E. (C), 1970-
Kerr, Mrs. A.P. (Lab), 1964-70
*Knight, Mrs. J.C.J. (C), 1966-

Lawrence, Miss A.S. (Lab), 1923-24 and 1926-31
Lee, Miss J. (Lab), 1929-31 and 1945-70
*Lestor, Miss J. (Lab), 1966-83 and 1987-
Lloyd George, Lady Megan (L), 1929-51 and (Lab), 1957-66

McAliskey, Mrs. B.J.[2] (Unity then Ind Soc), 1969-74(F)
McAlister, Mrs. M.A. (Lab), 1958-59
McCurley, Mrs. A.A. (C), 1983-87
Macdonald, Mrs. M. (SNP), 1973-74(F)
McDonald, Miss O.A. (Lab), 1976-87
McElhone, Mrs. H.M. (Lab), 1982-83
McKay, Mrs. M. (Lab), 1964-70
McLaughlin, Mrs. F.P.A. (C), 1955-64
*Mahon, Mrs. A. (Lab), 1987-
Mann, Mrs. J. (Lab), 1945-59
Manning, Mrs. E.L. (Lab), February-October 193? and 1945-50
Markievicz, Countess[3] (SF), 1918-22
Maynard, Miss V.J. (Lab), 1974(O)-87
*Michie, Mrs. J.R. (L), 1987-
Middleton, Mrs. L.A. (Lab), 1945-51
Middleweek, Miss H.V., see Hayman, Mrs. H.V.
Miller, Mrs. M. (Lab), 1974(O)-77
Monks, Mrs. C.M. (C), 1970-74(F)
Mosley, Lady Cynthia (Lab), 1929-31
*Mowlam, Miss M. (Lab), 1987-

Nichol, Mrs. M.E. (Lab), 1945-50
*Nicholson, Miss E.H. (C), 1987-
Noel-Buxton, Lady (Lab), 1930-31 and 1945-50

Oppenheim, Mrs. S. (C), 1970-87

WOMEN MEMBERS OF PARLIAMENT 1918-1987 (Cont.)

Paton, Mrs. F.B. (Lab), 1945-50
*Peacock, Mrs. E.J. (C), 1983-
Phillipson, Mrs. M. (C), 1923-29
Phillips, Dr. Marion (Lab), 1929-31
Pickford, Hon. Mary A. (C), 1931-34
Picton-Turberville, Miss E. (Lab), 1929-31
Pike, Miss I.M.P. (C), 1956-74(F)
Pitt, Dame Edith (C), 1953-64
*Primarolo, Mrs. D. (Lab), 1987-

Quennell, Miss J.M. (C), 1960-74(O)
*Quin, Miss J.G. (Lab), 1987-

Rathbone, Mrs. B.F., see Wright, Mrs. B.F.
Rathbone, Miss E.F. (Ind), 1929-46
Rees, Mrs. D.M. (Lab), 1950-51
*Richardson, Miss J. (Lab), 1974(F)-
Ridealgh, Mrs. M. (Lab), 1945-50
*Roe, Mrs. M.A. (C), 1983-
*Ruddock, Mrs. J.M. (Lab), 1987-
*Rumbold, Mrs. A.C.R. (C), 1982-
Runciman, Mrs. H. (L), 1928-29
Runge, Mrs. N.C. (C), 1931-35

Shaw, Mrs. C.M. (Lab), 1945-46
Shaw, Mrs. H.B. (C), 1931-45
*Shephard, Mrs. G.P. (C), 1987-
Shields, Mrs. E.L. (L), 1986-87
*Short, Miss C. (Lab), 1983-
Short, Mrs. R. (Lab), 1964-87
Slater, Mrs. H. (Lab), 1953-66
Summerskill, Dr. Edith (Lab), 1938-61
Summerskill, Dr. Hon. Shirley C.W. (Lab), 1964-83

Tate, Mrs. M.C. (C), 1931-45
*Taylor, Mrs. W.A. (Lab), 1974(O)-83 and 1987-
Terrington, Lady (L), 1923-24
*Thatcher, Mrs. M.H. (C), 1959-
Tweedsmuir, Lady (C), 1946-66

Vickers, Dame Joan (C), 1955-74(F)

*Walley, Miss J.L. (Lab), 1987-
Ward, Dame Irene (C), 1931-45 and 1950-74(F)
Ward, Mrs. S.A. (C), 1931-35
White, Mrs. E.L. (Lab), 1950-70
*Widdecombe, Miss A.N. (C), 1987-
Wilkinson, Miss E.C. (Lab), 1924-31 and 1935-47
Williams, Mrs. S.V.T.B. (Lab), 1964-79 and (SDP), 1981-83
Wills, Mrs. E.A. (Lab), 1945-50
*Winterton, Mrs. J.A. (C), 1983-
Wintringham, Mrs. M. (L), 1921-24
*Wise, Mrs. A. (Lab), 1974(F)-79 and 1987-
Wright, Mrs. B.F. (C), 1941-45
Wright, Miss S.R.R. (Lab), 1979-83

[1] The first woman to take her seat (December 1, 1919) in the House of Commons.
[2] The youngest woman to have been elected. Miss Devlin (as she was at the time) was twenty-one years of age and had been born on April 23, 1947. She was elected on April 18, 1969.
[3] The first woman to be elected (December 28, 1918) but she did not take her seat in the House of Commons.

Table 11.01 EUROPEAN ELECTION 1979

	Total votes	% share of total votes	Candidates	Elected	Forfeited Deposits[1]
ENGLAND					
C	5,817,992	53.4	66	54	0
L	1,444,204	13.2	66	0	34
Lab	3,536,261	32.6	66	12	0
Others	86,310	0.8	21	0	21
Total	**10,884,767**	**100.0**	**219**	**66**	**55**
WALES					
C	259,729	36.6	4	1	0
L	67,962	9.6	4	0	4
Lab	294,978	41.5	4	3	0
PC	83,399	11.7	4	0	3
Others	4,008	0.6	2	0	2
Total	**710,076**	**100.0**	**18**	**4**	**9**
SCOTLAND					
C	430,772	33.7	8	5	0
L	178,433	13.9	8	0	5
Lab	421,968	33.0	8	2	1
SNP	247,836	19.4	8	1	0
Others	–	–	0	–	–
Total	**1,279,009**	**100.0**	**32**	**8**	**6**
NORTHERN IRELAND[2]					
UDUP	170,688	29.8	1	1	0
UPNI	3,712	0.6	1	0	1
UU	125,169	21.9	2	1	0
Others	38,198	6.7	1	0	0
(Total 'Loyalist')	(337,767)	(59.0)	(5)	(2)	(1)
APNI	39,026	6.8	1	0	0
L	932	0.2	1	0	1
Rep	4,418	0.8	2	0	2
SDLP	140,622	24.6	1	1	0
Others	49,474	8.6	3	0	2
Total	**572,239**	**100.0**	**13**	**3**	**6**
UNITED KINGDOM					
C	6,508,493	48.4	78	60	0
L	1,690,599	12.6	78	0	42
Lab	4,253,207	31.6	78	17	1
PC	83,399	0.6	4	0	3
SNP	247,836	1.9	8	1	0
Others	662,557	4.9	36[3]	3[4]	29
Total	**13,446,091**	**100.0**	**282**	**81**	**75**

[1] The deposit of £600 was forfeited if a candidate in Great Britain failed to poll more than one-eighth of the total votes cast, exclusive of spoilt papers. In Northern Ireland the deposit was forfeited if the number of votes credited to any candidate at any stage of the count did not exceed one-quarter of the "quota" figure (i.e. the minimum number of votes required to secure election). The "quota" was calculated by dividing the number of valid ballot-papers by one more than the number of seats to be filled and increasing the resulting figure by one.

[2] Elections were conducted by the single transferable vote system of proportional representation. Figures given are of first preference votes.

[3] Including all candidates in Northern Ireland and 5 UACM, 3 EP, 1 EFP, 1 IMG, 1 MK, 1 WR & EFP.

[4] The three members for the Northern Ireland constituency (1 SDLP, 1 UDUP, 1 UU).

Table 11.02   MISCELLANEOUS STATISTICS 1979

BY-ELECTION

1979	T'out	C%	Lab%	L%	Others%
London, South-West (20/9)	19.4	41.2	32.7	23.9	2.2

ELECTORATE AND TURNOUT

	Total Electorate	Turnout %
ENGLAND	34,261,421	31.8
WALES	2,063,898	34.4
SCOTLAND	3,801,010	33.6
N. IRELAND	1,028,837	55.6
UNITED KINGDOM	**41,155,166**	**32.7**

The Electoral Register was eight months old.

CANDIDATES' EXPENSES

	£		£
Agents	124,635	Rooms	23,279
Clerks	20,494	Miscellaneous	71,600
Printing	1,066,327	Personal Expenses	45,993
Meetings	12,488		

Total £1,364,816   Average £4,840

The maximum a candidate could spend was limited to £5,000 plus 2p per elector. Personal expenses were excluded from this limit.

Note: For an explanation of the headings used above see footnotes [1] to [7], Table 3.02.

LIBERALS AND NATIONALISTS IN SECOND PLACE
Nine Liberals came second in seats won by eight Conservatives and one Scottish Nationalist.

MINORITY VOTES
Of the 79 constituencies, 27 (34.6%) were won on a minority vote. The party totals were Conservative 16; Labour 10; Scottish Nationalist 1.

PARTY VOTES AS PERCENTAGES OF THE ELECTORATE

C	Lab	L	Others	Non-voters
15.8	10.4	4.1	2.4	67.3

PARTY VOTES AS PERCENTAGES OF TWO-PARTY VOTES

C	Lab
60.5	39.5

MISCELLANEOUS STATISTICS 1979 (Cont.)

PARTY VOTES AS PERCENTAGES OF THREE-PARTY VOTES

C	Lab	L
52.3	34.1	13.6

POLLING DISTRICTS AND STATIONS

Polling Districts: 32,400   Polling Stations: 46,477

POSTAL BALLOT PAPERS

	No. of postal ballot papers issued	No. of covering envelopes returned before close of poll	No. rejected[1]	No. of postal ballot papers included at the start of the count
ENGLAND	657,901	430,987	12,857	418,130
WALES	55,930	36,888	1,711	35,177
SCOTLAND	75,003	48,531	1,375	47,156
N. IRELAND	39,733	33,179	912	32,267
UNITED KINGDOM	828,567	549,585	16,855	532,730

[1] Number of cases in which the covering envelope or its contents were marked "empty", "rejected", "declaration rejected" or "vote rejected".

The number of issued postal ballot papers as a percentage of the total electorate was 2.0%.
The number returned as a percentage of the number issued was 66.3%.
The number of covering envelopes rejected as a percentage of the number returned was 3.1%.
The number included at the start of the count as a percentage of the total poll was 4.0%.

RETURNING OFFICERS' EXPENSES

Total: £11,260,618   Average per constituency: £142,539

The cost of the free delivery of election addresses, poll-cards and postal ballot-papers (which the Post Office recovers from the Treasury) was £3,673,634.

SPOILT BALLOT PAPERS

	Want of official mark	Voting for more than one candidate	Writing or mark by which voter could be identified	Unmarked or void for uncertainty	Total	Average per constituency
ENGLAND	1,593	8,876	4,986	14,140	29,595	448
WALES	274	1,737	209	646	2,866	717
SCOTLAND	294	370	76	1,258	1,998	333
N. IRELAND	357	12,084	13	1,320	13,774	13,774
UNITED KINGDOM	2,518	23,067	5,284	17,364	48,233	611

SPONSORSHIP OF LABOUR CANDIDATES AND MEPs

Of the 78 candidates, four were sponsored by the Co-operative Party of whom two were elected. The remaining 74 candidates were sponsored by European Selection Organisations (amalgamations of Constituency Labour Parties).

MISCELLANEOUS STATISTICS 1979 (Cont.)

TYPES OF CONTESTS
Of the 78 single-member constituencies, 48 were contested by three candidates; 26 by four candidates; three by five candidates and one by six candidates.

TIME-TABLE
Election date announced: April 7, 1978
Nominations closed: May 12, 1979
Polling day: Thursday, June 7, 1979
Results declared: 49 constituencies overnight June 10/11; 29 on June 11; one (Northern Ireland) on June 12.
Parliament assembled: July 17, 1979

WOMEN CANDIDATES AND MEPs
Of the total candidates 29 (10.3%) were women. The party totals were: Conservative 10; Labour 8; Liberal 8; Independent 2, Scottish Nationalist 1.

Of the total MEPs 11 (13.6%) were women. The party totals were: Conservative 6; Labour 4; Scottish Nationalist 1.

Table 11.03 EUROPEAN ELECTION 1984

	Total votes	% share of total votes	Candidates	Elected	Forfeited Deposits[1]
ENGLAND					
C	4,879,964	43.7	66	42	0
Lab	3,963,213	35.4	66	24	0
L	1,206,908	10.8	33	0	1
SDP	1,035,998	9.3	33	0	2
(Total L/SDP)	(2,242,906)	(20.1)	(66)	(0)	(3)
Others	88,705	0.8	24	0	24
Total	**11,174,788**	**100.0**	**222**	**66**	**27**
WALES					
C	214,086	25.4	4	1	0
Lab	375,982	44.5	4	3	0
L	61,756	7.3	2	0	0
SDP	85,191	10.1	2	0	0
(Total L/SDP)	(146,947)	(17.4)	(4)	(0)	(0)
PC	103,031	12.2	4	0	2
Others	4,266	0.5	1	0	1
Total	**844,312**	**100.0**	**17**	**4**	**3**
SCOTLAND					
C	332,771	25.7	8	2	0
Lab	526,066	40.7	8	5	0
L	89,481	6.9	4	0	1
SDP	112,301	8.7	4	0	0
(Total L/SDP)	(201,782)	(15.6)	(8)	(0)	(1)
SNP	230,594	17.8	8	1	2
Others	2,560	0.2	1	0	1
Total	**1,293,773**	**100.0**	**33**	**8**	**4**
NORTHERN IRELAND[2]					
UDUP	230,251	33.6	1	1	0
UPUP	20,092	2.9	1	0	1
UU	147,169	21.5	1	1	0
(Total 'Loyalist')	(397,512)	(58.0)	(3)	(2)	(1)
APNI	34,046	5.0	1	0	1
NIEP	2,172	0.3	1	0	1
SDLP	151,399	22.1	1	1	0
SF	91,476	13.3	1	0	0
TWP	8,712	1.3	1	0	1
Total	**685,317**	**100.0**	**8**	**3**	**4**
UNITED KINGDOM					
C	5,426,821	38.8	78	45	0
L	1,358,145	9.7	39	0	2
SDP	1,233,490	8.8	39	0	2
(Total L/SDP)	(2,591,635)	(18.5)	(78)	(0)	(4)
Lab	4,865,261	34.8	78	32	0
PC	103,031	0.7	4	0	2
SNP	230,594	1.6	8	1	2
Others	780,848	5.6	34[3]	3[4]	30
Total	**13,998,190**	**100.0**	**280**	**81**	**38**

EUROPEAN ELECTION 1984 (Cont.)

[1] The deposit of £600 was forfeited if a candidate in Great Britain failed to poll more than one-eighth of the total votes cast, exclusive of spoilt papers. In Northern Ireland the deposit was forfeited if the number of votes credited to any candidate at any stage of the count did not exceed one-quarter of the "quota" figure (i.e. the minimum number of votes required to secure election). The "quota" was calculated by dividing the number of valid ballot-papers by one more than the number of seats to be filled and increasing the resulting figure by one.

[2] Elections were conducted by the single transferable vote system of proportional representation. Figures given are of first preference votes.

[3] Including all candidates in Northern Ireland and 15 EP, 1 CNP, 1 WR.

[4] The three members for the Northern Ireland constituency (1 SDLP, 1 UDUP, 1 UU).

Table 11.04 MISCELLANEOUS STATISTICS 1984

BY-ELECTION

	T'out	Lab%	C%	L%
1987				
Midlands West (5/3)	28.6	39.2	36.5	24.3

ELECTORATE AND TURNOUT

	Total Electorate	Turnout %
ENGLAND	35,392,982	31.6
WALES	2,124,967	39.7
SCOTLAND	3,911,128	33.1
N. IRELAND	1,064,045	64.4
UNITED KINGDOM	**42,493,122**	**32.9**

The Electoral Register was eight months old.

CANDIDATES' EXPENSES

	£		£
Agents	180,773	Rooms	51,784
Clerks	28,223	Miscellaneous	186,943
Printing	1,819,284	Personal Expenses	69,427
Meetings	22,791		

Total £2,359,225   Average £8,426

The maximum a candidate could spend was limited to £8,000 plus 3.5p per elector. Personal expenses were excluded from this limit.

Note: For an explanation of the headings used above see footnotes [1] to [7], Table 3.02.

LIBERALS AND NATIONALISTS IN SECOND PLACE

Seven Liberals and six Social Democratic Party candidates came second in seats won by Conservatives. One Scottish Nationalist came second in a seat won by Labour.

MINORITY VOTES

Of the 79 constituencies, 43 (54.4%) were won on a minority vote. The party totals were Conservative 25; Labour 17 and Scottish Nationalist 1.

PARTY VOTES AS PERCENTAGE OF THE ELECTORATE

C	Lab	L/SDP	Others	Non-voters
12.8	11.4	6.1	2.6	67.1

PARTY VOTES AS A PERCENTAGE OF TWO-PARTY VOTES

C	Lab
52.7	47.3

MISCELLANEOUS STATISTICS 1984 (Cont.)
PARTY VOTES AS PERCENTAGES OF THREE-PARTY VOTES

C	Lab	L/SDP
42.1	37.8	20.1

POLLING DISTRICTS AND STATIONS

Polling Districts: 33,579   Polling Stations: 43,916

POSTAL BALLOT PAPERS

	No. of postal ballot papers issued	No. of covering envelopes returned before close of poll	No. rejected[1]	No. of postal ballot papers included at the start of the count
ENGLAND	474,654	290,082	14,825	275,257
WALES	37,729	23,536	2,066	21,470
SCOTLAND	42,138	24,482	916	23,566
N. IRELAND	31,791	27,176	1,122	26,054
UNITED KINGDOM	**586,312**	**365,276**	**18,929**	**346,347**

[1] Number of cases in which the covering envelope or its contents were marked "empty", "rejected", "declaration rejected" or "vote rejected".

The number of issued postal ballot papers as a percentage of the total electorate was 1.4%.
The number returned as a percentage of the number issued was 62.3%.
The number of covering envelopes rejected as a percentage of the number returned was 5.2%.
The number included at the start of the count as a percentage of the total poll was 2.5%.

RETURNING OFFICERS' EXPENSES

Total: £18,694,392   Average per constituency: £236,638

The cost of the free delivery of election addresses, poll-cards and postal ballot-papers (which the Post Office recovers from the Treasury) was £6,937,506.

SPOILT BALLOT PAPERS

	Want of official mark	Voting for more than one candidate	Writing or mark by which voter could be identified	Unmarked or void for uncertainty	Total	Average per constituency
ENGLAND	922	8,067	2,206	9,923	21,118	320
WALES	204	1,449	118	536	2,307	577
SCOTLAND	358	394	189	748	1,689	211
N. IRELAND	166	1,757	38	9,593	11,654	11,654
UNITED KINGDOM	**1,650**	**11,667**	**2,551**	**20,800**	**36,768**	**465**

SPONSORSHIP OF LABOUR CANDIDATES AND MEPs

Of the 78 candidates, six were sponsored by the Co-operative Party of whom three were elected. The remaining 72 candidates were sponsored by European Selection Organisations (amalgamations of constituency Labour Parties).

MISCELLANEOUS STATISTICS 1984 (Cont.)

TYPES OF CONTESTS

Of the 78 single-member constituencies, 46 were contested by three candidates; 27 by four candidates; four by five candidates and one by six candidates.

———————————

TIME-TABLE

Election date announced: May 25, 1983
Nominations closed: May 15, 1984
Polling day: Thursday, June 14, 1984
Results declared: 61 constituencies overnight June 17/18; 17 on June 18; one (Northern Ireland) on June 19.
Parliament assembled: July 24, 1984.

———————————

WOMEN CANDIDATES AND MEPs

Of the total candidates 51 were women. The party totals were Conservative 13; Labour 11; SDP/Liberal Alliance 12; Ecology Party 9; Scottish Nationalist 3; Independent 2; Wessex Regionalist 1.

Of the total MEPs 12 (14.8%) were women. The party totals were Conservative 6; Labour 5; Scottish Nationalist 1.

———————————

Table 11.05 SEATS IN THE EUROPEAN PARLIAMENT

Country	Seats
Belgium	24
Denmark	16
France	81
Germany	81
Greece (from 1981)	24
Ireland	15
Italy	81
Luxembourg	6
Netherlands	25
United Kingdom	81
TOTAL	**434**

Table 12.01 TURNOUT AT LOCAL GOVERNMENT ELECTIONS [ENGLAND] 1945-1987

1945-1972

	Counties[1]	County Boroughs	Non-County Boroughs and Urban Districts[1]	Rural Districts	London County Council[2]	London Metropolitan Boroughs[3]
1945	–	45.4	47.4[4]	–	–	35.1
1946	29.5	42.4	40.4[4]	45.7	26.4	–
1947	–	52.6	49.6[4]	36.0	–	–
1948	–	–	–	44.2	–	–
1949	42.4	52.3	48.4	49.5	40.7	38.3
1950	–	45.3	47.6	46.2	–	–
1951	–	44.3	45.5	44.9	–	–
1952	42.7	49.8	50.4	49.5	43.4	–
1953	–	45.2	48.4	47.3	–	39.9
1954	–	42.6	45.4	47.0	–	–
1955	37.0	43.6	45.0	48.2	32.4	–
1956	–	37.5	41.3	41.3	–	30.9
1957	–	39.8	43.9	45.1	–	–
1958	33.2	40.1	42.4	43.3	31.5	–
1959	–	40.8	44.2	42.0	–	32.1
1960	–	35.2	40.1	37.3	–	–
1961	35.1	40.5	41.5	42.4	36.4	–
1962	–	40.1	45.1	41.5	–	32.3
1963	–	41.2	45.9	41.2	–	–
1964	38.3[5]	40.3	45.7	43.3	44.2	35.7
1965	27.9[6]	37.6	42.7	38.2	–	–
1966	–	35.3	41.9	36.0	–	–
1967	36.9	40.1	41.9	40.7	41.1	–
1968	–	35.6	40.2	35.7	–	35.9
1969	–	35.4	40.7	36.0	–	–
1970	32.5	37.3	39.7	40.3	35.2	–
1971	–	39.1	42.2	35.7	–	38.7
1972	–	36.6	40.3	38.0	–	–

1973-1987

	Metro Counties	Non-Metro Counties	Metro Districts	Non-Metro Districts	Greater London Council	Greater London Boroughs
1973	37.1	42.6	33.4	38.6	37.0	–
1974	–	–	–	–	–	36.3
1975	–	–	32.7	–	–	–
1976	–	–	38.1	44.3	–	–
1977	40.2	42.3	–	–	43.4	–
1978	–	–	37.2[7]	42.4[7]	–	42.9
1979	–	–	74.7[7]	76.6[7]	–	–
1980	–	–	36.3	38.9	–	–
1981	39.5	43.7	–	–	44.4	–
1982	–	–	38.8	41.8	–	43.9
1983	–	–	42.0	45.6	–	–
1984	–	–	40.8	40.2	–	–
1985	–	41.5	–	–	–	–
1986	–	–	39.9	41.9	–	45.5
1987	–	–	44.7	47.8	–	–

TURNOUT AT LOCAL GOVERNMENT ELECTIONS [ENGLAND] 1945-1987 (Cont.)

[1] Excluding London.

[2] Greater London Council from 1964.

[3] Greater London Boroughs from 1964.

[4] Urban District Council elections were held in the spring of 1946, 1947 and 1948 but the figures of electorate and votes cast were not shown separately in the *Statistical Review* so the turn-out percentages for 1945, 1946 and 1947 are not completely accurate as they include the Urban District elections which took place in the following years.

[5] Excluding Essex, Kent and Surrey.

[6] Essex, Kent and Surrey only.

[7] A Parliamentary General Election was held on the same day as the District Council elections.

[8]

Sources: 1945-73: *Registrar-General's Statistical Review of England and Wales, Part 2. Tables, Civil* (until 1957), *Population* (from 1958).

1974-79: *Electoral Statistics* (Office of Population Censuses and Surveys).

Note: The official collection of local government election data was discontinued by the Home Office from 1979 but resumed again in 1988. From 1980 until 1987 Parliamentary Research Services collected similar data and the figures given for these years were compiled from the figures provided to PRS by Returning Officers.

Table 12.02 TURNOUT AT LOCAL GOVERNMENT ELECTIONS [WALES] 1945-1987

1945-1972

	Counties	County Boroughs	Non-County Boroughs and Urban Districts	Rural Districts
1945	—	50.4	61.5[1]	—
1946	51.8	45.2	49.2[1]	65.3
1947	—	54.5	53.3[1]	85.5
1948	—	—	—	72.3
1949	53.6	52.1	56.8	65.1
1950	—	48.6	53.9	80.4
1951	—	45.6	53.7	68.6
1952	55.8	53.2	61.6	68.9
1953	—	47.5	55.2	92.4
1954	—	46.4	54.8	62.5
1955	54.7	47.9	57.6	65.4
1956	—	41.1	49.3	92.3
1957	—	46.8	53.5	60.7
1958	54.4	46.9	54.2	64.7
1959	—	45.5	51.1	81.7
1960	—	40.8	48.2	59.3
1961	51.0	44.5	57.3	61.9
1962	—	41.7	49.1	—
1963	—	43.5	53.6	57.0
1964	48.9	43.6	53.7	60.0
1965	—	40.3	47.9	—
1966	—	40.4	47.6	62.9
1967	46.9	45.3	54.1	60.8
1968	—	40.0	49.4	81.9
1969	—	39.8	50.5	63.0
1970	45.6	44.1	50.7	55.5
1971	—	41.1	48.4	75.7
1972	—	39.1	47.6	81.3

1973-1987

	Counties	Districts		Counties	Districts
1973	55.0	50.0	1981	48.6	—
1974	—	—	1982	—	—
1975	—	—	1983	—	46.3
1976	—	52.9	1984	—	43.2
1977	51.0	—	1985	45.2	—
1978	—	—	1986	—	40.0
1979	—	76.9[2]	1987	—	51.4
1980	—	—			

[1] Urban District Council elections were held in the spring of 1946, 1947 and 1948 but the figures of electorate and votes cast were not shown separately in the *Statistical Review* so the turnout percentages for 1945, 1946 and 1947 are not completely accurate as they include the Urban District elections which took place in the following years.

[2] A Parliamentary General Election was held on the same day as the District Council elections.

Sources: See Table 12.01.

Table 12.03 TURNOUT AT LOCAL GOVERNMENT ELECTIONS [SCOTLAND] 1945-1987

1945-1973

	Counties[1]	Counties of Cities	Large Burghs	Small Burghs	Districts
1945	54.6	43.1	54.5	58.6	55.3
1946	—	37.9	50.9	54.6	—
1947	—	52.3	58.9	58.5	—
1948	—	—	—	—	—
1949	60.6	48.6	53.1	51.6	62.8
1950	—	40.7	48.1	50.2	—
1951	—	37.6	47.0	49.1	—
1952	60.3	45.1	50.7	52.2	58.2
1953	—	37.4	45.3	50.3	—
1954	—	38.0	46.8	49.3	—
1955	58.5	46.4	36.0	50.2	57.4
1956	—	32.6	42.8	49.9	—
1957	—	31.1	42.2	50.2	—
1958	60.0	33.6	44.6	50.4	59.6
1959	—	37.1	45.2	51.6	—
1960	—	37.0	40.8	48.5	—
1961	57.8	40.9	43.8	50.1	54.6
1962	—	38.9	45.8	50.5	—
1963	—	38.6	40.9	50.2	—
1964	56.0	40.5	45.0	51.9	53.5
1965	—	36.1	42.0	49.7	—
1966	—	35.6	40.9	48.3	—
1967	54.9	41.2	44.6	48.9	54.9
1968	—	44.4	48.7	51.6	—
1969	—	36.7	41.8	45.1	—
1970	53.6	39.4	43.8	46.9	53.3
1971	—	40.0	43.9	47.7	—
1972	—	39.7	44.0	46.5	—
1973	45.1	32.3	37.4	39.0	44.1

1974-1987

	Regions & Islands	Districts		Regions & Islands	Districts
1974	50.1	52.1	1981	—	—
1975	—	—	1982	43.2	—
1976	—	—	1983	—	—
1977	—	48.2	1984	—	44.8
1978	45.0	—	1985	—	—
1979	—	—	1986	53.2	—
1980	—	46.2	1987	—	—

[1] Landward areas only.

Source: *Registrar-General for Scotland, Annual Report, Part 2*
          Population and Vital Statistics (1968-84)
          Scottish Home and Health Department 1986-

Table 12.04   TURNOUT AT LOCAL GOVERNMENT ELECTIONS [SUMMARY] 1945-1987

	England	Wales	Scotland
1945	45.5[1]	57.7[1]	50.9
1946	36.8[1]	52.1[1]	44.8
1947	50.8[1]	53.9[1]	55.1
1948	44.2	72.3	—
1949	46.4	56.1	52.1
1950	46.6	51.3	44.2
1951	45.0	50.0	42.2
1952	47.5	59.5	50.5
1953	46.0	51.4	41.6
1954	44.1	50.6	41.9
1955	41.0	56.0	43.7
1956	38.5	45.4	37.9
1957	42.0	49.9	36.8
1958	38.0	54.4	42.0
1959	41.4	48.2	41.4
1960	37.8	44.6	39.8
1961	38.9	53.5	45.2
1962	41.6	45.4	42.4
1963	43.7	48.8	41.3
1964	41.1	50.9	45.4
1965	38.7	44.5	40.2
1966	38.4	44.3	39.6
1967	39.8	50.8	45.7
1968	37.3	45.1	47.0
1969	37.8	45.3	39.9
1970	36.3	48.5	44.1
1971	40.1	44.8	42.6
1972	38.3	43.4	42.2
1973	38.7	52.5	33.0
1974	36.3	—	50.5
1975	32.7	—	—
1976	42.3	52.9	—
1977	41.9	51.0	48.2
1978	39.9	—	45.0
1979	76.0[2]	76.9[2]	—
1980	37.4	—	46.2
1981	42.8	48.6	—
1982	41.0	—	43.2
1983	44.5	46.3	—
1984	40.0	43.2	44.8
1985	41.5	45.2	—
1986	41.9	40.0	53.2
1987	45.0	51.4	—

[1] Including Urban District council elections held in the spring of 1946, 1947 and 1948. See footnote [4] to Table 12.01 and footnote [1] to Table 12.02.
[2] A Parliamentary General Election was held on the same day as the District Council elections.

Sources: See Tables 12.01 and 12.03.

Table 12.05 NUMBER OF COUNCILLORS RETURNED [ENGLAND] 1945-1987

1945-1972

a: Total returned　　　　　b: Returned unopposed　　　　　c: % of unopposed

	Counties (excluding London)			County Boroughs			Non-County Boroughs and Urban Districts (excluding London)			Rural Districts			London County Council (Greater London Council from 1964)			London Metropolitan Boroughs (Greater London Boroughs from 1964)		
	a	b	c	a	b	c	a	b	c	a	b	c	a	b	c	a	b	c
1945	–	–	–	1,952	153	7.8	8,343	546	6.5	–	–	–	–	–	–	1,251	139	11.1
1946	3,037	1,268	41.8	1,182	117	9.9	4,097	592	14.4	10,043	6,077	60.5	124	16	12.9	–	–	–
1947	–	–	–	1,123	94	8.4	3,949	516	13.1	1,317	953	72.4	–	–	–	–	–	–
1948	–	–	–	–	–	–	–	–	–	1,163	727	62.5	–	–	–	–	–	–
1949	3,060	1,554	50.8	1,251	92	7.4	5,826	1,170	20.1	10,052	6,795	67.6	129	0	0.0	1,370	99	7.2
1950	–	–	–	1,178	164	13.9	4,177	903	21.6	1,491	1,034	69.3	–	–	–	–	–	–
1951	–	–	–	1,277	160	12.5	4,129	1,074	26.0	1,340	992	74.0	–	–	–	–	–	–
1952	2,522[1]	1,387	55.0	1,211	142	11.7	5,855	1,405	24.0	10,146	6,915	68.2	129	0	0.0	1,356	91	6.7
1953	–	–	–	1,329	192	14.4	4,215	1,121	26.6	1,404	1,065	75.9	–	–	–	–	–	–
1954	–	–	–	1,268	205	16.2	4,329	1,227	28.3	1,423	1,063	74.7	–	–	–	–	–	–
1955	3,124	1,829	58.5	1,268	229	18.1	6,042	1,806	29.9	10,043	7,369	73.4	126	0	0.0	1,356	86	6.3
1956	–	–	–	1,245	237	19.0	4,294	1,347	31.4	1,418	1,130	79.7	–	–	–	–	–	–
1957	–	–	–	1,219	270	22.1	4,274	1,389	32.5	1,424	1,104	77.5	–	–	–	–	–	–
1958	3,172	1,866	58.8	1,292	233	18.0	5,971	1,825	30.6	10,100	7,664	75.9	126	0	0.0	1,336	101	7.6
1959	–	–	–	1,232	202	16.4	4,280	1,302	30.4	1,464	1,121	76.6	–	–	–	–	–	–
1960	–	–	–	1,223	153	12.5	4,314	1,327	30.8	1,473	1,114	75.6	–	–	–	–	–	–
1961	3,203	1,894	59.1	1,233	154	12.5	6,000	1,593	26.6	10,202	7,632	74.8	126	0	0.0	1,336	63	4.7
1962	–	–	–	1,231	122	9.9	4,318	1,147	26.6	1,447	1,049	72.5	–	–	–	–	–	–
1963	–	–	–	1,231	123	10.0	4,342	962	22.2	1,509	1,045	69.3	–	–	–	–	–	–
1964	2,727	1,412	51.8	1,208	105	8.7	5,404	1,260	23.3	10,202	7,135	69.9	100	0	0.0	1,859	18	1.0
1965	217	27	12.4	1,245	121	9.7	3,897	973	25.0	1,486	1,032	69.4	–	–	–	–	–	–
1966	–	–	–	1,444	112	7.8	3,806	783	20.6	1,590	1,043	65.6	–	–	–	–	–	–
1967	2,961	1,467	49.5	1,464	51	3.5	5,088	944	18.6	10,097	6,809	67.4	100	0	0.0	1,863	30	1.6
1968	–	–	–	1,475	84	5.7	3,723	829	22.3	1,502	1,072	71.4	–	–	–	–	–	–
1969	–	–	–	1,344	84	6.3	3,683	800	21.7	1,535	1,028	67.0	–	–	–	–	–	–
1970	2,979	1,537	51.6	1,299	66	5.1	5,118	1,081	21.1	10,207	7,158	70.1	100	0	0.0	1,863	15	0.8
1971	–	–	–	1,341	46	3.4	3,720	722	19.4	1,463	1,047	71.6	–	–	–	–	–	–
1972	–	–	–	1,273	38	3.0	3,681	890	24.2	1,520	1,025	67.4	–	–	–	–	–	–

NUMBER OF COUNCILLORS RETURNED [ENGLAND] 1945-1987 (Cont.)
1973-1987

	Metropolitan Counties			Non-Metropolitan Counties			Metropolitan Districts			Non-Metropolitan Districts			Greater London Council			Greater London Boroughs		
	a	b	c	a	b	c	a	b	c	a	b	c	a	b	c	a	b	c
1973	601	22	3.7	3,127	396	12.7	2,511	66	2.6	13,544	1,665	12.3	92	0	0.0	—	—	—
1974	—	—	—	—	—	—	—	—	—	—	—	—	—	—	—	1,867	22	1.2
1975	—	—	—	—	—	—	806	21	2.6	—	—	—	—	—	—	—	—	—
1976	—	—	—	—	—	—	851	13	1.5	13,591	2,204	16.2	—	—	—	—	—	—
1977	598	6	1.0	3,126	373	11.9	—	—	—	—	—	—	92	0	0.0	1,905	0	0.0
1978	—	—	—	—	—	—	938	7	0.7	675	47	7.0	—	—	—	—	—	—
1979	—	—	—	—	—	—	987	9	0.9	12,160	2,269	18.7	—	—	—	—	—	—
1980	—	—	—	—	—	—	1,364	11	0.8	1,619	109	6.7	—	—	—	—	—	—
1981	600	2	0.3	3,093	121	3.9	—	—	—	—	—	—	92	0	0.0	1,914	2	0.1
1982	—	—	—	—	—	—	1,339	5	0.4	1,588	50	3.1	—	—	—	—	—	—
1983	—	—	—	—	—	—	845	7	0.8	10,345	1,376	13.3	—	—	—	—	—	—
1984	—	—	—	—	—	—	850	14	1.6	1,906	91	4.8	—	—	—	—	—	—
1985	—	—	—	3,002	61	2.0	—	—	—	—	—	—	—	—	—	—	—	—
1986	—	—	—	—	—	—	861	25	2.9	1,939	52	2.7	—	—	—	1,914	3	0.2
1987	—	—	—	—	—	—	807	13	1.6	9,180	778	8.5	—	—	—	—	—	—

Sources: See Table 12.01

Table 12.06 NUMBER OF COUNCILLORS RETURNED [WALES] 1945-1987

1945-1972

a: Total returned   b: Returned unopposed   c: % of unopposed

Year	Counties			County Boroughs			Non-County Boroughs and Urban Districts			Rural Districts		
	a	b	c	a	b	c	a	b	c	a	b	c
1945	–	–	–	67	4	59.7	1,000	90	9.0	–	–	–
1946	701	396	56.5	48	5	10.4	367	104	28.3	1,112	531	47.8
1947	–	–	–	48	4	8.3	383	80	20.9	29	27	93.1
1948	–	–	–	–	–	–	–	–	–	29	18	62.1
1949	701	472	67.3	47	8	17.0	879	281	32.0	1,228	706	57.5
1950	–	–	–	47	7	14.9	381	159	41.7	38	34	89.5
1951	–	–	–	47	16	34.0	363	148	40.8	43	28	65.1
1952	497[1]	355	71.4	77	18	23.4	831	293	35.3	1,313	785	59.8
1953	–	–	–	47	15	31.9	391	190	48.6	34	33	97.1
1954	–	–	–	49	16	32.7	402	207	51.5	40	36	90.0
1955	714	579	81.1	47	14	29.8	917	385	42.0	1,369	923	67.4
1956	–	–	–	53	24	45.3	407	240	59.0	32	31	96.9
1957	–	–	–	49	20	40.8	393	260	66.2	40	34	85.0
1958	714	578	81.0	50	17	34.0	906	386	42.6	1,361	949	69.7
1959	–	–	–	50	12	24.0	395	219	55.4	34	33	97.1
1960	–	–	–	49	12	24.5	404	216	53.5	41	31	75.6
1961	714	582	81.5	59	11	18.6	921	380	41.3	1,367	924	67.6
1962	–	–	–	52	7	13.5	403	215	53.3	32	32	100.0
1963	–	–	–	52	6	11.5	403	182	45.2	38	32	84.2
1964	716	557	77.8	53	6	11.3	875	324	37.0	1,351	941	69.7
1965	–	–	–	52	10	19.2	405	185	45.7	33	33	100.0
1966	–	–	–	53	8	15.1	393	190	48.3	41	34	82.9
1967	717	489	68.2	61	4	6.6	930	306	32.9	1,321	847	64.1
1968	–	–	–	55	3	5.5	406	165	40.6	28	26	92.9
1969	–	–	–	56	1	1.8	393	183	46.6	42	34	81.0
1970	724	487	67.3	55	0	0.0	892	325	36.4	1,337	874	65.4
1971	–	–	–	55	4	7.3	410	183	44.6	31	30	96.8
1972	–	–	–	56	6	10.7	403	209	51.9	40	38	95.0

NUMBER OF COUNCILLORS RETURNED [WALES] 1945-1987
1973-1987

	Counties			Districts		
	a	b	c	a	b	c
1973	577	109	18.9	1,521	281	18.5
1974	–	–	–	–	–	–
1975	–	–	–	–	–	–
1976	–	–	–	1,510	316	20.9
1977	577	122	21.1	–	–	–
1978	–	–	–	–	–	–
1979	–	–	–	1,516	396	26.1
1980	–	–	–	–	–	–
1981	578	122	21.1	–	–	–
1982	–	–	–	–	–	–
1983	–	–	–	1,268	304	24.0
1984	–	–	–	76	6	7.9
1985	559	145	25.9	–	–	–
1986	–	–	–	81	2	2.5
1987	–	–	–	1,232	282	22.9

Sources: See Table 12.01

Table 12.07 NUMBER OF COUNCILLORS RETURNED [SCOTLAND] 1945-1987

1945-1973

a: Total returned b: Returned unopposed c: % of unopposed

	Counties			Counties of Cities			Large Burghs			Small Burghs			Districts		
	a	b	c	a	b	c	a	b	c	a	b	c	a	b	c
1945	–	–	–	133	33	24.8	248	21	8.5	1,122	116	10.3	–	–	–
1946	937	531	56.7	87	15	17.2	149	16	10.7	666	136	20.4	1,345	987	73.4
1947	–	–	–	86	11	12.8	144	18	12.5	662	165	24.9	–	–	–
1948															
1949	934	616	66.0	204	14	6.9	162	15	9.3	683	232	34.0	1,231	982	79.8
1950	–	–	–	89	8	9.0	178	30	16.9	679	263	38.7	–	–	–
1951	–	–	–	87	19	21.8	157	30	19.1	641	268	41.8	–	–	–
1952	941	691	73.4	112	16	14.3	153	40	26.1	660	266	40.3	1,260	1,064	84.4
1953	–	–	–	84	15	17.9	139	34	24.5	676	297	43.9	–	–	–
1954	–	–	–	113	15	13.3	162	54	33.3	648	300	46.3	–	–	–
1955	956	714	74.7	86	12	14.0	157	36	22.9	704	349	49.6	1,290	1,115	86.4
1956	–	–	–	86	12	14.0	156	32	20.5	669	334	49.9	–	–	–
1957	–	–	–	85	9	10.6	155	31	20.0	678	375	55.3	–	–	–
1958	949	739	77.9	85	13	15.3	143	38	26.6	690	351	50.9	1,297	1,134	87.4
1959	–	–	–	84	12	14.3	140	45	32.1	673	330	49.0	–	–	–
1960	–	–	–	85	12	14.1	160	42	26.3	663	356	53.7	–	–	–
1961	951	752	79.1	109	16	14.7	158	43	27.2	684	387	56.6	1,301	1,129	86.8
1962	–	–	–	87	2	2.3	167	28	16.8	666	365	54.8	–	–	–
1963	–	–	–	85	1	1.2	140	25	17.9	676	288	42.6	–	–	–
1964	943	728	77.2	109	1	0.9	154	28	18.2	688	291	42.3	1,285	1,095	85.2
1965	–	–	–	86	3	3.5	175	22	12.6	697	310	44.5	–	–	–
1966	–	–	–	85	6	7.1	142	22	15.5	667	302	45.3	–	–	–
1967	950	640	67.4	87	1	1.1	148	21	14.2	685	288	42.0	1,278	1,022	80.0
1968	–	–	–	85	0	0.0	148	16	10.8	686	257	37.5	–	–	–
1969	–	–	–	84	0	0.0	151	23	15.2	695	243	35.0	–	–	–
1970	950	642	67.6	88	0	0.0	151	21	13.9	678	265	39.1	1,297	1,033	79.6
1971	–	–	–	84	0	0.0	151	16	10.6	680	284	41.8	–	–	–
1972	–	–	–	84	0	0.0	148	18	12.2	682	329	48.2	–	–	–
1973	950	741	78.0	88	0	0.0	151	27	17.9	670	352	52.5	1,290	1,117	86.6

NUMBER OF COUNCILLORS RETURNED [SCOTLAND] 1945-1987 (Cont.)
1974-1987

	Regions and Islands			Districts		
	a	b	c	a	b	c
1974	507	77	15.2	1,110	223	20.1
1975	–	–	–	–	–	–
1976	–	–	–	–	–	–
1977	–	–	–	1,114	247	22.2
1978	508	134	26.4	–	–	–
1979	–	–	–	–	–	–
1980	–	–	–	1,123	289	25.7
1981	–	–	–	–	–	–
1982	520	110	21.2	–	–	–
1983	–	–	–	–	–	–
1984	–	–	–	1,150	247	21.5
1985	–	–	–	–	–	–
1986	524	89	17.0	–	–	–
1987	–	–	–	–	–	–

Source: See Table 12.03

Table 12.08 NUMBER OF COUNCILLORS RETURNED [SUMMARY] 1945-1987

1945-1972

a: Total returned   b: Returned unopposed   c: % of unopposed

	England			Wales			Scotland		
	a	b	c	a	b	c	a	b	c
1945	11,546	838	7.3	1,067	94	8.8	1,503	170	11.3
1946	18,483	8,070	43.7	2,228	1,036	46.5	3,184	1,685	52.9
1947	6,389	1,563	24.5	460	111	24.1	892	194	21.7
1948	1,163	727	62.5	29	18	62.1	—	—	—
1949	21,688	9,710	44.8	2,855	1,467	51.4	3,214	1,859	57.8
1950	6,846	2,101	30.7	466	200	42.9	946	301	31.8
1951	6,746	2,226	33.0	453	192	42.4	885	317	35.8
1952	19,863	9,849	49.6	2,718	1,451	53.4	3,126	2,077	66.4
1953	8,304	2,469	29.7	472	238	50.4	899	346	38.5
1954	7,020	2,495	35.5	491	259	52.7	923	369	40.0
1955	20,603	11,233	54.5	3,047	1,901	62.4	3,193	2,226	69.7
1956	8,313	2,800	33.7	492	295	60.0	911	378	41.5
1957	6,917	2,763	39.9	482	314	65.1	918	415	45.2
1958	20,661	11,588	56.1	3,031	1,930	63.7	3,164	2,275	71.9
1959	8,312	2,726	32.8	479	264	55.1	897	387	43.1
1960	7,010	2,594	37.0	494	259	52.4	908	410	45.2
1961	20,764	11,273	54.3	3,061	1,897	62.0	3,203	2,327	72.7
1962	8,332	2,381	28.6	487	254	52.2	920	395	42.9
1963	7,082	2,130	30.1	493	220	44.6	901	314	34.9
1964	21,500	9,930	46.2	2,995	1,828	61.0	3,179	2,143	67.4
1965	6,845	2,153	31.5	490	228	46.5	958	335	35.0
1966	6,840	1,938	28.3	487	232	47.6	894	330	36.9
1967	19,710	9,271	47.0	3,029	1,646	54.3	3,148	1,972	62.6
1968	8,563	2,015	23.5	489	194	39.7	919	273	29.7
1969	6,562	1,912	29.1	491	218	44.4	930	266	28.6
1970	19,703	9,842	50.0	3,008	1,686	56.1	3,164	1,961	62.0
1971	8,387	1,830	21.8	496	217	43.8	915	300	32.8
1972	6,474	1,953	30.2	499	253	50.7	914	347	38.0

NUMBER OF COUNCILLORS RETURNED [SUMMARY] 1945-1987 (Cont.)
1973-1987

	England			Wales			Scotland		
	a	b	c	a	b	c	a	b	c
1973	19,875	2,149	10.8	2,098	390	18.6	3,149	2,237	71.0
1974	1,867	22	1.2	–	–	–	1,617	300	18.6
1975	806	21	2.6	–	–	–	–	–	–
1976	14,442	2,217	15.4	1,510	316	20.9	–	–	–
1977	3,816	379	9.9	577	122	21.1	1,114	247	22.2
1978	3,518	54	1.5	–	–	–	508	134	26.4
1979	13,147	2,278	17.3	1,516	396	26.1	–	–	–
1980	2,982	120	4.0	–	–	–	1,123	289	25.7
1981	3,693	123	3.3	578	122	21.1	–	–	–
1982	2,927	55	1.9	–	–	–	520	110	21.2
1983	11,190	1,383	12.4	1,268	304	24.0	–	–	–
1984	2,756	105	3.8	76	6	7.9	1,150	247	21.5
1985	3,002	61	2.0	559	145	25.9	–	–	–
1986	2,800	77	2.8	81	2	2.5	524	89	17.0
1987	9,987	791	7.9	1,232	282	22.9	–	–	–

Sources: See Tables 12.01 and 12.03

Table 12.09 LOCAL ELECTIONS CALENDAR 1973-1996

Type of Authority and Number	1973 (Whole councils)	1974 (Whole councils)	1 May 1975	6 May 1976	5 May 1977 (E & W) 3 May 1977 (Scotland)	4 May 1978 (E & W) 2 May 1978 (Scotland)	3 May 1979	1 May 1980
English & Welsh County Councils (45 + 8 = 53), Metropolitan (6) & Non-Metropolitan (47)	12 April				Whole council			
Greater London Council	12 April				Whole council			
London Borough Councils (32)		2 May				Whole council		
English Metropolitan District Councils (36)	10 May		1/3 council	1/3 council		1/3 council	Whole (3) or 1/3 council	Whole (10) or 1/3 council
English Non-Metropolitan District Councils (296)	7 June			Whole council		1/3 council (44) or none	1/3 council (44) or whole council	1/3 council (102) whole council (1) or none
Welsh District Councils (37)	10 May			Whole council			Whole council	
Scottish Regional (9) & Islands Councils (3)		7 May				Whole council		
Scottish District Councils (53)		7 May			Whole council			Whole council

LOCAL ELECTIONS CALENDAR 1973-1996 (Cont.)

Type of Authority and Number	7 May 1981	6 May 1982	5 May 1983	3 May 1984	2 May 1985	8 May 1986[1]	7 May 1987	5 May 1988
English & Welsh County Councils (45 + 8 = 53), Metropolitan (6) & Non-Metropolitan (47)[2]	Whole council				Whole council			
Greater London Council[2]	Whole council							
London Borough Councils (32)		Whole council				Whole council		
English Metropolitan District Councils (36)		Whole (10) or 1/3 council	1/3 council	1/3 council		1/3 council	1/3 council	1/3 council
English Non-Metropolitan District Councils (296)		1/3 council (103) or none	1/3 council (103) or whole	1/3 council (123) or none		1/3 council (122) Whole council (1) or none	1/3 (116) or whole council	1/3 council (117) or none
Welsh District Councils (37)			Whole council	1/3 council (6) or none		1/3 council (6) or none	1/3 (4) or whole council	1/3 council (5) or none
Scottish Regional (9) & Islands Councils (3)		Whole council				Whole council		
Scottish District Councils (53)				Whole council				Whole council

[1] Polling was postponed from 1 May owing to the Jewish Passover
[2] The six Metropolitan County Councils and the Greater London Council were abolished on 31 March 1986 and no elections were held in 1985

LOCAL ELECTIONS CALENDAR 1973-1996 (Cont.)

Type of Authority and Number	4 May 1989	3 May 1990	2 May 1991	7 May 1992	6 May 1993	5 May 1994	4 May 1995	2 May 1996
English & Welsh County Councils (39 + 8 = 47)	Whole council				Whole council			
London Borough Councils (32)		Whole council				Whole council		
English Metropolitan District Councils (36)		1/3 council	1/3 council	1/3 council		1/3 council	1/3 council	1/3 council
English Non-Metropolitan District Councils (296)		1/3 council or none	1/3 council or whole council	1/3 council or none		1/3 council or none	1/3 council or whole council	1/3 council or none
Welsh District Councils (37)		1/3 council or none	1/3 council or whole council	1/3 council or none		1/3 council or none	1/3 council or whole council	1/3 council or none
Scottish Regional (9) and Islands Councils (3)		Whole council				Whole council		
Scottish District Councils (53)				Whole council				Whole council

The dates of polling (the first Thursday in May) are provisional and can be altered by the Secretary of State for the Home Department.
It is now no longer possible to indicate the number of non-metropolitan districts in England and Wales electing by thirds as councils can opt to change from thirds to whole council and from whole council to thirds and the numbers will change from year to year.

Table 13.01 REFERENDUM ON NORTHERN IRELAND REMAINING PART OF THE UNITED KINGDOM — March 8, 1973

Question:
Do you want Northern Ireland to remain part of the United Kingdom?
or
Do you want Northern Ireland to be joined with the Republic of Ireland,
outside the United Kingdom?

Electorate	T'out %	Remain part of UK	%	Joined with Republic	%	Spoilt Ballot Papers
1,018,712	58.7	591,820	98.9	6,463	1.1	5,973

Source: House of Commons Papers 1974-75 (Cmnd. 5875) xxviii, 1.

Table 13.02 REFERENDUM ON UNITED KINGDOM MEMBERSHIP OF THE EUROPEAN ECONOMIC COMMUNITY — June 5, 1975

Question:
Do you think that the United Kingdom should stay in the European Community (The Common Market)?

	Civilian Electorate	Civilian T'out%[1]	Yes	%	No	%	Service Votes	Spoilt Ballot Papers
ENGLAND	33,356,208	64.6	14,918,009	68.7	6,812,052	31.3	207,465	42,161
Avon	665,484	68.7	310,145	67.8	147,024	32.2	499	635
Bedfordshire	326,566	67.9	154,338	69.4	67,969	30.6	829	385
Berkshire	443,472	66.4	215,184	72.6	81,221	27.4	2,666	571
Buckinghamshire	346,348	69.5	180,512	74.3	62,578	25.7	2,643	357
Cambridgeshire	375,753	62.9	177,789	74.1	62,143	25.9	3,840	354
Cheshire	633,614	65.5	290,714	70.1	123,839	29.9	128	663
Cleveland	392,672	60.2	158,982	67.3	77,079	32.7	47	308
Cornwall	298,706	66.8	137,828	68.5	63,478	31.5	2,321	572
Cumbria	349,596	64.8	162,545	71.9	63,564	28.1	83	415
Derbyshire	653,005	64.1	286,614	68.6	131,452	31.4	NIL	687
Devon	676,378	68.0	334,244	72.1	129,179	27.9	4,239	991
Dorset	429,752	68.3	217,432	73.5	78,239	26.5	3,200	976
Durham	444,783	61.5	175,284	64.2	97,724	35.8	24	453
East Sussex	511,437	65.8	249,780	74.3	86,198	25.7	104	775
Essex	1,010,317	67.7	463,505	67.6	222,085	32.4	2,648	1,119
Gloucestershire	347,218	68.4	170,931	71.7	67,465	28.3	1,304	504
Greater London	5,250,343	60.8	2,201,031	66.7	1,100,185	33.3	114,900	6,874
Greater Manchester	1,932,717	64.1	797,316	64.5	439,191	35.5	82	2,843
Hampshire	975,440	68.0	484,302	71.0	197,761	29.0	20,142	1,379
Hereford and Worcester	419,866	66.4	203,128	72.8	75,779	27.2	867	642
Hertfordshire	662,177	70.2	326,943	70.4	137,266	29.6	621	1,239
Humberside	607,890	62.4	257,826	67.8	122,199	32.2	1,207	765
Isles of Scilly	1,447	75.0	802	74.5	275	25.5	NIL	8
Isle of Wight	86,381	67.5	40,837	70.2	17,375	27.8	NIL	116
Kent	1,035,313	67.4	493,407	70.4	207,358	29.6	3,653	1,120
Lancashire	1,000,755	66.4	455,170	68.6	208,821	31.4	460	1,302
Leicestershire	590,780	67.2	291,500	73.3	106,004	26.7	1,557	835
Lincolnshire	370,518	63.7	180,603	74.7	61,011	25.3	6,149	445
Merseyside	1,147,920	62.7	465,625	64.8	252,712	35.2	138	1,602
Norfolk	485,229	63.8	218,883	70.1	93,198	29.9	3,016	605
Northamptonshire	351,653	66.7	162,803	69.5	71,322	30.5	166	507
Northumberland	212,846	65.0	95,980	69.2	42,645	30.8	401	231
North Yorkshire	468,998	64.3	234,040	76.3	72,805	23.7	5,853	738
Nottinghamshire	705,183	63.1	297,191	66.8	147,461	33.2	550	1,052
Oxfordshire	355,977	67.7	179,938	73.6	64,643	26.4	4,065	449
Salop	249,463	62.0	113,044	72.3	43,329	27.7	1,860	238
Somerset	293,191	67.7	138,830	69.6	60,631	30.4	1,251	300
South Yorkshire	954,539	62.4	377,916	63.4	217,792	36.6	941	1,060
Staffordshire	706,230	64.3	306,518	67.4	148,252	32.6	973	657
Suffolk	397,626	64.9	187,484	72.2	72,251	27.8	1,993	472
Surrey	720,440	70.1	386,369	76.2	120,576	23.8	2,518	770
Tyne and Wear	872,253	62.7	344,069	62.9	202,511	37.1	110	469
Warwickshire	327,967	68.0	156,303	69.9	67,221	30.1	879	391
West Midlands	1,972,987	62.5	801,913	65.1	429,207	34.9	NIL	2,153
West Sussex	464,396	68.6	242,890	76.2	75,928	23.8	750	719
West Yorkshire	1,485,749	63.6	616,730	65.4	326,993	34.6	65	1,860
Wiltshire	344,833	67.8	172,791	71.7	68,113	28.3	7,723	555

REFERENDUM ON UNITED KINGDOM MEMBERSHIP
OF THE EUROPEAN ECONOMIC COMMUNITY (Cont.)

	Civilian Electorate	Civilian T'out%[1]	Yes	%	No	%	Service Votes	Spoilt Ballot Papers
WALES	2,011,136	66.7	869,135	64.8	472,071	35.2	3,855	4,339
Clwyd	272,798	65.8	123,980	69.1	55,424	30.9	554	515
Dyfed	241,415	67.5	109,184	67.6	52,264	32.4	980	491
Gwent	314,369	68.2	132,557	62.1	80,992	37.9	NIL	808
Gwynedd	167,706	64.3	76,421	70.6	31,807	29.4	694	240
Mid Glamorgan	390,175	66.6	147,348	56.9	111,672	43.1	NIL	900
Powys	76,531	67.9	38,724	74.3	13,372	25.7	272	170
South Glamorgan	275,324	66.7	127,932	69.5	56,224	30.5	1,355	705
West Glamorgan	272,818	67.4	112,989	61.6	70,316	38.4	NIL	510
SCOTLAND	3,688,799	61.7	1,332,186	58.4	948,039	41.6	9,295	6,451
Borders	74,834	63.2	34,092	72.3	13,053	27.7	NIL	160
Central	188,613	64.1	71,986	59.7	48,568	40.3	32	331
Dumfries and Galloway	101,703	61.5	42,608	68.2	19,856	31.8	60	179
Fife	235,166	63.3	84,239	56.3	65,260	43.7	1,255	589
Grampian	321,140	57.4	108,520	58.2	78,071	41.8	2,625	507
Highland	127,925	58.7	40,802	54.6	33,979	45.4	NIL	257
Lothian	548,369	63.6	208,133	59.5	141,456	40.5	2,002	960
Orkney	13,157	48.2	3,911	61.8	2,419	38.2	NIL	15
Shetland	13,411	47.1	2,815	43.7	3,631	56.3	163	29
Strathclyde	1,759,889	61.7	625,959	57.7	459,073	42.3	2,191	2,951
Tayside	282,160	63.8	105,728	58.6	74,567	41.4	666	422
Western Isles	22,432	50.1	3,393	29.5	8,106	70.5	301	51
NORTHERN IRELAND	1,028,451	47.5	259,251	52.1	237,911	47.9	10,579	1,589
UNITED KINGDOM	40,084,594	64.0	17,378,581	67.2	8,470,073	32.8	231,194	54,540

[1] In calculating this figure the service votes have been *deducted* from and the spoilt ballot papers *added* to the total valid votes cast.

Special arrangements were made to enable members of the forces and their spouses to vote irrespective of whether or not they were included in the electoral register as service voters. At the time of the Referendum there were about 119,000 service voters on the register and the Ministry of Defence claimed that their scheme enfranchised 370,200 servicemen and their spouses. Of the 119,000 service voters on the register it would seem that most of them would be eligible to vote under the special arrangements and therefore the actual service electorate must have been in the region of 380,000 to 400,000 giving a turnout of between 57% and 60%.

The following explanatory notes were issued by the National Counting Officer in respect of service electors and the counting of their ballot papers:—

The persons who have a service qualification are
(a) members of the forces;
(b) Crown servants serving in a post outside the UK;
(c) staff of the British Council employed in a post outside the UK; and
(d) the wife, or husband, of any person in the three preceding categories if residing outside the UK to be with him, or her.

REFERENDUM ON UNITED KINGDOM MEMBERSHIP
OF THE EUROPEAN ECONOMIC COMMUNITY (Cont.)

For the purpose of the referendum (5 June) special arrangements are being made for members of the forces whether stationed in the UK or abroad, and their spouses when residing abroad, to vote in their units, whether or not their homes have been included in the current register of service voters. A corollary of this provision is that, in the case of any member of the forces, or his or her spouse when overseas, who *is* registered as a service voter on the current register and has appointed a proxy, the proxy will not be allowed to vote on his behalf in the referendum. The great majority of servicemen and women, and their spouses overseas, will be voting under the special forces arrangements. Those stationed in the UK, however, who are on the register as service voters, will still be entitled to vote in person or by post, even though their proxies will not be allowed to vote on their behalf. This facility is likely to be taken advantage of by persons who, having left the forces since the current register was compiled, will not benefit from the special forces voting arrangements, and a small number of servicemen in the UK on leave.

The special arrangements will not apply to service voters who are Crown servants, British Council staff or their spouses who will be entitled to vote in person, by post or by proxy at their own polling stations in the ordinary way, and nowhere else.

The votes cast under the special forces arrangements will be counted with the rest of the civilian votes. Votes cast in forces units in the UK will be counted with the votes for the county in which that unit is situated. Votes cast in forces units outside the UK will be counted with the votes for the G.L.C. In announcing the total number of ballot papers he has counted each counting officer will declare what number of these represent ballot papers resulting from the special forces voting arrangements. He will not, however, be able to make a similar breakdown in respect of the totals of valid votes. This is deliberate to prevent separate "Yes" and "No" totals becoming available for the forces alone.

The position regarding service voters will therefore be that some will be voting (in person, by post, or by proxy) in the ordinary way: others will be voting under the special forces voting arrangements. The persons voting under the special forces arrangements will include some who are registered as service voters and many others who are not. In these circumstances it would be misleading to give separate voter totals because there is no way of establishing what proportion of these will have alternative special voting arrangements open to them and how they will exercise their choice.

Source: House of Commons Papers 1974-75 (Cmnd. 6105) ix, 645.

Table 13.03 REFERENDUM ON DEVOLUTION FOR WALES — March 1, 1979

Question:
Do you want the provisions of the Wales Act 1978 to be put into effect?

	Electorate	T'out %	Yes	%	No	%	Spoilt Ballot Papers
Clwyd	284,639	51.1	31,384	21.6	114,119	78.4	227
Dyfed	247,431	64.6	44,849	28.1	114,947	71.9	463
Gwent	319,387	55.3	21,369	12.1	155,389	87.9	189
Gwynedd	171,051	63.4	37,363	34.4	71,157	65.6	276
Mid Glamorgan	394,264	58.6	46,747	20.2	184,196	79.8	929
Powys	80,817	66.0	9,843	18.5	43,502	81.5	175
South Glamorgan	282,907	58.7	21,830	13.1	144,186	86.9	595
West Glamorgan	275,853	57.5	29,663	18.7	128,834	81.3	455
TOTAL	**2,056,349**[1]	**58.3**	**243,048**	**20.3**	**956,330**	**79.7**	**3,309**

[1] A provision of the Wales Act was that not less than 40% of persons entitled to vote voted "Yes" in the referendum. The Secretary of State for Wales estimated that of the total electorate on March 1, 14,900 had died; 800 were convicted prisoners in prisons and 2,600 were students and nurses registered at more than one address. The official estimated number of the electorate was therefore reduced to 2,038,049 and of this the total "Yes" vote was 11.9% and the "No" vote was 46.9%. The turnout was increased to 58.8%.

Source: Welsh Office

Table 13.04 REFERENDUM ON DEVOLUTION FOR SCOTLAND — March 1, 1979

Question:
Do you want the provisions of the Scotland Act 1978 to be put into effect?

	Electorate	T'out %	Yes	%	No	%	Spoilt Ballot Papers
Borders	77,565	66.4	20,746	40.3	30,780	59.7	92
Central	197,772	65.9	71,296	54.7	59,105	45.3	198
Dumfries and Galloway	105,202	64.1	27,162	40.3	40,239	59.7	114
Fife	246,097	65.3	86,252	53.7	74,436	46.3	254
Grampian	343,527	57.2	94,944	48.3	101,485	51.7	415
Highland	136,445	64.7	44,973	51.0	43,274	49.0	90
Lothian	567,255	65.9	187,221	50.1	186,421	49.9	324
Orkney	13,937	54.1	2,104	27.9	5,439	72.1	17
Shetland	14,882	50.3	2,020	27.0	5,466	73.0	18
Strathclyde	1,769,077	62.5	596,519	54.0	508,599	46.0	1,302
Tayside	293,188	63.0	91,482	49.5	93,325	50.5	282
Western Isles	22,365	49.9	6,218	55.8	4,933	44.2	27
TOTAL	**3,787,312**[1]	**63.0**	**1,230,937**	**51.6**	**1,153,502**	**48.4**	**3,133**

[1] A provision of the Scotland Act was that not less than 40% of persons entitled to vote voted "Yes" in the referendum. The Secretary of State for Scotland estimated that of the total electorate on March 1, 26,400 had died; 2,000 were convicted prisoners in prison and 11,800 were students and nurses registered at more than one address. The official estimated number of the electorate was therefore reduced to 3,747,112 and of this total the "Yes" vote was 32.8% and the "No" vote 30.8%. The turnout was increased to 63.6%.

Source: The Certificate of the Chief Counting Officer (Cmnd. 7530 of 1979-80).

Table 14.01 GENERAL ELECTION TIME-TABLE 1832-1910

Year	Parliament Dissolved[1]	First Nomination	First Contest	Last Contest[2]	Parliament Assembled
1832	December 3	December 8	December 10	January 8 (1833)	January 29
1835	December 29 (1834)	January 5	January 6	February 6	February 19
1837	July 17	July 22	July 24	August 18	November 15
1841	June 23	June 28	June 29	July 22	August 19
1847	July 23	July 28	July 29	August 26	November 18
1852	July 1	July 6	July 7	July 31	November 4
1857	March 21	March 26	March 27	April 24	April 30
1859	April 23	April 27[1]	April 28	May 18	May 31
1865	July 6	July 10	July 11	July 24	February 1 (1866)
1868	November 11	November 16	November 17	December 7	December 10
1874	January 26	January 29[2]	January 31	February 17	March 5
1880	March 24	March 30	March 31	April 27	April 29
1885	November 18	November 23	November 24	December 18	January 12 (1886)
1886	June 26	June 30	July 1	July 27	August 5
1892	June 28	July 1	July 4	July 26	August 4
1895	July 8	July 12	July 13	August 7	August 12
1900	September 25	September 28	October 1	October 24	December 3
1906	January 8	January 11	January 12	February 8	February 13
1910(J)	January 10	January 14	January 15	February 10	February 15
1910(D)	November 28	December 2	December 3	December 19	January 31 (1911)

Between 1705 and 1832 General Elections took place in the following years. The dates given are those of the first and last elections to each Parliament. 1705 (May 7-June 6); 1708 (April 30-July 7); 1710 (October 2-November 16); 1713 (August 22-November 12); 1715 (January 22-March 9); 1722 (March 19-May 9); 1727 (August 14-October 17); 1734 (April 22-June 6); 1741 (April 30-June 11); 1747 (June 26-August 4): 1754 (April 13-May 20); 1761 (March 25-May 5); 1768 (March 16-May 6); 1774 (October 5-November 10); 1780 (September 6-October 18); 1784 (March 30-May 10); 1790 (June 16-July 28); 1796 (May 25-June 29); 1802 (July 5-August 28); 1806 (October 29-December 17); 1807 (May 4-June 9); 1812 (October 5-November 10); 1818 (June 15-July 25); 1820 (March 6-April 14); 1826 (June 7-July 12); 1830 (July 29-September 1); 1831 (April 28-June 1).

[1] The Septennial Act of 1715 fixed the duration of a Parliament at seven years.
[2] The length of time between the first and last contested election is somewhat distorted by the fact that it was usual for the polling in the University constituencies and in Orkney and Shetland to be held a week or so after the other constituencies had completed polling. If University constituencies and Orkney and Shetland are excluded, the last polls were held on the following dates: 1832—January 1, 1833; 1835—January 27; 1837—August 18; 1841—July 22; 1847—August 18; 1852—July 28; 1857—April 24; 1859—May 18; 1865—July 24; 1868—November 30; 1874—February 17; 1880—April 14; 1885—December 9; 1886—July 17; 1892—July 19; 1895—July 29; 1900—October 15; 1906—January 29; 1910(J)—January 31; 1910(D)—December 19.

Table 14.02 GENERAL ELECTION TIME-TABLE 1918-1987

Year	Election Date Announced[1]	Parliament Dissolved[2]	Nominations Closed	Polling Day[3]	Parliament Assembled
1918	November 14	November 25	December 4	Saturday, December 14[4]	February 4 (1919
1922	October 23	October 26	November 4	Wednesday, November 15	November 20
1923	November 13	November 16	November 26	Thursday, December 6	January 8 (1924)
1924	October 9	October 9	October 18	Wednesday, October 29	December 2
1929	April 24	May 10	May 20	Thursday, May 30	June 25
1931	October 6	October 7	October 16	Tuesday, October 27	November 3
1935	October 23	October 25	November 4	Thursday, November 14	November 26
1945	May 23	June 15	June 25	Thursday, July 5[5]	August 1
1950	January 11	February 3	February 13	Thursday, February 23	March 1
1951	September 19	October 5	October 15	Thursday, October 25	October 31
1955	April 15	May 6	May 16	Thursday, May 26	June 7
1959	September 8	September 18	September 28	Thursday, October 8	October 20
1964	September 15	September 25	October 5	Thursday, October 15	October 27
1966	February 28	March 10	March 21	Thursday, March 31	April 18
1970	May 18	May 29	June 8	Thursday, June 18	June 29
1974(F)	February 7	February 8	February 18	Thursday, February 28	March 6
1974(O)	September 18	September 20	September 30	Thursday, October 10	October 22
1979	March 29	April 7	April 23	Thursday, May 3	May 9
1983	May 9	May 13	May 23	Thursday, June 9	June 15
1987	May 11	May 18	May 27	Thursday, June 11	June 17

[1] The method of informing the country of a Dissolution has been as follows:

Announcement made by the Leader of the House of Commons: General Election of 1918.

Announcement by the Prime Minister in the House of Commons: General Elections of 1923, 1924, 1929, 1931, 1935.

Official announcement issued to the press during a parliamentary recess: General Elections of 1922, 1945, 1950, 1959, 1964, 1974(O).

Official announcement issued to the press during a parliamentary session: General Elections of 1966, 1970, 1974(F), 1979, 1983, 1987.

Broadcast (sound radio) by the Prime Minister during a parliamentary recess: General Elections of 1951 and 1955.

[2] The Parliament Act of 1911 fixed the duration of a Parliament at five years.

[3] The date of polling did not apply to the University constituencies (where the poll remained open for five days), Orkney and Shetland (where the poll remained open for two days until 1929), or in a few cases where polling in a constituency was postponed due to the death of a candidate after the close of nominations.

[4] The counting of votes did not take place until December 28 as the ballot papers of His Majesty's Forces serving on the Western Front (who had been allowed to vote by post) had to be collected and dispatched to Britain.

[5] Due to the appointed polling day falling during the local holiday week in several constituencies, polling was delayed in twenty-two constituencies until July 12 and in one constituency until July 19. The counting of votes did not take place until July 26 as the ballot papers of His Majesty's Forces serving in certain countries overseas (who had been allowed to vote by post) had to be collected and dispatched to Britain by air.

Table 14.03 SEATS IN THE HOUSE OF COMMONS 1832-1987

	1832-1868[1]	1868-1885[2]	1885-1918[3]	1918-1922[4]	1922-1945[5]	1945-1950[6]	1950-1955[7]	1955 1974(F)[8]	1974(F)-1983[9]	Since 1983[10]
London Boroughs	18	22	59	62	62	62	43	42	92	84
English Boroughs	304	263	166	193	193	216	248	247	212	194
English Counties	142	170	231	230	230	232	215	222	212	245
ENGLAND	464	455	456	485	485	510	506	511	516	523
Welsh Boroughs	15	16	12	11	11	11	10	10	10	6
Welsh Counties	17	17	22	24	24	24	26	26	26	32
WALES	32	33	34	35	35	35	36	36	36	38
Scottish Burghs	23	26	31	33	33	33	32	32	29	29
Scottish Counties	30	32	39	38	38	38	39	39	42	43
SCOTLAND	53	58	70	71	71	71	71	71	71	72
Irish Boroughs	39	39	16	21	4	4	4	4	4	4
Irish Counties	64	64	85	80	8	8	8	8	8	13
IRELAND[11]	103	103	101	101	12	12	12	12	12	17
THE UNIVERSITIES[12]	6	9	9	15	12	12	0	0	0	0
UNITED KINGDOM	658	658	670	707	615	640	625	630	635	650

[1] Representation of the People Acts (England and Wales/Scotland/Ireland), 1832. In 1844 Sudbury (2 seats) was disfranchised reducing the number of Members to 656. In 1852 St. Albans (2 seats) was disfranchised reducing the number of Members to 654. By the Appropriation of Seats (Sudbury and St. Albans) Act, 1861 two of these seats were allocated immediately to Birkenhead and Lancashire, Southern, and the remaining two seats were given to Yorkshire, West Riding from the Dissolution of Parliament in 1865. The number of Members was thus restored to 656 in 1861 and 658 in 1865.

[2] Representation of the People Acts (England and Wales/Scotland/Ireland), 1868. In 1870 Beverley (2 seats), Bridgwater (2 seats), Cashel (1 seat) and Sligo (1 seat) were disfranchised reducing the number of Members to 652. In June 1885, Macclesfield (2 seats) and Sandwich (2 seats) were disfranchised reducing the number of Members to 648.

[3] Redistribution of Seats Act, 1885.

[4] Representation of the People Act, 1918.

[5] Government of Ireland Act, 1920.

[6] House of Commons (Redistribution of Seats) Act, 1944.

[7] Representation of the People Act, 1948.

[8] Statutory Instruments, 1955, Nos. 2-31 and 165-186.

[9] Statutory Instruments, 1970, Nos. 1674, 1675, 1678, 1680.

[10] Statutory Instruments, 1982, No. 183; 1983, Nos. 417, 418, 422.

[11] The whole of Ireland until 1922, thereafter Northern Ireland only.

[12] The University seats were divided as follows: 1832-68 — England 4; Ireland 2. 1868-1918 — England 5; Scotland 2; Ireland 2. 1918-50 — England 7, Wales 1; Scotland 3; Ireland (until 1922) 4; Northern Ireland (from 1922) 1.

Table 14.04 MINISTERS DEFEATED 1918-1987

Election[1]	Ministry at Dissolution	Cabinet Ministers	Ministers not in the Cabinet	Law Officers	Junior Ministers[2]
1918	COALITION	0	0	0	0
1922	CONSERVATIVE	1	0	1	4
1923	CONSERVATIVE	2	2	1	2
1924	LABOUR	1	0	0	7
1929	CONSERVATIVE	1	0	2	5
1931	NATIONAL[3]	0	0	1	3
1935	NATIONAL	2	0	0	0
1945	NATIONAL[4]	5	8	0	19
1950	LABOUR	1	0	1	5
1951	LABOUR	0	0	0	2
1955	CONSERVATIVE	0	0	0	0
1959	CONSERVATIVE	0	0	0	2
1964	CONSERVATIVE	2	1	0	3
1966	LABOUR	0	0	0	0
1970	LABOUR	1	3	0	10
1974(F)	CONSERVATIVE	1	0	0	2
1974(O)	LABOUR	0	0	0	0
1979	LABOUR	1	0	0	7
1983	CONSERVATIVE	0	0	0	2
1987	CONSERVATIVE	0	0	1	4

[1] At by-elections the following Ministers were defeated:
Sir A.S.T. Griffith-Boscawen (C), Minister of Agriculture and Fisheries (Dudley, 1921).
T.A. Lewis (L), Lord Commissioner of the Treasury (Glamorgan, Pontypridd, 1922).
Sir A.S.T. Griffith-Boscawen (C), Minister of Health (Surrey, Mitcham, 1923).
J.W. Hills (C), Financial Secretary to the Treasury (Liverpool, Edge Hill, 1923).
Hon. G.F. Stanley (C), Under-Secretary of State for the Home Department (Willesden, East, 1923).
P.C. Gordon Walker (Lab), Secretary of State for Foreign Affairs (Leyton, 1965).
With the exception of Sir A.S.T. Griffith-Boscawen who, after his defeat at Dudley in 1921, retained office and was elected at another by-election one month later, all defeated Ministers subsequently resigned office.
[2] Including the Treasurer, Comptroller and Vice-Chamberlain of H.M. Household.
[3] The defeated members of the former Labour Government were:—
    Cabinet Ministers, 13; Ministers not in the Cabinet, 1; Junior Ministers, 20.
[4] The defeated members of the former Coalition Government were:—
    Ministers not in the Cabinet, 10; Law Officers, 1; Junior Ministers, 14.

Table 14.05 SEATS VACANT AT DISSOLUTIONS 1886-1987

1886
No seat vacant

1892
Essex, Epping (C)
Lambeth, Norwood (C)
Pembroke and Haverfordwest Boroughs (C)
Swansea Town (L)

1895
No seat vacant

1900
Armagh, South (N)

1906
Cambridge University (C)
Montgomeryshire (L)

1910 (J)
Ipswich (L)
Kensington, South (C)
Liverpool, Exchange (L)
Middlesex, Uxbridge (C)
Portsmouth (L)
Tipperary, Mid (N)

1910 (D)
Carmarthenshire, Western (L)
Kerry, East (Ind N)
Lancashire, Clitheroe (Lab)

1918
Belfast, North (C)
Cork, North-East (Ind N)
Fulham (C)
Staffordshire, Western (C)
Surrey, Kingston (C)
Surrey, Reigate (Nat P)

1922
Roxburghshire and Selkirkshire (Co L)

1923
Ayrshire and Bute, Kilmarnock (L)
Glasgow, Central (C)
University of Wales (NL)
Warwickshire, Warwick and Leamington (C)

1924
London University (C)

1929
Buckinghamshire, Aylesbury (C)
Cambridge University (C)
Carlisle (C)
Lancashire, Ince (Lab)
Nottinghamshire, Mansfield (Lab)
Preston (one seat) (C)
Willesden, East (C)
Yorkshire, Thirsk and Malton (C)

1931
Gateshead[1] (Lab)
Yorkshire, Hemsworth (Lab)

[1] Member died on the day of Dissolution

1935
Derbyshire, Clay Cross (Lab)
Essex, Harwich (NL)
Hammersmith, North (Lab)
Holborn[1] (C)
Lancashire, Farnworth (C)
Roxburghshire and Selkirkshire (C)

1945
Antrim (one seat) C
Bradford, East (C)
Bristol, North (NL)
Cardiganshire (L)
Hythe (C)
Wednesbury (Lab)
Yorkshire, Rother Valley (Lab)

1950
Deptford (Lab)
Durham, Chester-le-Street (Lab)
Islington, North (Lab)
Manchester, Ardwick (Lab)
Rotherham (Lab)
Sheffield, Hillsborough (Lab)
Sheffield, Park (Lab)

1951
Droylsden (Lab)
Lanarkshire, Lanark (C)
Lincolnshire, Grantham (C)

1955
Glasgow, Pollok (C)
Kent, Gravesend (Lab)
Norwich, South (C)

1959
Birmingham, Sparkbrook (Lab)
Kensington, South (C)
Lancashire, Clitheroe (C)
Midlothian (Lab)
Nottingham, North (Lab)
Yorkshire, Richmond (C)

1964
Ashton-under-Lyne (Lab)
Bebington (C)
Berkshire, Newbury (C)
Blackpool, South (C)
Cheshire, Runcorn (C)
Edinburgh, Pentlands (C)
Norfolk, North (Lab)
Northamptonshire, Kettering (Lab)
Renfrewshire, West (NL & C)
Salford, West (Lab)
Shoreditch and Finsbury (Lab)
Southgate (C)
Surrey, Woking (C)
Westmorland (C)

1966
Birmingham, Edgbaston (C)
Cornwall, Falmouth and Camborne (Lab)

SEATS VACANT AT DISSOLUTIONS 1886-1987 (Cont.)

1970
Northumberland, Morpeth (Lab)
Twickenham (C)

1974 (F)
Worcestershire, South (C)

1974 (O)
Newcastle upon Tyne, East (Lab)
Swansea, East (Lab)

1979
Abingdon (C)
Batley and Morley (Lab)
Chipping Barnet (C)
Derbyshire, North-East (Lab)

1983
Cardiff, North-West (C)
Rhondda (Lab)

1987
Deptford (Lab)
Kirkcaldy (Lab)

Table 14.06   THE WEATHER ON POLLING DAY 1918-1987

Election	Weather
1918	Rain over the whole country with thunderstorms in the North.
1922	Quiet weather with low temperatures. Fog in many places.
1923	Fog in central England and Southern Scotland but fine elsewhere.
1924	Wet and very windy.
1929	Fine in the North but cloudy in the South.
1931	Unsettled in Scotland and Northern Ireland but fine elsewhere.
1935	Unsettled with strong winds in the West and South-West.
1945	Clear and fair.
1950	Sunny and mild until evening then heavy rain.
1951	Light fog and frost in the morning but clearing and remaining generally fair.
1955	Generally fine and sunny but with some showers in the evening.
1959	A dry autumn day.
1964	Rain over much of the country.
1966	Mild day with only a trace of rain anywhere except in the North of Scotland.
1970	Fine everywhere.
1974(F)	Some rain in all parts of the country but especially in the South-West.
1974(O)	Cloudy with showers in some parts but few instances of heavy rain.
1979	Fair. The only appreciable rain was reported from Scotland and the West Country.
1983	Cloudy with light showers in most areas. Warm.
1987	Generally cool. Frequent showers, sometimes heavy with thunderstorms in many areas but mainly dry and sunny in western districts.

Sources: 1918-35 and 1983- Meteorological Office
1945-79 Nuffield College studies of British General Elections

Table 14.07 THE FIRST RESULT 1918-1987

Since 1918 when polling in all constituencies at a General Election took place on the same day, there has always been keen competition between Returning Officers to provide the first result declared.

The following constituencies provided the first result of each General Election and from 1950 the actual time of declaration is given.

Election	Constituency	Election	Constituency
1918	Salford, North	1959	Billericay (9.57 p.m.)
1922	Wallasey	1964	Cheltenham (10.00 p.m.)
1923	Manchester, Exchange	1966	Cheltenham (10.04 p.m.)
1924	Salford, South	1970	Guildford (11.10 p.m.)
1929	Oxford	1974(F)	Guildford (11.10 p.m.)
1931	Hornsey	1974(O)	Guildford (11.10 p.m.)
1935	Cheltenham	1979	Glasgow, Central (11.34 p.m.)
1945	Salford, South	1983	Torbay (11.10 p.m.)
1950	Salford, West (10.45 p.m.)	1987	Torbay (11.02 p.m.)
1951	Salford, West (10.21 p.m.)		
1955	Cheltenham (10.08 p.m.)		
	Salford, West (10.08 p.m.)		

Note: Close of poll extended in 1970 from 9.00 p.m. to 10.00 p.m.

Sources: The Press Association, *The Times,* local newspapers.

Table 14.08   THE OVERNIGHT RESULTS 1950-1987

Since 1950 an increasing number of constituencies have commenced counting immediately after polling finished instead of waiting until the next morning. The following is a summary of the strength of the parties and of gains and losses when all the overnight counts had been completed.

Election	Total Results	STATE OF PARTIES C	Lab	L*	Others	PARTY GAINS AND LOSSES C +	−	Lab +	−	L* +	−	Others +	−
1950	264	102^1	163	1	0	—		—		—		—	
1951	319	145^2	175	2	1	11	1	0	12	1	0	1	0
1955	357	176	179	2	0	9	0	0	8	0	0	0	1
1959	388	205	180	3	0	21	4	3	21	1	0	0	0
1964	430	181	247	2	0	4	49	52	4	0	2	0	1
1966	461	151	304	5	1	0	43	42	1	2	1	1	0
1970	418	188	227	2	1	54	6	9	51	0	3	1	4
1974(F)	442	177	255	5	5	2	12	10	5	2	1	4	0
1974(O)	493	185	294	5	9	1	21	20	1	0	2	5	2
1979	514	258	245	7	4	52	6	11	47	0	1	0	9
1983	572	352	199	17	4	8	1	1	6	1	3	0	0
1987	595	348	225	16	6	12	27	25	6	2	8	4	2

[1] Including 2 unopposed
[2] Including 4 unopposed
*SDP/Liberal Alliance 1983-87

Table 14.09 UNOPPOSED RETURNS 1832-1987

Election	Total Seats	C	Lab	L	N	Others	Total	%
1832	658	66	—	109	—	14	189	28.7
1835	658	121	—	154	—	0	275	41.8
1837	658	121	—	115	—	0	236	35.9
1841	658	212	—	113	—	12	337	51.2
1847	656	213	—	136	—	18	367	55.9
1852	654	160	—	95	—	0	255	39.0
1857	654	148	—	176	—	4	328	50.2
1859	654	196	—	183	—	0	379	58.0
1865	658	142	—	161	—	0	303	46.0
1868	658	91	—	121	—	0	212	32.2
1874	652	125	—	52	10	0	187	28.7
1880	652	58	—	41	10	0	109	16.7
1885	670	10	—	14	19	0	43	6.4
1886	670	118	—	40	66	0	224	33.4
1892	670	40	—	13	9	1	63	9.4
1895	670	132	—	11	46	0	189	28.2
1900	670	163	0	22	58	0	243	36.3
1906	670	13	0	27	73	1	114	17.0
1910(J)	670	19	0	1	55	0	75	11.2
1910(D)	670	72	3	35	53	0	163	24.3
1918	707	41	11	27	1	27	107	15.1
1922	615	42	4	10	1	0	57	9.3
1923	615	35	3	11	1	0	50	8.1
1924	615	16	9	6	1	0	32	5.2
1929	615	4	0	0	3	0	7	1.1
1931	615	56	6[1]	5	0	0	67	10.9
1935	615	26	13	0	0	1	40	6.5
1945	640	1	2	0	0	0	3	0.5
1950	625	2	0	0	0	0	2	0.3
1951	625	4	0	0	0	0	4	0.6
1955	630	0	0	0	0	0	0	—
1959	630	0	0	0	0	0	0	—
1964	630	0	0	0	0	0	0	—
1966	630	0	0	0	0	0	0	—
1970	630	0	0	0	0	0	0	—
1974(F)	635	0	0	0	0	0	0	—
1974(O)	635	0	0	0	0	0	0	—
1979	635	0	0	0	0	0	0	—
1983	650	0	0	0	0	0	0	—
1987	650	0	0	0	0	0	0	—

[1] Including one unendorsed

Table 14.10   ANALYSIS OF CONSTITUENCIES 1832-1949

1832–1868[1]

	4 Members	3 Members	2 Members	1 Member	Total
London Boroughs	1	0	7	0	8
English Boroughs	0	0	126	52	178
English Counties	0	7	60	1	68
ENGLAND	1	7	193	53	254
Welsh Boroughs	0	0	0	15	15
Welsh Counties	0	0	4	9	13
WALES	0	0	4	24	28
Scottish Burghs	0	0	2	19	21
Scottish Counties	0	0	0	30	30
SCOTLAND	0	0	2	49	51
Irish Boroughs	0	0	6	27	33
Irish Counties	0	0	32	0	32
IRELAND	0	0	38	27	65
THE UNIVERSITIES	0	0	3	0	3
UNITED KINGDOM	1	7	240	153	401

1868–1885[2]

	4 Members	3 Members	2 Members	1 Member	Total
London Boroughs	1	0	9	0	10
English Boroughs	0	4	80	91	175
English Counties	0	7	74	1	82
ENGLAND	1	11	163	92	267
Welsh Boroughs	0	0	1	14	15
Welsh Counties	0	0	4	9	13
WALES	0	0	5	23	28
Scottish Burghs	0	1	2	19	22
Scottish Counties	0	0	0	32	32
SCOTLAND	0	1	2	51	54
Irish Boroughs	0	0	6	27	33
Irish Counties	0	0	32	0	32
IRELAND	0	0	38	27	65
THE UNIVERSITIES	0	0	3	3	6
UNITED KINGDOM	1	12	211	196	420

1885–1918

	4 Members	3 Members	2 Members	1 Member	Total
London Boroughs	0	0	1	57	58
English Boroughs	0	0	20	126	146
English Counties	0	0	0	231	231
ENGLAND	0	0	21	414	435
Welsh Boroughs	0	0	1	10	11
Welsh Counties	0	0	0	22	22
WALES	0	0	1	32	33
Scottish Burghs	0	0	1	29	30
Scottish Counties	0	0	0	39	39
SCOTLAND	0	0	1	68	69
Irish Boroughs	0	0	1	14	15
Irish Counties	0	0	0	85	85
IRELAND	0	0	1	99	100
THE UNIVERSITIES	0	0	3	3	6
UNITED KINGDOM	0	0	27	616	643

ANALYSIS OF CONSTITUENCIES 1832-1949 (Cont.)

1918—1922

	4 Members	3 Members	2 Members	1 Member	Total
London Boroughs	0	0	1	60	61
English Boroughs	0	0	10	173	183
English Counties	0	0	0	230	230
ENGLAND	0	0	11	463	474
Welsh Boroughs	0	0	0	11	11
Welsh Counties	0	0	0	24	24
WALES	0	0	0	35	35
Scottish Burghs	0	0	1	31	32
Scottish Counties	0	0	0	38	38
SCOTLAND	0	0	1	69	70
Irish Boroughs	0	0	1	19	20
Irish Counties	0	0	0	80	80
IRELAND	0	0	1	99	100
THE UNIVERSITIES	0	1	4	4	9
UNITED KINGDOM	0	1	17	670	688

1922—1945

	4 Members	3 Members	2 Members	1 Member	Total
London Boroughs	0	0	1	60	61
English Boroughs	0	0	10	173	183
English Counties	0	0	0	230	230
ENGLAND	0	0	11	463	474
Welsh Boroughs	0	0	0	11	11
Welsh Counties	0	0	0	24	24
WALES	0	0	0	35	35
Scottish Burghs	0	0	1	31	32
Scottish Counties	0	0	0	38	38
SCOTLAND	0	0	1	69	70
Irish Boroughs	0	0	0	4	4
Irish Counties	0	0	3	2	5
IRELAND	0	0	3	6	9
THE UNIVERSITIES	0	1	3	3	7
UNITED KINGDOM	0	1	18	576	595

1945—1949

	4 Members	3 Members	2 Members	1 Member	Total
London Boroughs	0	0	1	60	61
English Boroughs	0	0	10	196	206
English Counties	0	0	0	232	232
ENGLAND	0	0	11	488	499
Welsh Boroughs	0	0	0	11	11
Welsh Counties	0	0	0	24	24
WALES	0	0	0	35	35
Scottish Burghs	0	0	1	31	32
Scottish Counties	0	0	0	38	38
SCOTLAND	0	0	1	69	70
Irish Boroughs	0	0	0	4	4
Irish Counties	0	0	3	2	5
IRELAND	0	0	3	6	9
THE UNIVERSITIES	0	1	3	3	7
UNITED KINGDOM	0	1	18	601	620

From 1950 all constituencies returned one MP.

[1] For details of the changes which took place between 1832 and 1868 see Table 14.03 footnote[1].
[2] For details of the changes which took place between 1868 and 1885 see Table 14.03 footnote[2].

Table 14.11 SINGLE MEMBER SEATS WON ON A
MINORITY VOTE 1885-1987

Election	C	Lab	L[1]	Others	Total	% of seats[2]
1885	8	0	9	5	22	51.2
1886	0	0	0	0	0	—
1892	6	0	1	3	10	31.3
1895	5	0	8	2	15	51.7
1900	2	0	1	1	4	50.0
1906	11	2	9	5	27	58.7
1910(J)	8	0	21	1	30	65.2
1910(D)	1	0	10	2	13	76.5
1918	50	17	21	9	97	37.6
1922	89	54	28	3	174	74.0
1923	90	65	46	2	203	79.6
1924	80	33	7	4	124	54.4
1929	151	118	40	1	310	65.5
1931	21	4[2]	8	1	34	30.1
1935	32	17	7	2	58	37.9
1945	92	71	2	9	174	51.3
1950	106	76	5	0	187	36.7
1951	25	14	0	0	39	31.0
1955	25	11	1	0	37	26.2
1959	47	31	2	0	80	31.1
1964	154	71	7	0	232	53.2
1966	131	43	11	0	185	46.7
1970	68	48	6	2	124	27.9
1974(F)	234	150	9	15	408	68.3
1974(O)	224	131	11	14	380	59.8
1979	107	83	6	10	206	32.6
1983	165	141	15	15	336	51.7
1987	142	109	19	13	283	43.5

[1] SDP/Liberal Alliance 1983-87
[2] Single-member seats with three or more candidates

Table 14.12 **SINGLE MEMBER SEATS WON ON A MAJORITY OF THE ELECTORATE 1918-1987**

Election	C	Lab	L[1]	Others	Total	% of contested seats
1918	15	0	3	16	34	6.0
1922	7	8	1	0	16	3.0
1923	0	7	1	0	8	1.5
1924	41	6	2	1	50	9.2
1929	0	26	0	0	26	4.6
1931	204	10	9	20	243	46.6
1935	25	20	1	3	49	9.0
1945	0	80	0	0	80	13.4
1950	45	106	1	0	152	24.4
1951	84	128	2	0	214	34.5
1955	53	52	1	0	106	16.8
1959	53	54	0	0	107	16.8
1964	2	52	0	0	54	8.6
1966	1	54	0	0	55	8.7
1970	0	20	0	0	20	3.2
1974(F)	0	22	0	0	22	3.5
1974(O)	0	10	0	0	10	1.6
1979	5	12	0	0	17	2.7
1983	0	1	0	0	1	0.2
1987	3	12	0	0	15	2.3

[1]SDP/Liberal Alliance 1983-87

Table 14.13 **TYPES OF CONTESTS 1885-1987**

Election	SINGLE MEMBER SEATS WITH CANDIDATES NUMBERING:										Total Seats
	One	Two	Three	Four	Five	Six	Seven	Eight	Nine	Eleven	
1885	35	538	39	4	0	0	0	0	0	0	616
1886	212	400	4	0	0	0	0	0	0	0	616
1892	57	527	30	2	0	0	0	0	0	0	616
1895	181	406	29	0	0	0	0	0	0	0	616
1900	229	379	7	1	0	0	0	0	0	0	616
1906	108	462	45	1	0	0	0	0	0	0	616
1910(J)	69	501	46	0	0	0	0	0	0	0	616
1910(D)	153	446	16	1	0	0	0	0	0	0	616
1918	101	311	211	36	10	1	0	0	0	0	670
1922	48	293	212	22	1	0	0	0	0	0	576
1923	41	280	254	1	0	0	0	0	0	0	576
1924	30	318	223	5	0	0	0	0	0	0	576
1929	5	98	447	26	0	0	0	0	0	0	576
1931	54	409	99	14	0	0	0	0	0	0	576
1935	34	389	146	7	0	0	0	0	0	0	576
1945	3	259	291	42	6	0	0	0	0	0	601
1950	2	113	405	100	5	0	0	0	0	0	625
1951	4	495	122	4	0	0	0	0	0	0	625
1955	0	489	133	8	0	0	0	0	0	0	630
1959	0	373	238	19	0	0	0	0	0	0	630
1964	0	194	379	53	4	0	0	0	0	0	630
1966	0	234	349	44	2	1	0	0	0	0	630
1970	0	185	328	103	13	1	0	0	0	0	630
1974(F)	0	38	370	191	32	3	1	0	0	0	635
1974(O)	0	0	346	238	44	7	0	0	0	0	635
1979	0	3	173	300	118	28	12	0	1	0	635
1983	0	0	251	250	99	31	12	5	1	1	650
1987	0	0	351	236	51	11	1	0	0	0	650

Table 14.14 **THE ILLITERATE VOTE 1880-1910**

Election	England	Wales	Scotland	Ireland	Total	% of electors voting
1880	27,490	2,136	*	5,312	34,938	2.1
1885	74,909	5,521	7,708	98,404	186,542	4.3
1886	35,541	3,046	4,836	36,722	80,145	2.9
1892	42,480	3,629	4,577	84,919	135,605	3.1
1895	24,852	3,669	4,062	40,357	72,940	2.0
1906	18,596	1,162	2,041	12,510	34,309	0.7
1910(J)	15,657	1,494	2,044	22,515	41,710	0.7

*No figures available.

Voters who were illiterate, or incapacitated by blindness or other physical cause, could have their ballot papers marked for them by Presiding Officers at polling stations. Statistics were only published from 1880 until 1910(J).

Source: Returns of Illiterate Voters (Home Office).

Table 14.15 POLLING DISTRICTS AND STATIONS 1950-1987

Election	Polling Districts[1]	Polling Stations[2]
1950	25,304	48,243
1951	26,348	48,212
1955	27,797	49,510
1959	28,951	49,817
1964	30,255	49,637
1966	30,470	49,565
1970	30,864	49,687
1974(F)	31,287	48,631
1974(O)	31,171	48,384
1979	33,086	48,035
1983	34,247	46,903
1987	35,042	46,566

[1] Each constituency is divided into a number of polling districts by the local authority (in Scotland by the Returning Officer).

[2] Each constituency polling district is further divided into a number of polling stations for the accommodation of electors. A separate room or separate booth may contain a separate polling station, or several polling stations may be constructed in the same room or booth. A Presiding Officer and clerks are appointed and separate equipment is provided for each polling station.

Source: Returns of Election Expenses (Home Office).

Table 14.16 LIBERALS AND NATIONALISTS IN SECOND PLACE 1950-1987

The following table shows the number of constituencies (contested by *both* Conservative and Labour candidates) in which Liberal or Nationalist candidates took second place in the poll.

Election	L	PC	SNP
1950	17	0	0
1951	9	0	0
1955	11	1	1
1959	26	1	1
1964	55	0	1
1966	26	1	3
1970	26	8	9
1974(F)	145	7	17
1974(O)	102	6	42
1979	82	1	13
1983	312	1	7
1987	261[1]	1[2]	13[3]

[1] Held by 230 Conservatives, 31 Labour
[2] Held by Labour
[3] Held by 10 Labour, 3 Conservatives

SDP/Liberal Alliance 1983-87

Table 14.17 CONSTITUENCY BOUNDARY CHANGES 1945-1987

Election	Unchanged	%	Minor changes	%	Major changes	%
1945[1]	562	87.8	31	4.8	47	7.4
1950[2]	80	12.8	8	1.3	537	85.9
1951[3]	584	93.4	41	6.6	0	–
1955[2]	382	60.6	72	11.4	176	28.0
1959[3]	615	97.6	15	2.4	0	–
1964[3]	566	89.8	64	10.2	0	–
1974(F)[2]	210	33.1	109	17.2	316	49.7
1983[2]	66	10.4	43	6.8	526	82.8
1987[3]	556	85.5	92	14.2	2	0.3

[1] Review of twenty abnormally large constituencies and the creation of an additional twenty-five seats in the House of Commons.

[2] Review of all constituency boundaries.

[3] Review of certain constituencies to bring the boundaries into line with changes which had taken place in local government boundaries.

Premanent Boundary Commissions (for England, Wales, Scotland and Northern Ireland) were created in 1944 and prior to the 1945 election they carried out a review of twenty abnormally large constituencies in England. Initial reports were published between September and December 1947 and the First Periodical Reports appeared between August and November 1954. The original rules laid down that each Commission must report not less than three or more than seven years from the date of their previous report but this was altered in 1958 to between ten and fifteen years. The Second Periodical Reports were published in June 1969 and the Third Periodical Reports between November 1982 and February 1983.

As regards what constitutes a major or minor change, the figures in each category prior to 1974 are based on the Commissioners reports but modified as a result of information from other sources. Since 1974 it has been possible to obtain the number of electors involved in each change and only changes involving less than 5% of the electorate have been classed as minor. Boundary changes involving no electors have been classed as unchanged.

With the limited information available prior to 1974 it is possible that some minor changes should have been classed as major or unchanged so the figures for the redistributions of 1950 and 1955 should be treated with caution.

Table 14.18 ELECTORAL QUOTAS 1946-1976

In considering boundary changes, the Boundary Commissions apply an electoral quota which is a figure obtained by dividing the total electorate by the number of constituencies existing at the time the Commissions begin their reviews. So far as practicable each constituency should have an electorate close to the electoral quota but the length of time between the start of the reviews, the reports and final approval by Parliament means that the quota may have altered considerably.
Until 1965 the quota was calculated for Great Britain as a whole but since then it has been related to each part of the United Kingdom.
The following table shows the electoral quota used by each Commission.

Commenced review	Effective from General Election	ELECTORAL QUOTA			
		England	Wales	Scotland	N. Ireland
1946	1950	57,697	57,697	57,697	71,457
1953[1]	1955	55,670	55,670	55,670	72,913
1965	1974(F)	58,759	50,367	47,745	74,952
1976[2]	1983	65,753	58,753	53,649	61,206

[1] 1954 in Northern Ireland
[2] 1978 in Scotland and 1981 in Wales

Table 14.19 SPOILT BALLOT PAPERS 1880-1987

	Want of official mark	Voting for more than one candidate	Writing or mark by which voter could be identified	Unmarked or void for uncertainty	Total	Average per constituency
1880						
ENGLAND	—	—	—	—	7,905	31
WALES	—	—	—	—	531	19
SCOTLAND	—	—	—	—	1,797	33
IRELAND	—	—	—	—	1,551	27
UNITED KINGDOM	—	—	—	—	**11,784**[1]	29
1924						
ENGLAND & WALES	1,997	4,418	8,334	9,415	24,164	49
SCOTLAND	864	436	1,647	3,038	5,985	88
N. IRELAND	24	507	298	626	1,455	146
UNITED KINGDOM	**2,885**	**5,361**	**10,279**	**13,079**	**31,604**	**54**
1950						
SCOTLAND	1,849	986	1,136	1,295	5,266	74
1951						
SCOTLAND	1,193	646	1,254	1,574	4,667	66
1955						
SCOTLAND	921	671	1,158	1,841	4,591	65
1959						
SCOTLAND	927	796	878	1,615	4,216	59
1964						
ENGLAND	1,750	12,289	5,358	12,087	31,484	62
WALES	234	1,137	275	921	2,567	71
SCOTLAND	823	1,063	887	1,929	4,702	66
N. IRELAND	19	997	267	1,037	2,320	193
UNITED KINGDOM	**2,826**	**15,486**	**6,787**	**15,974**	**41,073**	**65**
1966						
ENGLAND	1,203	8,847	7,145	21,913	39,108	77
WALES	198	1,036	309	1,737	3,280	91
SCOTLAND	652	852	790	2,894	5,188	73
N. IRELAND	8	784	281	1,250	2,323	194
UNITED KINGDOM	**2,061**	**11,519**	**8,525**	**27,794**	**49,899**	**79**
1970						
ENGLAND	1,414	10,406	6,588	14,809	33,217	65
WALES	78	1,547	258	635	2,518	70
SCOTLAND	623	1,208	354	1,251	3,436	48
N. IRELAND	3	983	341	849	2,176	181
UNITED KINGDOM	**2,118**	**14,144**	**7,541**	**17,544**	**41,347**	**66**

SPOILT BALLOT PAPERS 1880-1987 (Cont.)

	Want of official mark	Voting for more than one candidate	Writing or mark by which voter could be identified	Unmarked or void for uncertainty	Total	Average per constituency
1974(F)						
ENGLAND	2,063	8,651	6,386	15,108	32,208	62
WALES	197	1,134	255	585	2,171	60
SCOTLAND	824	657	333	1,403	3,217	45
N. IRELAND	92	1,772	346	2,446	4,656	388
UNITED KINGDOM	**3,176**	**12,214**	**7,320**	**19,542**	**42,252**[2]	**67**
1974(O)						
ENGLAND	2,095	8,543	4,599	9,892	25,129	49
WALES	225	1,201	214	502	2,142	60
SCOTLAND	582	983	196	869	2,630	37
N. IRELAND	36	2,765	1,000	4,004	7,805	650
UNITED KINGDOM	**2,938**	**13,492**	**6,009**	**15,267**	**37,706**[3]	**59**
1979						
ENGLAND	2,034	63,622	5,064	26,640	97,360	189
WALES	293	5,081	307	3,964	9,645	268
SCOTLAND	804	852	316	1,359	3,331	47
N. IRELAND	151	2,960	114	4,287	7,512	626
UNITED KINGDOM	**3,282**	**72,515**	**5,801**	**36,250**	**117,848**[4]	**186**
1983						
ENGLAND	1,698	21,551	3,875	12,666	39,790	76
WALES	166	3,042	190	686	4,084	107
SCOTLAND	709	639	564	965	2,877	40
N. IRELAND	246	2,706	64	1,337	4,353	256
UNITED KINGDOM	**2,819**	**27,938**	**4,693**	**15,654**	**51,104**	**79**
1987						
ENGLAND	1,463	9,770	4,093	11,987	27,213	52
WALES	76	1,374	158	653	2,261	60
SCOTLAND	599	381	485	1,055	2,520	35
N. IRELAND	270	2,691	240	1,650	4,851	285
UNITED KINGDOM	**2,408**	**14,216**	**4,976**	**15,345**	**36,945**	**57**

With the exceptions of the General Elections of 1880 and 1924, statistics relating to spoilt ballot papers were not compiled (except in Scotland from 1950) until the General Election of 1964.

[1] No returns from ten constituencies in England and seven in Ireland.
[2] No returns from two constituencies in England.
[3] No return from one constituency in England.
[4] The increased number of spoilt ballot papers in England and Wales at this election was due to local government elections being held on the same day and electors being asked to mark two ballot papers.

Sources: 1880: House of Commons Papers, 1881 (25), lxxiv, 285
1924: House of Commons Papers, 1926 (49) xxii, 619
1950 onwards: Returns compiled by the Home Office and the Scottish Home and Health Department.

Table 14.20 ELECTION PETITIONS 1832-1964

	Void Elections[1]	Undue Elections[2]	Elections upheld[3]	Petitions withdrawn[4]	Total
General Elections					
1832	7	10	23	8	48
1835	5	7	9	13	34
1837	1	13	40	31	85
1841	10	15	11	36	72
1847	17	1	11	22	51
1852	30	3	29	60	122
1857	7	2	24	39	72
1859	10	1	23	26	60
1865	14	2	19	34	69
1868	21	1	43	37	102
1874	16	3	8	9	36
1880	19	0	15	19	53
1885	4	1	4	3	12
1886	0	2	2	0	4
1892	5	1	6	1	13
1895	2	0	6	2	10
1900	2	0	3	2	7
1906	2	0	3	1	6
1910(J)	3	0	1	1	5
1910(D)	5	1	4	3	13
1922	1	0	1	0	2
1923	1	0	0	0	1
1929	0	0	1	0	1
1955	0	1	0	0	1
1959	0	0	1	0	1
1964	0	0	1	0	1
Total	**182**	**64**	**288**	**347**	**881**
By-Elections					
1832-35	1	1	3	1	6
1835-37	0	4	4	2	10
1837-41	5	2	10	1	18
1841-47	4	2	6	8	20
1847-52	6	1	4	10	21
1852-57	4	1	7	15	27
1857-59	1	0	0	2	3
1859-65	2	1	6	11	20
1865-68	2	1	2	3	8
1868-74	5	2	8	4	19
1874-80	6	1	5	3	15
1880-85	4	1	3	0	8
1892-95	2	0	1	0	3
1895-1900	0	0	0	1	1
1955-59	0	1	0	0	1
1959-64	0	1	0	0	1
Total	**42**	**19**	**59**	**61**	**181**

ELECTION PETITIONS 1832-1964 (Cont.)

The details of the petition trials since 1918 are as follows:

Date	Constituency	Allegations	Result
April 1923	Derbyshire, North Eastern	Irregularities in the reception, rejection and counting of votes	Election upheld
May 1923	Northumberland, Berwick-upon-Tweed	Exceeding maximum permitted election expenses	Void election
May 1924	Oxford	Exceeding maximum permitted election expenses	Void election
October 1929	Plymouth, Drake	Bribery, etc.	Election upheld
September 1955	Fermanagh and South Tyrone	Elected member disqualified as a felon	Undue election
October 1955	Mid-Ulster	Elected member disqualified as a felon	Undue election
April 1960	Kensington, North	Irregularities by the Returning Officer	Election upheld
July 1961	Bristol, South-East	Elected member disqualified as a Peer	Undue election
December 1964	Perthshire and Kinross-shire, Kinross and West Perthshire	Corrupt and illegal practices (failure to include cost of party political broadcasts in return of election expenses)	Election upheld

[1] A 'void' election was one in which the result was quashed and a new writ issued.

[2] An 'undue' election was one in which the Committee or Election Court found the successful candidate not duly elected and ruled that another candidate was entitled to be declared elected. This category includes double returns. See Appendix 14.

[3] An election 'upheld' was one in which the Committee of Election Court dismissed the petition and found the Member duly elected.

[4] A 'withdrawn' petition includes a number of cases in which petitions lapsed due to a legal technicality or the Dissolution of Parliament. Also included in this category are some instances of petitioners failing to appear for the hearing. Petitions which were withdrawn after a hearing or trial commenced are not included in this category but are treated as elections upheld.

Sources: *Journals of the House of Commons*
O'Malley and Hardcastle's Reports on Election Petitions, Vols. 1-7.
The Table, Vol. 24, pp. 59-76 (Fermanagh and South Tyrone: Mid Ulster).
All England Law Reports, 1960, Vol. 2, p. 150 and *Weekly Law Reports,* 1960, Vol. 1, p. 762 (Kensington, North).
All England Law Reports, 1961, Vol. 3, p. 354 and *Weekly Law Reports,* 1961, Vol. 3, p. 577 (Bristol, South-East).
Scots Law Times, 1965, p. 186 (Kinross and West Perthshire).
House of Lords Record Office.
Public Record Office.
Royal Courts of Justice.

Table 14.21 **VOTES PER SEAT WON 1974-1987**

	1974(F)	1974(O)	1979	1983	1987
C	39,974	37,771	40,407	32,777	36,597
Lab	38,690	35,916	42,871	40,464	43,798
L[1]	432,823	411,285	392,164	842,793	333,711
PC	85,687	55,440	66,272	62,655	41,200
SNP	90,454	76,329	252,130	165,988	138,824
Others	68,450	76,402	86,718	56,686	50,440

[1] SDP/Liberal Alliance 1983-87

Table 14.22 VOTES CAST FOR WINNERS AND LOSERS 1974-1987

1974 (February)

	WINNERS			LOSERS		
	Candidates	Votes	% of Total Votes	Candidates	Votes	% of Total Votes
C	297	7,279,384	23.2	326	4,592,796	14.6
Lab	301	7,151,965	22.8	322	4,493,651	14.3
L	14	312,372	1.0	503	5,747,147	18.3
PC	2	21,926	0.1	34	149,448	0.5
SNP	7	113,496	0.4	63	519,684	1.7
Others	14	406,581	1.3	252	551,712	1.8
Total	635	15,285,724	48.8	1,500	16,054,438	51.2

1974 (October)

	Candidates	Votes	% of Total Votes	Candidates	Votes	% of Total Votes
C	277	6,284,720	21.5	345	4,177,845	14.3
Lab	319	7,264,542	24.9	304	4,192,537	14.4
L	13	249,539	0.9	606	5,097,165	17.4
PC	3	47,492	0.2	33	118,829	0.4
SNP	11	173,655	0.6	60	665,962	2.3
Others	12	415,844	1.4	269	500,974	1.7
Total	635	14,435,792	49.5	1,617	14,753,312	50.5

1979

	Candidates	Votes	% of Total Votes	Candidates	Votes	% of Total Votes
C	339	9,558,212	30.6	283	4,139,711	13.3
Lab	269	6,348,058	20.3	354	5,184,160	16.6
L	11	236,118	0.8	566	4,077,686	13.1
PC	2	26,695	0.1	34	105,849	0.3
SNP	2	28,438	0.1	69	475,821	1.5
Others	12	341,912	1.1	635	698,702	2.2
Total	635	16,539,433	53.0	1,941	14,681,929	47.0

1983

	Candidates	Votes	% of Total Votes	Candidates	Votes	% of Total Votes
C	397	10,087,462	32.9	236	2,924,854	9.6
Lab	209	4,274,800	13.9	424	4,182,134	13.6
L[1]	23	454,019	1.5	610	7,326,930	23.9
PC	2	28,017	0.1	36	97,292	0.3
SNP	2	28,548	0.1	70	303,427	1.0
Others	17	342,837	1.1	552	620,817	2.0
Total	650	15,215,683	49.6	1,928	15,455,454	50.4

1987

	Candidates	Votes	% of Total Votes	Candidates	Votes	% of Total Votes
C	376	10,559,017	32.4	257	3,201,566	9.8
Lab	229	5,418,705	16.7	404	4,611,102	14.2
L[1]	22	411,598	1.3	611	6,930,035	21.3
PC	3	49,310	0.2	35	74,289	0.2
SNP	3	58,508	0.2	68	357,965	1.1
Others	17	405,424	1.2	300	452,059	1.4
Total	650	16,902,562	52.0	1,675	15,627,016	48.0

[1] SDP/Liberal Alliance

Appendix 1 REASONS FOR HOLDING GENERAL ELECTIONS 1832-1987

1832 To elect a new Parliament subsequent to the passing of the First (Electoral) Reform Act.

1835 Viscount Melbourne resigned as Prime Minister and was succeeded by Sir Robert Peel who immediately asked for a Dissolution.

1837 Death of William IV.

1841 Request by the Prime Minister after a defeat in the House of Commons.

1847 Request by the Prime Minister for a Dissolution on Parliament nearing the end of its statutory term of seven years.

1852 Lord John Russell resigned as Prime Minister after a defeat in the House of Commons. He was succeeded by the Earl of Derby who four months later requested a Dissolution.

1857 Request by the Prime Minister for a Dissolution after a defeat in the House of Commons.

1859 Request by the Prime Minister for a Dissolution after a defeat in the House of Commons.

1865 Request by the Prime Minister for a Dissolution on Parliament nearing the end of its statutory term of seven years.

1868 To elect a new Parliament subsequent to the passing of the Second (Electoral) Reform Act.

1874 Request by the Prime Minister for a Dissolution on Parliament nearing the end of its statutory term of seven years.

1880 Request by the Prime Minister for a Dissolution on Parliament nearing the end of its statutory term of seven years.

1885 Resignation of the Liberal Government and request for a Dissolution after a defeat in the House of Commons on an amendment to the Finance Bill. The Marquess of Salisbury formed a minority Conservative Government but within five months he requested a Dissolution.

1886 Resignation of the Liberal Government and request for a Dissolution after a defeat in the House of Commons on the Irish Home Rule Bill.

1892 Request by the Prime Minister for a Dissolution on Parliament nearing the end of its statutory term of seven years.

1895 Resignation of the Liberal Government after a defeat in the House of Commons on the issue of the supply of cordite to the Army. The Marquess of Salisbury formed a minority Conservative Government and immediately requested a Dissolution.

1900 Request by the Prime Minister for a Dissolution to obtain a renewal of the electors' confidence in the Government at a time when it appeared that the South African War was drawing to a close.

1906 Resignation of the Conservative Government after a series of defeats in by-elections and internal disputes over tariff reform. Sir Henry Campbell-Bannerman formed a minority Liberal Government and immediately requested a Dissolution.

1910(J) Request by the Prime Minister for a Dissolution after the House of Lords had rejected the Finance Bill.

1910(D) Request by the Prime Minister for a Dissolution after a Constitutional Conference of Liberal and Conservative members had failed to agree on proposals to limit the power of the House of Lords.

1918 End of World War 1. Parliament should have been dissolved in 1915 but its life was extended due to the war.

1922 David Lloyd George resigned as Prime Minister of a Coalition Government and Andrew Bonar Law formed a Conservative Government and immediately asked for a Dissolution.

1923 Andrew Bonar Law resigned as Prime Minister and was succeeded by Stanley Baldwin who within six months asked for a Dissolution to obtain a mandate for tariff reforms.

REASONS FOR HOLDING GENERAL ELECTIONS 1832-1987 (Cont.)

1924	Resignation of the Labour Government and request for a Dissolution after a defeat in the House of Commons on the issue of the Government's decision not to prosecute J.R. Campbell, editor of a Communist Party journal, under the Incitement to Mutiny Act.
1929	Request by the Prime Minister for a Dissolution on Parliament nearing the end of its statutory term of five years.
1931	Resignation of the Labour Government and formation of a National Government by James Ramsay MacDonald who six weeks later asked for a Dissolution in order to obtain a new mandate.
1935	Request by the Prime Minister for a Dissolution on Parliament nearing the end of its statutory term of five years.
1945	End of War in Europe. Parliament should have been dissolved in 1940 but its life was extended due to the war.
1950	Request by the Prime Minister for a Dissolution on Parliament nearing the end of its statutory term of five years.
1951	Request by the Prime Minister for a Dissolution to obtain a renewal of the electors' confidence in the Government and an adequate parliamentary majority.
1955	Sir Winston Churchill resigned as Prime Minister and was succeeded by Sir Anthony Eden who immediately asked for a Dissolution.
1959	Request by the Prime Minister for a Dissolution on Parliament nearing the end of its statutory term of five years.
1964	Request by the Prime Minister for a Dissolution on Parliament nearing the end of its statutory term of five years.
1966	Request by the Prime Minister for a Dissolution to obtain a renewal of the electors' confidence in the Government and an adequate parliamentary majority.
1970	Request by the Prime Minister for a Dissolution on Parliament nearing the end of its statutory term of five years.
1974(F)	Request by the Prime Minister for a Dissolution to obtain a renewal of the electors' confidence in the Government on the eve of a strike by the National Union of Mineworkers.
1974(O)	Request by the Prime Minister for a Dissolution to obtain a renewal of the electors' confidence in the Government and an overall parliamentary majority.
1979	Resignation of the Labour Government and a request for a Dissolution following a defeat in the House of Commons on a motion of no confidence.
1983	Request by the Prime Minister for a Dissolution on Parliament nearing the end of its statutory term of five years.
1987	Request by the Prime Minister for a Dissolution on Parliament nearing the end of its statutory term of five years.

Appendix 2 PRINCIPAL CHANGES IN THE ELECTORAL SYSTEM 1832-1987

Date[1]

June 1832   *Representation of the People Act* (known as the "First Reform Act"). Modest reform of electoral law, extension of the franchise and re-distribution of seats.

August 1867   *Representation of the People Act* (sometimes called the "Second Reform Act"). Extension of the franchise and re-distribution of seats.

July 1868   *Parliamentary Elections Act.* Removed the trial of election petitions from a House of Commons committee to the Courts.

July 1872   *Ballot Act.* Introduced voting by secret ballot.

August 1883   *Corrupt and Illegal Practices Prevention Act.* Placed a maximum limit on election expenses incurred by candidates.

December 1884   *Representation of the People Act* (sometimes called the "Third Reform Act"). Extension of the franchise and re-distribution of seats.

February 1918   *Representation of the People Act.* Abolition of property qualification for voting. Women enfranchised at age 30 and over. Charges of Returning Officers no longer to be paid by candidates. All polls at General Elections to be held on the same day. Postal and proxy voting introduced for servicemen. Candidates required to lodge £150 deposit on nomination which was forfeited if they failed to poll more than one-eighth of the total votes cast. Candidates entitled to free postage on their election addresses or leaflets. Redistribution of seats.

March 1922   *Irish Free State (Agreement) Act.* No further writs to be issued for constituencies in Ireland other than Northern Ireland.

October 1924   First use of radio for broadcasts by the party leaders during a General Election campaign.

July 1926   *Re-Election of Ministers Act (1919) Amendment Act.* Removed the necessity for Ministers of the Crown to seek re-election on accepting office.

July 1928   *Representation of the People (Equal Franchise) Act.* Women enfranchised at age 21 and over. Male and female adult suffrage achieved.

July 1948   *Representation of the People Act.* All plural voting and university constituencies abolished. Extension of postal voting to civilians. Limit on the number of cars which candidates could use on polling day. Redistribution of seats.

December 1949   *Electoral Registers Act.* Persons coming of age between November and June each year to be included in the electoral register, marked by the symbol 'Y' and eligible to vote at any election from October onwards.

October 1951   First use of television for broadcasts by the party leaders during a General Election campaign.

December 1958   *Representation of the People (Amendment Act).* Removal of the restriction on the number of cars which candidates could use on polling day.

July 1963   *Peerage Act.* Peers allowed to disclaim Peerages for life and thus become eligible for membership of the House of Commons.

April 1969   *Representation of the People Act.* Extension of the franchise to persons at age 18 and over. Close of poll extended from 9.00 p.m. to 10.00 p.m.

July 1981   *Representation of the People Act.* Disqualified convicted persons serving sentences of more than 12 months in the British Islands or the Republic of Ireland from nomination to or membership of the House of Commons.

July 1985   *Representation of the People Act.* Extended the franchise to British citizens who are resident outside the UK to qualify as 'overseas electors' in the constituency for which they were last registered for a period of 5 years. Extended absent voting to holidaymakers and raised the deposit to £500 but reduced the threshold to one-twentieth of the total votes cast.

[1] The dates given are those on which the relative Acts came into force but frequently major changes in election law were not effective until the Dissolution of the Parliament then in being or until the coming into force of a Statutory Instrument.

Appendix 3 ELECTION RECORDS 1918-1987

The following records have been established since the introduction of universal suffrage in 1918. University seats and those in Ireland from 1918-22 have been ignored in compiling the records.

Largest Majorities — General Elections (Over 50,000)
Sir A.C. Rawson (Brighton[1], C), 1931 62,253
G.C. Tryon (Brighton[1], C), 1931 62,041
C.C. Craig (Antrim[1], C), 1924. 58,354
R.W.H. O'Neill (Antrim[1], C), 1924. 58,250
Sir P. Cunliffe-Lister (Middlesex, Hendon, C), 1931 51,000
G.B.H. Currie (Down, North, C), 1959. 50,734
S.K. Cunningham (Antrim, South, C), 1959. 50,041

Largest Majorities — By-Elections (Over 30,000)
United Kingdom — Rev. I.R.K. Paisley (Antrim, North, UDUP), January 23, 1986 33,024
Great Britain — E.E. Gates (Lancashire, Middleton and Prestwich, C), May 22, 1940 31,618

Smallest Majorities — General Elections (Under 10)
A.J. Flint (Derbyshire, Ilkeston, N. Lab) 1931 2
F.D. Acland (Devon, Tiverton, L), 1923 3
T.W. Stamford (Leeds, West, Lab), 1924. 3
Sir H. Nicholls, Bt. (Northamptonshire, Peterborough, C), 1966 3
G.G. Jones (Carmarthen, Lab), 1974(F) 3
Lord Colum Crichton-Stuart (Cheshire, Northwich, C), 1929 4
Hon. G.R. Ward (Worcester, C), 1945 4
L. Ropner (Durham, Sedgefield, C), 1923 6
E.L. Gandar-Dower (Caithness and Sutherland, C), 1945 6
F.J. Privett (Portsmouth, Central, C), 1922 7
D.H. Hobden (Brighton, Kemptown, Lab), 1964 7
D.H. Spencer (Leicester, South, C), 1983 7
P.A. Tyler (Cornwall, Bodmin, L), 1974(F) 9

Smallest Majorities — By-Elections (Under 50)
Sir H.C. Lowther (Cumberland, Penrith and Cockermouth, Co C), May 13, 1921 31
O.W. Nicholson (Westminster, Abbey, C), March 19, 1924 43

Largest Number of Votes Cast for a Candidate — General Elections (Over 65,000)
Sir A.C. Rawson (Brighton[1], C), 1931 75,205
G.C. Tryon (Brighton[1], C), 1931 74,993
Sir R. Blair (Middlesex, Hendon, C), 1935. 69,762
C.F. Entwistle (Bolton[1], C), 1931 66,385
Sir P. Cunliffe-Lister (Middlesex, Hendon, C), 1931 66,305

Largest Number of Votes Cast for a Candidate — By-Elections (Over 50,000)
C.H. Mullan (Down[1], C), June 6, 1946. 50,699

Smallest Number of Votes Cast for a Candidate — General Elections (Under 25)
B.C. Wedmore (Finchley, Ind), 1983 13
W.G. Boaks (Devon North, Ind), 1979 20
Mrs. K. Purie-Harwell (Battersea, Ind), 1983 22

Smallest Number of Votes Cast for a Candidate — By-Elections (Under 10)
W.G. Boaks (Glasgow, Hillhead, Ind), March 25, 1982. 5
E.L. Bevan (Bermondsey, Ind Lab), February 24, 1983 8

Highest Turnout — General Election
United Kingdom — Fermanagh and South Tyrone, 1951 . . . . 93.4%
Great Britain — Lancashire, Darwen, 1924. . . . . 92.7%

ELECTION RECORDS 1918-1987 (Cont.)

Lowest Turnout — General Election
Lambeth, Kennington, 1918[2] 29.7%

Lowest Turnout — By-Election
Poplar, South Poplar, August 12, 1942[3] 9.3%

[1] Two-member seat.

[2] Polling had been delayed in this constituency due to the death of the Conservative candidate. This plus the fact that the 1918 electoral register was notoriously inaccurate helps to explain the very low turnout.

[3] If war-time by-elections are excluded, the 24.9% poll at the Shoreditch and Finsbury by-election on November 27, 1958, is the lowest turnout recorded.

Appendix 4 ELECTION PRECEDENTS 1918-1987

By-Elections

The ebb and flow of political support between General Elections was dramatically shown by the following by-election results:

Kent, Dartford (27/3/20). A Coalition majority of 9,370 at the previous (1918) General Election was turned into a Labour majority of 9,048.

Fulham, East (25/10/33). A Conservative majority of 14,521 at the previous (1931) General Election was turned into a Labour majority of 4,840.

Kent, Orpington (14/3/62). A Conservative majority of 14,760 at the previous (1959) General Election was turned into a Labour majority of 7,855.

Leyton (21/1/65). A Labour majority of 7,926 at the previous (1964) General Election was turned into a Conservative majority of 205.

Walthamstow, West (21/9/67). A Labour majority of 8,725 at the previous (1966) General Election was turned into a Conservative majority of 62.

Dudley (28/3/68). A Labour majority of 10,022 at the previous (1966) General Election was turned into a Conservative majority of 11,656.

Warwickshire, Meriden (28/3/68). A Labour majority of 4,581 at the previous (1966) General Election was turned into a Conservative majority of 15,263.

Birmingham, Ladywood (26/6/69). A Labour majority of 5,315 at the previous (1966) General Election was turned into a Liberal majority of 2,713.

Swindon (30/10/69). A Labour majority of 10,443 at the previous (1966) General Election was turned into a Conservative majority of 478.

Worcestershire, Bromsgrove (27/5/71). A Labour majority of 1,868 at the previous (1970) General Election was turned into a Conservative majority of 10,874.

Rochdale (26/10/72). A Labour majority of 5,171 at the previous (1970) General Election was turned into a Liberal majority of 5,093.

Sutton and Cheam (7/12/72). A Conservative majority of 12,696 at the previous (1970) General Election was turned into a Liberal majority of 7,417.

Isle of Ely (26/7/73). A Conservative majority of 9,606 at the previous (1970) General Election was turned into a Liberal majority of 1,470.

Yorkshire, Ripon (26/7/73). A Conservative majority of 12,064 at the previous (1970) General Election was turned into a Liberal majority of 946.

Northumberland, Berwick-upon-Tweed (8/11/73). A Conservative majority of 7,145 at the previous (1970) General Election was turned into a Liberal majority of 57.

Walsall, North (4/11/76). A Labour/Co-operative majority of 15,885 at the previous (October 1974) General Election was turned into a Conservative majority of 4,379.

Workington (4/11/76). A Labour majority of 9,551 at the previous (October 1974) General Election was turned into a Conservative majority of 1,065.

Birmingham, Stechford (31/3/77). A Labour majority of 11,923 at the previous (October 1974) General Election was turned into a Conservative majority of 1,949.

Ashfield (28/4/77). A Labour majority of 22,915 at the previous (October 1974) General Election was turned into a Conservative majority of 264.

Ilford, North (2/3/78). A Labour majority of 778 at the previous (October 1974) General Election was turned into a Conservative majority of 5,497.

Liverpool, Edge Hill (29/3/79). A Labour majority of 6,171 at the previous (October 1974) General Election was turned into a Liberal majority of 8,133.

Crosby (26/11/81). A Conservative majority of 19,272 at the previous (1979) General Election was turned into a Social Democratic Party majority of 5,289.

Bermondsey (24/2/83). A Labour majority of 19,338 at the previous (1979) General Election was turned into a Liberal majority of 9,319.

Portsmouth, South (14/6/84). A Conservative majority of 12,335 at the previous (1983) General Election was turned into a Social Democratic Party majority of 1,341.

Ryedale (8/5/86). A Conservative majority of 16,142 at the previous (1983) General Election was turned into a Liberal majority of 4,940.

See also under the heading Nationalists

ELECTION PRECEDENTS 1918-1987 (Cont.)

Candidates

Anglesey is a constituency which appears to attract candidates with the same surname. At the General Election of 1955 the Labour, Liberal and Conservative candidates all shared Hughes as their surname. At the General Election of 1964 the Conservative, Liberal and Plaid Cymru candidates all had the surname of Jones.

At Bermondsey, Rotherhithe at the General Election of 1918 and at Lincoln at the General Election of 1950, the successful candidates each polled exactly the same number of votes as the combined total votes of their opponents.

There is only one instance of eleven candidates contesting a single seat at a General Election. This was at Finchley in 1983.

There is only one instance of seventeen candidates contesting a single seat at a by-election. This was at Chesterfield on March 1, 1984.

At the General Election of October 1974, H. Smith and T.L. Keen of the Campaign for a More Prosperous Britain contested respectively twelve and eleven constituencies each. Smith polled a total of 2,192 votes and Keen 2,036.

Two candidates, W.G. Boaks (Ind) and W.E. Gladstone (L formerly C) were candidates at twenty-eight elections. Boaks first contested a seat at the General Election of 1951 and his last contest was at a by-election in October 1982. In all the contests he polled only a total of 1,772 votes — his highest was 240 and the lowest was 5. He forfeited his deposit each time. He died aged 81 in April 1986.

W.E. Gladstone fought eighteen contested elections and was returned unopposed ten times. He was only defeated on three occasions and the elections covered the period 1832-92 and fifteen General Elections and eight by-elections. He died in May 1898 aged 88.

Counts

Brighton, Kemptown and Northamptonshire, Peterborough claim the joint record for recounts — seven.

At Brighton, Kemptown at the General Election of 1964, the Labour candidate D.H. Hobden was returned with a majority of seven votes after seven recounts.
No official figures of the recounts were issued but from local press reports it appears that the first count resulted in a Labour majority of 302 but there was a discrepancy in the number of ballot papers counted of about 400. On the first recount the Labour majority was reduced to thirty-eight. A second recount put the Conservative candidate ahead by one vote but the Labour lead was restored in the third, fourth and fifth recounts with majorities of twenty-nine, ten, and six. At 2.40 a.m. the count was adjourned until 9 a.m. when two further recounts both gave the Labour candidate a majority of seven votes. The result was finally declared just after 10 a.m. There were 60 spoilt ballot-papers.

At Northamptonshire, Peterborough at the General Election of 1966 the Conservative candidate, Sir Harmar Nicholls, Bt., was returned with a majority of three votes after seven recounts. The first count gave the Labour candidate a majority of 163 and the first recount produced the same result. Uncounted ballot-papers were then discovered in a ballot-box and the second recount gave Labour a majority of two votes. Third and fourth recounts reversed the position and gave Sir Harmar majorities of two and then six votes. A fifth recount put Labour back in the lead by a single vote but a sixth recount showed Sir Harmar ahead once again, this time with a majority of two votes. The seventh and final recount added another vote to Sir Harmar's majority.
There were thirty-eight spoilt ballot-papers and counting started at 9.00 a.m. but the result was not declared until 5.30 p.m.

Probably the longest time taken to count ballot-papers and declare a result can be claimed by Derbyshire, North-Eastern. At the General Election of 1922 the count commenced at 10 a.m. on the day after polling and continued until shortly after 1 a.m. the following morning when it was adjourned until 10 a.m. The result was finally declared, after three recounts and four adjustments, at 1.15 p.m. The final outcome was a majority of five votes for the Labour candidate but after a recount and scrutiny by an Election Court the majority was increased to fifteen votes. The total time taken to count the votes and declare the result was approximately 18¼ hours.

ELECTION PRECEDENTS 1918-1987 (Cont.)

Electorate
The constituency with the largest ever electorate was Essex, Romford. At the General Election of 1935 there were 167,939 electors on the Register. At the same election Middlesex, Hendon claimed 164,786 electors. When the last pre-war Electoral Register was published in 1939 the figures had risen to 208,609 at Hendon and 207,101 at Romford. Both constituencies were divided in the redistribution which took place in 1945.

The constituency with the smallest electorate was the City of London, a two-member seat. At the General Election of 1945 there were only 10,851 electors on the Register of whom 6,608 qualified for a vote on account of business premises in the constituency.
Southwark, North holds the record for the smallest electorate in a single-member seat — 14,108 electors at the General Election of 1945.

Expenses
James Maxton (Glasgow, Bridgeton, ILP) created a record when he retained his seat at the General Election of 1935 and only spent £54 in election expenses.

Forfeited Deposits
The Scottish Universities by-election (22-27/11/46) created an unusual record when out of five candidates, four forfeited their deposits.

From November 1947 until December 1954 no Liberal candidate was able to save his deposit at a by-election.

At both the Bermondsey (24/2/83) and Chesterfield (1/3/84) by-elections fourteen candidates lost their deposits. At Bermondsey there were sixteen candidates and at Chesterfield seventeen.

Minorities
At each of the ten General Elections from 1918 to 1951, the successful candidate in the Lancashire, Darwen constituency was returned on a minority vote.

At the General Election of 1922, the successful Conservative candidate at Portsmouth, Central polled only 26.9% of the total votes cast.

Nationalists
The Scottish National Party and Plaid Cymru have each gained surprise victories at by-elections —

At Lanarkshire, Motherwell on April 12, 1945, Dr. Robert McIntyre (SNP) won the seat from Labour with a majority of 617 votes. The Labour majority at the previous (1935) General Election had been 430 over a Conservative but at the by-election Dr. McIntyre had a straight fight with Labour due to the electoral truce which existed during the war. The constituency had not previously been contested by a Scottish Nationalist.

At Lanarkshire, Hamilton on November 2, 1967, Mrs. Winifred Ewing (SNP) won the seat from Labour with a majority of 1,799. The Labour majority at the previous (1966) General Election had been 16,576 in a straight-fight with a Conservative. The Scottish National Party had not contested the seat since 1959 when their candidate had forfeited his deposit.

At Glasgow, Govan on November 8, 1973, Mrs. Margo Macdonald (SNP) won the seat from Labour with a majority of 571. The Labour majority at the previous (1970) General Election had been 7,142 and the SNP candidate had forfeited his deposit.

At Carmarthenshire, Carmarthen on July 14, 1966, Gwynfor Evans (PC) won the seat from Labour with a majority of 2,436. The Labour majority at the previous (1966) General Election had been 9,233 in a four-cornered contest in which Evans had secured third place.

Polling days
The polling at a General Election has been on a Thursday since 1935. Prior to that it was a Tuesday in 1931; a Wednesday in 1922 and 1924; a Thursday in 1923 and 1929; a Saturday in 1918.

By-elections are now normally held on a Thursday but in 1958 the Pontypool by-election was held on a Monday; in 1965 the Saffron Walden poll was held on a Tuesday; in 1978 (because the Returning Officer wished to avoid a clash with the television coverage of the opening match in the World Cup football competition) the Hamilton by-election was held on a Wednesday; in 1956 the Newport by-election was held on a Friday; in 1951 the Harrow, West by-election was held on a Saturday.

ELECTION PRECEDENTS 1918-1987 (Cont.)

Postal Votes

The record for the largest number of postal ballot-papers issued and included in a count is held by Fermanagh and South Tyrone. At the General Election of 1974(O) the number issued was 9,911 (13.9% of the electorate) of which 8,979 (14.2% of the total poll) were included in the count.

If Northern Ireland is excluded, Devon, North holds the record. At the General Election of 1974(O) the number issued was 4,109 (5.6% of the electorate) of which 3,298 (5.6% of the total poll) were included in the count.

Glasgow, Bridgeton holds the record for the smallest postal vote. At the General Election of 1950 there were only 115 postal ballot-papers issued and 91 counted. At the General Election of 1966 the number issued increased to 127 but the number included in the count fell to a record low figure of 87.

Spoilt ballot papers

Since statistics relating to spoilt ballot-papers were first compiled for the United Kingdom in 1964, the record for the highest number of spoilt papers is held by Belfast, West. At the General Election of 1979, 2,283 were rejected of which 1,913 were unmarked or void for uncertainty.

If Northern Ireland is excluded, the highest number of spoilt papers was at Cardiff, West at the General Election of 1979 when the total was 2,253. Of this number, 2,123 were unmarked or void for uncertainty many of them having the word 'Conservative' written across them.

The lowest number of spoilt papers was at Edinburgh, Leith at the General Election of 1974(O) when only nine were rejected.

Turnout

There was so much local interest in the result of the Ashton-under-Lyne by-election (29/10/28) that the Mayor arranged for coloured rockets indicating the party of the successful candidate to be fired from the roof of the Town Hall. The by-election resulted in a Labour victory and yellow rockets (the local Labour colour) were fired which could be seen throughout the town by many people awaiting the result. Despite a steady downpour of rain throughout polling day the by-election achieved a turnout of 89.1%, a record for a by-election which has never been exceeded in Great Britain.

At the five General Elections from 1922 to 1931, the turnout at Lancashire, Darwen always exceeded 90.0%.

Camberwell, North holds the record for the smallest number of votes cast in a parliamentary election. At a by-election on March 30, 1944, two candidates polled a total of only 3,329 votes. The turnout was 11.2%.

Victory and Defeat

The most overwhelming victory ever recorded at a General Election was at Devon, North in 1959. The Conservative candidate received 98.0% of the total votes cast. At a by-election on May 22, 1940 at Lancashire, Middleton and Prestwich, the Conservative candidate received 98.7% of the total votes cast.

When the Liberals won Devon, Torrington (27/3/58) it was the first Liberal gain at a by-election for twenty-nine years. The previous occasion had been at Lincolnshire, Holland with Boston on March 21, 1929.

When Labour won Lewisham, North (14/2/57) from the Conservatives it was the first time that they had gained a seat from the Conservatives at a by-election for over seventeen years. The previous occasion had been at Lambeth, Kennington on May 24, 1939.

One of the most humiliating defeats ever suffered by a Government at a by-election took place at Kent, Dartford on March 27, 1920. At the previous (1918) General Election a Coalition Liberal candidate had won the seat in a straight-fight with Labour with a majority of 9,370. At the five-cornered by-election contest Labour gained the seat with a majority of 9,048, the Coalition candidate (this time a Conservative) taking third place. The Coalition vote fell from 71.4% to 15.5% and the Labour vote went up from 28.6% to 50.2%.

ELECTION PRECEDENTS 1918-1987 (Cont.)

When the Conservatives won Sunderland, South (13/5/53) it was the first occasion since 1924 that a Government had won a seat from the Opposition at a by-election and only two such previous victories had been recorded since 1918. These were Liverpool, West Toxteth (22/5/24) when Labour won the seat from the Conservatives, and Woolwich, East (2/3/21) when the Conservatives won the seat from Labour.

There has been only one occasion since 1953 that a Government has won a seat from the Opposition at a by-election. This was at Brighouse and Spenborough (17/3/60) when a National Liberal and Conservative candidate won the seat from Labour.

Women

Dame Irene Ward was a member of the House of Commons longer than any other woman. She was first elected for Wallsend in 1931 and retained her seat until defeated in 1945. In 1950 she was elected for Tynemouth and retired in 1974(F). She fought a total of twelve contested elections.

Lady Megan Lloyd George was a member of the House of Commons for a total of thirty-one years and fought ten contested elections. She was Liberal member for Anglesey from 1929 until she was defeated in 1951. In 1957 she was elected at a by-election as Labour member for Carmarthenshire, Carmarthen and retained the seat until her death in 1966.

Miss Jennie Lee was first elected for Lanarkshire, Northern at a by-election in 1929 but was defeated at the General Election of 1931. She was elected for Staffordshire, Cannock in 1945 and retained the seat until she was defeated in 1970. She fought thirteen elections, a record for a woman candidate.

At the General Election of 1983, of the five candidates who contested Sheffield, Central, four were women.

Appendix 5 HOURS OF POLL 1832-1987

ENGLAND AND WALES

COUNTIES

December 3, 1832-October 1, 1853:

Two days polling.
First day 9.00 a.m. to 4.00 p.m.;
second day eight consecutive hours
closing not later than 4.00 p.m.
[2 & 3 Wm. 4, c. 45]

October 2, 1853-November 17, 1885:

One day polling.
8.00 a.m. to 5.00 p.m.
[16 & 17 Vict., c. 15]

November 18, 1885-August 14, 1913:

One day polling.
8.00 a.m. to 8.00 p.m.
[48 & 49 Vict., c. 10]

August 15, 1913-February 2, 1950:

On request of any candidate poll could
open one hour earlier (i.e. 7.00 a.m.);
close one hour later (i.e. 9.00 p.m.) or
open one hour earlier and close one
hour later (i.e. 7.00 a.m. to 9.00 p.m.)
[3 & 4 Geo. 5, c. 6]

February 3, 1950-February 15, 1970:

One day polling.
7.00 a.m. to 9.00 p.m.
[12, 13 & 14 Geo. 6, c. 68]

February 16, 1970-

One day polling.
7.00 a.m. to 10.00 p.m.
[1969, c. 15]

BOROUGHS

December 3, 1832-August 24, 1835:

Two days polling.
First day seven consecutive hours;
second day eight consecutive hours
closing not later than 4.00 p.m.
[2 & 3 Wm. 4, c. 45]

August 25, 1835-February 24, 1878:

One day polling.
8.00 a.m. to 4.00 p.m.
[5 & 6 Wm. 4, c. 36]

February 25, 1878-July 27, 1884:

Close of poll in the ten London borough
constituencies extended to 8.00 p.m.
[41 & 42 Vict., c. 4]

July 28, 1884-November 17, 1885:

Close of poll in all borough constituencies
with over 3,000 electors extended to 8.00 p.m.
[47 & 48 Vict., c. 34]

November 18, 1885-

As county constituencies, q.v.

SCOTLAND

COUNTIES

December 3, 1832-June 13, 1853:

Two days polling.
First day 9.00 a.m. to 4.00 p.m.,
second day 8.00 a.m. to 4.00 p.m.
[2 & 3 Wm. 4, c. 65]

June 14, 1853-November 17, 1885:

One day polling.
8.00 a.m. to 4.00 p.m. except in Orkney
and Shetland where two days polling
was retained.
[16 & 17 Vict., c. 28]

BURGHS

December 3, 1832-September 8, 1835:

As counties, q.v.

September 9, 1835-July 27, 1884:

One day polling.
8.00 a.m. to 4.00 p.m.
[5 & 6 Wm. 4, c. 78]

July 28, 1884-

As England and Wales, q.v.

HOURS OF POLL 1832-1987 (Cont.)

Scotland (Cont.)

COUNTIES

November 18, 1885-June 15, 1926:

As England and Wales, q.v. but excluding
Orkney and Shetland where two days
polling was retained.
[*48 & 49 Vict., c. 10*]

June 16, 1926-

Polling in Orkney and Shetland
reduced to one day.
[*16 & 17 Geo. 5, c. 9*]

BURGHS

July 28, 1884-

As England and Wales, q.v.

IRELAND (Northern Ireland from 1922)

COUNTIES

December 3, 1832-March 15, 1851:

Five days polling.
First to fourth days 9.00 a.m. to 6.00 p.m.
(between April 15 and September 14) or
9.00 a.m. to 5.00 p.m. (between September
15 and April 14); fifth day 9.00 a.m. to
5.00 p.m.
[*1 Geo. 4, c. 11 & 2 & 3 Wm. 4, c. 88*]

March 16, 1851-December 31, 1862:

Two days polling.
First day 9.00 a.m. to 4.00 p.m.;
second day 8.00 a.m. to 4.00 p.m.
[*13 & 14 Vict., c. 68*]

January 1, 1863-July 27, 1884:

One day polling.
8.00 a.m. to 5.00 p.m.
[*25 & 26 Vict., c. 62*]

July 28, 1884-

As England and Wales, q.v.

BOROUGHS

December 3, 1832-July 21, 1847:

As counties, q.v.

July 22, 1847-July 27, 1884:

One day polling.
8.00 a.m. to 5.00 p.m.
[*10 & 11 Vict., c. 81*]

July 28, 1884-

As England and Wales, q.v.

Throughout this Appendix the citation of the relative Act of Parliament is shown in italic type
within square brackets.

Appendix 6 ACTS OF PARLIAMENT 1832-1987

The following is a list of all Acts relating to parliamentary elections and the registration of electors.

1832 (2 & 3 Will. 4)
c. 45	Representation of the People
c. 64	Parliamentary Boundaries
c. 65	Representation of the People [Scotland]
c. 69	Corporate Property (Elections)
c. 88	Representation of the People [Ireland]
c. 89	Parliamentary Boundaries [Ireland]

1833 (3 & 4 Will. 4)
c. 20	Stafford Election (Witnesses Indemnity)

1834 (4 & 5 Will. 4)
c. 17	Warwick Election (Witnesses Indemnity)
c. 18	Liverpool Election (Witnesses Indemnity)
c. 88	Parliamentary Registration [Scotland]

1835 (5 & 6 Will. 4)
c. 36	Parliamentary Elections (Borough Polls)
c. 78	Representation of the People (Amendment) [Scotland]

1836 (6 & 7 Will. 4)
c. 10	Stafford Election (Witnesses Indemnity)
c. 101	Parliamentary Registration
c. 102	Parliamentary Elections (County Polls)

1839 (2 & 3 Vict.)
c. 38	Election Petitions

1840 (3 & 4 Vict.)
c. 47	Parliamentary Elections (Returning Officers)
c. 81	Parliamentary Elections (Polls)

1841 (4 & 5 Vict.)
c. 57	Parliamentary Elections (Bribery)
c. 58	Controverted Elections (Trials)

1842 (5 & 6 Vict.)
c. 31	Harwich, etc. (Indemnity of Witnesses)
c. 52	Sudbury Disfranchisement (Witnesses Indemnity)
c. 73	Controverted Elections (Trials)
c. 74	University of Dublin Registration
c. 102	Parliamentary Elections (Bribery and Treating)

1843 (6 & 7 Vict.)
c. 11	Sudbury Disfranchisement (Witnesses Indemnity)
c. 18	Parliamentary Registration
c. 28	Parliamentary Registration [Ireland]
c. 47	Controverted Elections (Trials)
c. 97	Sudbury Bribery Commission

1844 (7 & 8 Vict.)
c. 53	Disfranchisement of Sudbury
c. 103	Controverted Elections (Trials)

1846 (9 & 10 Vict.)
c. 19	Parliamentary Elections (Polling Booths) [Ireland]
c. 30	Parliamentary Elections (Polls) [Ireland]
c. 44	Election of Members for Cheshire

1847 (10 & 11 Vict.)
c. 21	Parliamentary Elections (Soldiers)
c. 81	Parliamentary Elections (Polls) [Ireland]

ACTS OF PARLIAMENT 1832-1987 (Cont.)

1848 (11 & 12 Vict.)
c. 18   Controverted Elections (Trials)
c. 24   Disfranchisement of Freemen, Great Yarmouth
c. 90   Parliamentary Registration
c. 98   Controverted Elections (Trials)

1850 (13 & 14 Vict.)
c. 68   Parliamentary Elections (Polls) [Ireland]
c. 69   Parliamentary Registration [Ireland]

1851 (14 & 15 Vict.)
c. 106   St. Alban's Bribery Commission

1852 (15 & 16 Vict.)
c. 9   Disfranchisement of St. Alban's
c. 57   Election Commissioners

1853 (16 & 17 Vict.)
c. 15   Parliamentary Elections (County Polls)
c. 28   Parliamentary Elections (County Polls) [Scotland]
c. 58   Dublin Parliamentary Revising
c. 68   Parliamentary Elections (Polls)

1854 (17 & 18 Vict.)
c. 57   Returning Officers
c. 102   Corrupt Practices Prevention

1855 (18 & 19 Vict.)
c. 24   Parliamentary Elections [Scotland]

1856 (19 & 20 Vict.)
c. 58   Parliamentary Registration (Burghs) [Scotland]
c. 84   Corrupt Practices Prevention

1858 (21 & 22 Vict.)
c. 87   Corrupt Practices Prevention
c. 110   Election of Members during Recess

1859 (22 & 23 Vict.)
c. 48   Corrupt Practices Prevention

1860 (23 & 24 Vict.)
c. 99   Corrupt Practices Prevention

1861 (24 & 25 Vict.)
c. 53   Universities Elections (Ballot Papers)
c. 56   Dublin Revising Barristers
c. 60   Parliamentary Registration [Ireland]
c. 83   Parliamentary Registration [Scotland]
c. 112   Appropriation of Seats (Sudbury and St. Albans)
c. 122   Corrupt Practices Prevention

1862 (25 & 26 Vict.)
c. 62   County Elections [Ireland]
c. 92   Parliamentary Elections [Ireland]
c. 95   Parliamentary Elections (Polling Places)
c. 109   Corrupt Practices Prevention

1863 (26 & 27 Vict.)
c. 20   Elections in Recess
c. 29   Corrupt Practices Prevention

1864 (27 & 28 Vict.)
c. 22   Registration of County Voters [Ireland]
c. 34   House of Commons (Vacation of Seats)

ACTS OF PARLIAMENT 1832-1987 (Cont.)

1865 (28 & 29 Vict.)
c. 8   Controverted Elections (Trials)
c. 36   Parliamentary Registration (Counties)
c. 92   Parliamentary Elections (Ayr District of Burghs) [Scotland]

1866 (29 & 30 Vict.)
c. 54   Revising Barristers

1867 (30 & 31 Vict.)
c. 102   Representation of the People

1867 (31 & 32 Vict.)
c. 6   Parliamentary Elections (Suspension of Writs)

1868 (31 & 32 Vict.)
c. 41   Parliamentary Registration (Boroughs)
c. 46   Boundary
c. 48   Representation of the People [Scotland]
c. 49   Representation of the People [Ireland]
c. 58   Parliamentary Registration
c. 65   Universities Elections (Ballot Papers)
c. 112   Parliamentary Registration [Ireland]
c. 125   Parliamentary Elections (Petitions and Corrupt Practices)

1869 (32 & 33 Vict.)
c. 21   Election Commissioners Expenses
c. 65   Corrupt Practices (Freemen of Dublin City)

1870 (33 & 34 Vict.)
c. 21   Bridgwater and Beverley Disfranchisement
c. 25   Norwich Voters Disfranchisement
c. 38   Sligo and Cashel Disfranchisement
c. 54   Dublin Voters Disfranchisement

1871 (34 & 35 Vict.)
c. 61   Election Commissioners Expenses
c. 77   Norwich Voters Disfranchisement

1872 (35 & 36 Vict.)
c. 33   Parliamentary and Municipal Elections (Ballot)

1873 (36 & 37 Vict.)
c. 2   Polling Districts [Ireland]
c. 30   Registration of Voters [Ireland]
c. 70   Revising Barristers

1874 (37 & 38 Vict.)
c. 53   Revising Barristers

1875 (38 & 39 Vict.)
c. 84   Parliamentary Elections (Returning Officers)

1876 (39 & 40 Vict.)
c. 72   Norwich and Boston Corrupt Voters

1878 (41 & 42 Vict.)
c. 3   House Occupiers Disqualification Removal
c. 4   Parliamentary Elections (Metropolis)
c. 5   House Occupiers Disqualification Removal [Scotland]
c. 26   Parliamentary and Municipal Registration
c. 41   Parliamentary Elections, Returning Officers Expenses [Scotland]
c. 75   Arronmore Polling District [Ireland]

1879 (42 & 43 Vict.)
c. 75   Parliamentary Elections and Corrupt Practices

1880 (43 Vict.)
c. 18   Parliamentary Elections and Corrupt Practices

ACTS OF PARLIAMENT 1832-1987 (Cont.)

1880 (43 & 44 Vict.)
c. 6   House Occupiers in Counties Disqualification Removal [Scotland]

1881 (44 & 45 Vict.)
c. 40   Universities Elections Amendment [Scotland]
c. 42   Corrupt Practices (Suspension of Elections)

1882 (45 & 46 Vict.)
c. 68   Corrupt Practices (Suspension of Elections)

1883 (46 & 47 Vict.)
c. 46   Corrupt Practices (Suspension of Elections)
c. 51   Corrupt and Illegal Practices Prevention

1884 (47 & 48 Vict.)
c. 34   Elections (Hours of Poll)
c. 35   County of Dublin Jurors and Voters' Revision
c. 78   Corrupt Practices (Suspension of Elections)

1884 (48 & 49 Vict.)
c. 3   Representation of the People
c. 46   Medical Relief Disqualification Removal
c. 57   Revising Barristers
c. 66   Registration Appeals [Ireland]

1885 (48 & 49 Vict.)
c. 10   Elections (Hours of Poll)
c. 15   Registration
c. 16   Registration Amendment [Scotland]
c. 17   Parliamentary Registration [Ireland]
c. 23   Redistribution of Seats
c. 56   Parliamentary Elections Corrupt Practices
c. 62   Parliamentary Elections (Returning Officers)

1886 (49 & 50 Vict.)
c. 42   Revising Barristers
c. 43   Revising Barristers [Ireland]
c. 57   Parliamentary Elections (Returning Officers)
c. 58   Returning Officers [Scotland]

1889 (52 & 53 Vict.)
c. 19   Registration of County Electors (Extension of Time)

1890 (53 & 54 Vict.)
c. 58   Parliamentary Registration Expenses [Ireland]

1890 (54 & 55 Vict.)
c. 11   Electoral Disabilities Removal

1891 (54 & 55 Vict.)
c. 18   Registration of Electors
c. 49   Returning Officers [Scotland]

1895 (58 & 59 Vict.)
c. 40   Corrupt and Illegal Practices Prevention

1896 (59 & 60 Vict.)
c. 17   Glasgow Parliamentary Divisions

1900 (63 & 64 Vict.)
c. 8   Electoral Disabilities (Military Service) Removal

1908 (8 Edw. 7)
c. 14   Polling Arrangements (Parliamentary Boroughs)
c. 21   Registration
c. 35   Polling Districts and Registration of Voters [Ireland]

ACTS OF PARLIAMENT 1832-1987 (Cont.)

1913 (3 & 4 Geo. 5)
c. 6 Extension of Polling Hours

1914 (4 & 5 Geo. 5)
c. 25 Electoral Disabilities (Naval and Military Service) Removal

1915 (5 & 6 Geo. 5)
c. 50 Re-election of Ministers
c. 76 Elections and Registration

1916 (5 & 6 Geo. 5)
c. 100 Parliament and Registration

1916 (6 & 7 Geo. 5)
c. 22 Re-election of Ministers
c. 56 Re-election of Ministers (No. 2)

1918 (7 & 8 Geo. 5)
c. 64 Representation of the People
c. 65 Redistribution of Seats [Ireland]

1918 (8 & 9 Geo. 5)
c. 47 Parliament (Qualification of Women)
c. 50 Representation of the People

1919 (9 & 10 Geo. 5)
c. 2 Re-election of Ministers
c. 8 Representation of the People (Returning Officers' Expenses)
c. 10 Parliamentary Elections (Soldiers)

1920 (10 & 11 Geo. 5)
c. 15 Representation of the People
c. 35 Representation of the People (No. 2)
c. 67 Government of Ireland

1921 (11 & 12 Geo. 5)
c. 34 Representation of the People

1922 (12 & 13 Geo. 5)
c. 12 Representation of the People
c. 41 Representation of the People (No. 2)

1926 (16 & 17 Geo. 5)
c. 9 Economy (Miscellaneous Provisions)
c. 19 Re-election of Ministers

1928 (18 & 19 Geo. 5)
c. 12 Representation of the People (Equal Franchise)
c. 25 Representation of the People (Reading University)

1933 (23 & 24 Geo. 5)
c. 27 Blind Voters

1939 (2 & 3 Geo. 6)
c. 115 Local Elections and Register of Electors (Temporary Provisions)

1940 (4 & 5 Geo. 6)
c. 3 Local Elections and Register of Electors (Temporary Provisions)

1941 (4 & 5 Geo. 6)
c. 49 Local Elections and Register of Electors (Temporary Provisions)

1942 (5 & 6 Geo. 6)
c. 38 Local Elections and Register of Electors (Temporary Provisions)

1943 (6 & 7 Geo. 6)
c. 48 Parliament (Elections and Meetings)

ACTS OF PARLIAMENT 1832-1987 (Cont.)

1943 (7 & 8 Geo. 6)
c. 2   Local Elections and Register of Electors (Temporary Provisions)
c. 24   Parliamentary Electors (War-Time Registration)
c. 41   House of Commons (Redistribution of Seats)

1944 (8 & 9 Geo. 6)
c. 3   Local Elections and Register of Electors (Temporary Provisions)

1945 (8 & 9 Geo. 6)
c. 5   Representation of the People
c. 40   Postponement of Polling Day

1945 (9 & 10 Geo. 6)
c. 21   Elections and Jurors

1947 (10 & 11 Geo. 6)
c. 10   House of Commons (Redistribution of Seats)

1948 (11 & 12 Geo. 6)
c. 65   Representation of the People

1949 (12, 13 & 14 Geo. 6)
c. 66   House of Commons (Redistribution of Seats)
c. 68   Representation of the People
c. 86   Electoral Registers
c. 90   Election Commissioners

1953 (2 & 3 Eliz. 2)
c. 8   Electoral Registers

1957 (5 & 6 Eliz. 2)
c. 43   Representation of the People

1958 (6 & 7 Eliz. 2)
c. 26   House of Commons (Redistribution of Seats)

1958 (7 & 8 Eliz. 2)
c. 9   Representation of the People

1964
c. 31   Elections (Welsh Forms)

1969
c. 15   Representation of the People

1974
c. 10   Representation of the People
c. 13   Representation of the People (No. 2)

1975
c. 66   Recess Elections

1976
c. 29   Representation of the People (Armed Forces)

1977
c. 9   Representation of the People
c. 14   Returning Officers (Scotland)

1978
c. 10   European Assembly Elections
c. 32   Representation of the People

1979
c. 15   House of Commons (Redistribution of Seats)
c. 40   Representation of the People

1980
c. 3   Representation of the People

ACTS OF PARLIAMENT 1832-1987 (Cont.)

1981
c. 8   European Assembly Elections
c. 34   Representation of the People

1983
c. 2   Representation of the People

1985
c. 50   Representation of the People

1986
c. 56   Parliamentary Constituencies

Appendix 7 POLLING POSTPONED BY DEATH OF A CANDIDATE 1918-1987

Since 1918 when polling at a General Election took place on the same date in all constituencies (except in the Universities) the death of a candidate after nomination and prior to the day of election caused a postponement of the election and this has only occurred at six General Elections.

1918	F.A. Lucas the Conservative candidate for Lambeth, Kennington died three days before polling.
1923	C.F. White the Liberal candidate and former MP for Derbyshire, Western died two days before polling.
1929	H. Yates the Labour candidate for Warwickshire, Rugby died three days before polling.
1945	W. Windsor the Labour candidate and former MP for Kingston upon Hull, Central died six days before polling.
1950	E.L. Fleming the Conservative candidate for Manchester, Moss Side (and former MP for Manchester, Withington) died six days before polling.
1951	F. Collindridge the Labour candidate and former MP for Barnsley died nine days before polling.

Appendix 8 PARLIAMENTARY BOUNDARY COMMISSIONS 1831-1987

Until the creation of permanent Boundary Commissions in 1944, reviews of boundaries were undertaken from time to time by *ad hoc* Commissions and the following list gives the relevant dates of each report but it should be noted that irrespective of the date the boundary changes were implemented (by Act or Statutory Instrument) they did not come into effect until the Dissolution of the Parliament then in being.

Commenced review	Date of report	Date of Act or SI	Length of time (months)
ENGLAND			
August 8, 1831	February 10, 1832	July 11, 1832	11
August 16, 1867	February 5, 1868	July 13, 1868	11
December 5, 1884	February 10, 1885 and		
	April 22, 1885	June 25, 1885	6
May 14, 1917	September 27, 1917	February 6, 1918	9
October 26, 1944	March 29, 1945	June 11, 1945	8
January 31, 1946[1]	October 24, 1947	July 30, 1948	30
July 28, 1953	November 10, 1954	January 5, 1955 and	
		February 1, 1955	18
February 16, 1965	April 21, 1969	November 11, 1970	69
February 17, 1976	February 1, 1983	March 16, 1983	85
WALES			
August 8, 1831	February 10, 1832	July 11, 1832	11
August 16, 1867	February 5, 1868	July 13, 1868	11
December 5, 1884	February 10, 1885	June 25, 1885	6
May 14, 1917	September 27, 1917	February 6, 1918	9
January 31, 1946[1]	November 17, 1947	July 30, 1948	30
July 28, 1953	November 10, 1954	February 1, 1955	18
February 16, 1965	May 19, 1969	November 11, 1970	69
February 16, 1981	January 25, 1983	March 16, 1983	25
SCOTLAND			
November 8, 1831	February 21, 1832	July 17, 1832	8
December 5, 1884	February 10, 1885	June 25, 1885	6
May 16, 1917	September 28, 1917	February 6, 1918	9
January 31, 1946[1]	November 5, 1947	July 30, 1948	30
July 27, 1953	August 23, 1954	January 5, 1955	17
February 16, 1965	April 24, 1969	November 11, 1970	69
February 16, 1978	February 18, 1983	March 16, 1983	61
NORTHERN IRELAND			
January 31, 1946[1]	September 4, 1947	July 30, 1948	30
January ?, 1954[2]	November 10, 1954	Not applicable[3]	—
February 16, 1965	June 10, 1969	November 11, 1970	69
February 16, 1976	October 27, 1982	December 22, 1982	70

[1] The membership of the Commissions was published in *The Times* on January 4, 1946 and they held their first meeting on January 31 when it was announced that a review would now commence. No official notice of the commencement of the review was published in the *London Gazette*.

[2] No official notice of the commencement of the review was published in the *Belfast Gazette* and when the report was published it did not give the January date.

[3] The report recommended no change.

Appendix 9 ROYAL COMMISSIONS 1832-1906

Until 1906, the House of Commons appointed Royal Commissions from time to time to look into allegations of corruption in certain constituencies which had arisen through election petitions.

The following is a list of the Commissions with a reference to the House of Commons Bound Sets of Sessional Papers.

ENGLAND

Constituency	Appointed		Reported		Session	Paper No.	Volume No.	Page No.
Sudbury	Aug	1843[1]	Mar	1844	1844	538	xviii	247
St. Albans	Aug	1851[2]	Feb	1852	1852	1431	xxvii	1
Canterbury	May	1853	Jul	1853	1852-53	1658	xlvii	1
Kingston upon Hull	May	1853	Aug	1853	1854	1703	xxii	1
Cambridge	Jun	1853	Aug	1853	1852-53	1685	xlvi	1
Maldon	Jun	1853	Aug	1853	1852-53	1673	xlviii	1
Barnstaple	Jul	1853	Dec	1853	1854	1704	xxi	1
Tynemouth and North Shields	Jul	1853	Feb	1854	1854	1729	xxi	539
Gloucester	Aug	1859	Jan	1860	1860	2586	xxvii	1
Wakefield	Aug	1859	Jan	1860	1860	2601	xxviii	1
Berwick-upon-Tweed	Jul	1860	Feb	1861	1861	2766	xvii	1
Great Yarmouth	Jun	1866	Dec	1866	1867	3775	xxx	1
Lancaster	Jun	1866	Feb	1867	1867	3777	xxvii	1
Reigate	Jun	1866	Feb	1867	1867	3774	xxviii	1
Totnes	Jun	1866	Jan	1867	1867	3776	xxix	1
Beverley	Jun	1869	Jan	1870	1870	15	xxix	1
Bridgwater	Jun	1869	Dec	1869	1870	10 & 11	xxx	1 & 9
Norwich	Jun	1869	Feb	1870	1870	13	xxxi	1
Boston	May	1875	Feb	1876	1876	1441	xxviii	1
Norwich	Jul	1875	Mar	1876	1876	1442	xxvii	1
Boston	Sep	1880	Jan	1881	1881	2784	xxxviii	1
Canterbury	Sep	1880	Dec	1880	1881	2775	xxxix	1
Chester	Sep	1880	Mar	1881	1881	2824	xl	1
Gloucester	Sep	1880	Mar	1881	1881	2841	xli	1
Knaresborough	Sep	1880	Jan	1881	1881	2777	xlii	1
Macclesfield	Sep	1880	Mar	1881	1881	2853	xliii	1
Oxford	Sep	1880	Apr	1881	1881	2856	xliv	1
Sandwich	Sep	1880	Feb	1881	1881	2796	xlv	1
Worcester	Jul	1906	Nov	1906	1906	3268	xcv	473

IRELAND

Galway Borough	Aug	1857	Dec	1857	1857-58	2291	xxvi	309
Dublin Borough	Aug	1869[3]	May	1870	1870	93	xxxiii	1
Cashel	Jun	1869	Dec	1869	1870	9	xxxii	1
Sligo Borough	Jun	1869	Mar	1870	1870	48	xxxii	621

[1] By Act, 6 & 7 Vict.,c. 97

[2] By Act, 14 & 15 Vict.,c. 106

[3] By Act 32 & 33 Vict.,c. 65

Appendix 10 MEMBERS RETURNED FOR TWO OR MORE CONSTITUENCIES 1832-1918

The following is a list of double and treble elections at each General Election, i.e. where a candidate was elected for more than one constituency and had to choose which constituency he wished to represent.

The constituency prefixed with an asterisk is the one which the MP chose to represent.

1832
Viscount Lowther (C) Cumberland, Western
  *Westmorland

C.P. Thomson (L) Dover
  *Manchester

1841
D. O'Connell (R) *Cork County
  Meath County

1847
R. Cobden (L) Stockport
  *Yorkshire, West Riding

J. O'Connell (R) Kilkenny City
  *Limerick City

Hon. C.P. Villiers (L) Lancashire, Southern
  *Wolverhampton

1865
G. Hardy (C) Leominster
  *Oxford University

1874
P. Callan (HR) *Dundalk
  Louth County

1880
W.E. Gladstone (L) *Edinburghshire
  Leeds

Marquess of Radnor Boroughs
Hartington (L) *Lancashire, North-Eastern

C.S. Parnell (HR) *Cork City
  Mayo County
  Meath County

1885
E.D. Gray (N) Carlow County
  *Dublin, St. Stephen's Green

T.M. Healy (N) *Londonderry, South
  Monaghan, North

A. O'Connor (N) *Donegal, East
  Queen's, Ossory

T.P. O'Connor (N) Galway City
  *Liverpool, Scotland

1886
W.E. Gladstone (L) *Edinburghshire (Midlothian)
  Leith Burghs

J. McCarthy[1] (N) *Londonderry City
  Longford, North

T. Sexton (N) *Belfast, West
  Sligo, South

1892
W. O'Brien (N) *Cork City
  Cork, North-East

1895
M. Davitt (N) Kerry, East
  *Mayo, South

D. Kilbride (N) *Galway, North
  Kerry, South

E.F.V. Knox (N) Cavan, West
  *Londonderry City

1906
J. Devlin (N) *Belfast, West
  Kilkenny, North

P.A. McHugh (N) Leitrim, North
  *Sligo, North

1910(J)
W. O'Brien (Ind N) *Cork City
  Cork, North-East

1910(D)
R. Hazleton[2] (N) *Galway, North
  Louth, North

1918[3]
E. de Valera (SF) Clare, East
  Mayo, East

A. Griffith (SF) Cavan, East
  Tyrone, North-West

J.E. MacNeill (SF) Londonderry
  National University

W.L.J. Mellows (SF) Galway, East
  Meath, North

---

[1] Elected for Londonderry City as the result of a petition.
[2] Unseated on petition for Louth, North.
[3] The Sinn Fein MPs did not take their seats in the House of Commons.

Appendix 11 · BOROUGHS DISFRANCHISED FOR CORRUPTION 1832-1885

Borough	Date	Transferred to	Act
Sudbury	29/7/44	Suffolk, Western	7 & 8 Vict., c. 53
St. Albans	3/5/52	Hertfordshire	15 & 16 Vict., c. 9
Great Yarmouth	11/11/68	Norfolk, Northern Suffolk, Eastern	30 & 31 Vict., c. 102
Lancaster	11/11/68	Lancashire, Northern	30 & 31 Vict., c. 102
Reigate	11/11/68	Surrey, Mid	30 & 31 Vict., c. 102
Totnes	11/11/68	Devon, Southern	30 & 31 Vict., c. 102
Beverley	4/7/70	Yorkshire, East Riding	33 & 34 Vict., c. 21
Bridgwater	4/7/70	Somerset, Western	33 & 34 Vict., c. 21
Cashel	1/8/70	Tipperary County	33 & 34 Vict., c. 38
Sligo	1/8/70	Sligo County	33 & 34 Vict., c. 38
Macclesfield	25/6/85	Cheshire, Eastern	48 & 49 Vict., c. 23
Sandwich	25/6/85	Kent, Eastern	48 & 49 Vict., c. 23

Appendix 12 VOID ELECTIONS 1832-1987

The following is a list of constituencies in which on petition the election was declared void and a by-election would be held unless the House of Commons decided to suspend the issue of a new writ. The cause of the void election was bribery and/or corrupt practices unless otherwise stated. Double vacancies are indicated.

GENERAL ELECTIONS

Election	Constituency	Party
1832	●Carrickfergus	Conservative
	●Hertford	Conservative (2)
	Montgomery Boroughs	Conservative
	Oxford	Liberal
	*Tiverton	Liberal
	●Warwick	Conservative
1835	Carlow County	Conservative (2)
	*Drogheda	Liberal
	Ipswich	Conservative (2)
1837	*Marylebone	Liberal
1841	Athlone	Liberal
	Belfast	Conservative (2)
	Ipswich	Liberal (2)
	Newcastle-under-Lyme	Liberal
	Southampton	Conservative (2)
	●Sudbury	Liberal (2)
1847	Aylesbury	Conservative
	Bewdley	Conservative
	Carlisle	Liberal (1)
		Conservative (1)
	Cheltenham	Conservative
	Derby	Liberal (2)
	Great Yarmouth	Conservative (2)
	Harwich	Conservative
	Horsham	Liberal
	Kinsale	Conservative
	Lancaster	Liberal
	Leicester	Liberal (2)
	Lincoln	Liberal
	*Sligo Borough	Repealer
1852	Barnstaple	Conservative (2)
	Berwick-upon-Tweed	Liberal (2)
	Blackburn	Liberal
	Bridgnorth	Conservative
	Cambridge	Conservative (2)
	Canterbury	Conservative (2)
	Chatham	Conservative
	Clare	Liberal (2)
	Clitheroe	Liberal
	†Frome	Liberal
	Harwich	Conservative
	Huddersfield	Liberal
	Kingston upon Hull	Liberal (2)
	Lancaster	Liberal
	Liverpool	Conservative (2)
	Maidstone	Conservative
	Maldon	Conservative (2)
	Plymouth	Conservative

VOID ELECTIONS 1832-1987 (Cont.)

Election	Constituency	Party
1852 (cont.)	Rye	Liberal
	Sligo Borough	Liberal
	Taunton	Conservative
	Tynemouth and North Shields	Conservative
1857	*Beverley	Liberal
	Falkirk	Liberal
	Galway Borough	Liberal
	Great Yarmouth	Liberal (2)
	Mayo	Independent Opposition
	Oxford	Liberal
1859	Beverley	Conservative
	Clare	Liberal
	Dartmouth	Liberal
	Gloucester	Liberal (2)
	Kingston upon Hull	Conservative
	Norwich	Liberal (2)
	Roscommon	Conservative
	Wakefield	Liberal
1865	Bridgwater	Conservative
	†Cambridge	Conservative
	Devonport	Conservative (2)
	Helston	Liberal
	●Lancaster[1]	Liberal (2)
	Northallerton	Conservative
	Nottingham	Liberal (2)
	●Reigate[1]	Liberal
	●Totnes[1]	Liberal
	Windsor	Liberal (2)
1868	●Beverley[1]	Conservative (2)
	Bewdley	Conservative
	Blackburn	Conservative (2)
	Bradford	Liberal
	Brecon	Conservative
	●Bridgwater[1]	Liberal (2)
	●Cashel Borough[1]	Liberal
	Drogheda	Liberal
	Dublin Borough	Conservative
	Hereford	Liberal (2)
	Norwich	Conservative
	●Sligo Borough[1]	Conservative
	Stafford	Liberal (1) Conservative (1)
	Westbury	Conservative
	††Wexford Borough	Liberal
	Youghal	Liberal
1874	Dudley	Liberal
	Durham	Liberal (2)
	Durham, Northern	Liberal (2)
	††Hackney	Liberal (2)
	††Haverfordwest Boroughs	Liberal
	Kidderminster	Conservative
	Launceston	Conservative
	††Mayo	Home Ruler (2)
	Poole	Liberal
	Stroud	Liberal (2)
	Wakefield	Conservative

VOID ELECTIONS 1832-1987 (Cont.)

Election	Constituency	Party
1880	Bewdley	Liberal
	●Boston	Conservative (1)
		Liberal (1)
	†Bute	Liberal
	●Canterbury	Conservative (2)
	●Chester	Liberal (2)
	Dungannon	Liberal
	Evesham	Liberal
	●Gloucester	Liberal
	Gravesend	Liberal
	Knaresborough	Liberal
	Lichfield	Conservative
	●Macclesfield[1]	Liberal (2)
	Plymouth	Conservative
	Tewkesbury	Liberal
	Wallingford	Liberal
1885	Barrow in Furness	Liberal
	Ipswich	Liberal (2)
	Norwich	Conservative
1892	Northumberland, Hexham	Conservative
	Meath, North	Nationalist
	Meath, South	Nationalist
	Rochester	Conservative
	Walsall	Conservative
1895	Staffordshire, Lichfield	Liberal
	Southampton	Conservative
1900	Maidstone	Liberal
	Monmouth Boroughs	Conservative
1906	Cornwall, Bodmin	Liberal
	Worcester	Conservative
1910 (J)	Dorset, Eastern	Liberal
	Hartlepools, The	Liberal
	Kerry, East[2]	Independent Nationalist
1910 (D)	Cheltenham	Liberal
	Cork, East	Nationalist
	Kingston upon Hull, Central	Conservative
	Louth, North	Nationalist
	West Ham, North	Liberal
1922	Berwick-upon-Tweed	National Liberal
1923	Oxford	Liberal

BY-ELECTIONS

1832-35	Dungarvan (1834)	Liberal
1837-41	Maidstone (1838)	Conservative
	Cambridge (1839)	Conservative
	Ludlow (1839)	Liberal
	††Totnes[3] (1839)	Conservative (1)
		Liberal (1)
1841-47	Ipswich (1842)	Conservative (2)
	Nottingham (1842)	Conservative
	Durham (1843)	Conservative

VOID ELECTIONS 1832-1987 (Cont.)

Election	Constituency	Party
1847-52	††Rye (1847)	Liberal
	Cheltenham (1848)	Liberal
	Sligo Borough (1848)	Liberal
	Aylesbury (1850)	Liberal
	Harwich (March 1851)	Conservative
	††Harwich (May 1851)	Liberal
1852-57	Durham (1852)	Conservative
	Peterborough (1852)	Liberal
	Clitheroe (1853)	Liberal
	Barnstaple (1854)	Conservative
1857-59	Limerick Borough (1858)	Liberal
1859-65	†Norwich (1859)	Liberal
	Lisburn (1863)	Liberal
1865-68	Coventry (1867)	Liberal
	Bristol[2] (1868)	Conservative
1868-74	Longford County (1869)	Liberal
	Waterford Borough (1869)	Liberal
	Bristol (1870)	Liberal
	Mallow (1870)	Liberal
	Norwich (1870)	Conservative
1874-80	Galway Borough (1874)	Home Ruler
	St. Ives (1874)	Conservative
	Stroud (May 1874)	Conservative
	Stroud (July 1874)	Liberal
	Horsham (1875)	Liberal
	●Norwich (1875)	Liberal
1880-85	●Oxford (1880)	Conservative
	●Sandwich[1] (1880)	Conservative
	Wigtown Burghs (1880)	Conservative
	Wigan (1881)	Conservative
1892-95	**Gloucestershire, Cirencester (1892)	Conservative
	Pontefract (1893)	Liberal

*Lack of property qualification to be elected

**Tie after recount and scrutiny

†Disqualified from being elected

††Irregularity by Returning Officer

●Writ suspended. No by-election held

[1] Subsequently disfranchised. See Table 14.19

[2] Parliament Dissolved before a by-election could be held

[3] Double return. See Appendix 14

Appendix 13 UNDUE ELECTIONS 1832-1987

An 'undue' election is an election at which a Committee of the House of Commons or Election Court found the successful candidate not duly elected and ruled that another candidate was entitled to be declared elected. Double and treble returns are excluded but see Appendix 14.

GENERAL ELECTIONS

Election	Constituency	Won by	Awarded to	Date[1]
1832	Caernarvon Boroughs[2]	C	L	March 6, 1833
		L	C	May 22, 1833
	Coleraine	C	L	May 17, 1833
	Galway Borough	R	R	May 2, 1833
	Longford	R(2)	C(2)	April 2, 1833
	Mallow	R	L	April 24, 1833
	Petersfield	L	C	March 5, 1833
	Salisbury	C	L	May 6, 1833
	Southampton	C	L	April 2, 1833
1835	Canterbury	L	C	March 26, 1835
	Cork Borough	C(2)	L(2)	April 18, 1835
	*Cork County	L	C	June 5, 1835
	Dublin Borough	L(2)	C(2)	May 16, 1836
	Windsor	L	C	April 6, 1835
1837	Bedford	C	L	May 21, 1838
	Belfast	L(2)	C(2)	March 8, 1838
	Evesham	C	L	March 20, 1838
	Ipswich	L	C	February 26, 1838
	Kingston upon Hull	C	L	May 7, 1838
	Kinsale	L	C	April 11, 1838
	Norwich	C	L	May 14, 1838
	Petersfield	C	L	February 14, 1838
	Shaftesbury	L	C	April 3, 1838
	Stirlingshire	C	L	April 30, 1838
	Tralee	C	L	March 12, 1838
	Tynemouth and North Shields	L	L	February 23, 1838
1841	Athlone	C	L	June 10, 1842
	Clitheroe	L	C	March 21, 1842
	Flintshire	L	C	May 20, 1842
	Great Marlow	L	C	April 11, 1842
	Lewes	L	C	March 21, 1842
	Longford	R	C	April 18, 1842
	Lyme Regis	L	C	May 30, 1842
	**Wakefield	L	C	April 21, 1842
	Waterford Borough	C(2)	L(2)	June 10, 1842
	Weymouth and Melcombe Regis	C(2)	L(2)	April 4, 1842
	Wigan	C	L	April 11, 1842
1847	Dundalk	R	L	March 20, 1848
1852	Derby	C	L	March 9, 1853
	*Tavistock	L	L	February 21, 1853
1857	Sligo Borough	L	C	July 31, 1857
1865	Boston	L	L	March 21, 1866
	Bridgnorth	L	C	March 22, 1866
1868	Taunton	C	L	March 8, 1869
1874	Boston	L	C	June 23, 1874
	Wigtown Burghs	C	L	June 1, 1874[1]

UNDUE ELECTIONS 1832-1987 (Cont.)

Election	Constituency	Won by	Awarded to	Date[1]
1886	Yorkshire, Buckrose	L	C	January 27, 1887
	Londonderry Borough	C	N	January 27, 1887[1]
1892	Greenock	L	LU	August 9, 1892
1910(D)	Exeter	L	C	April 21, 1911
1955	**Fermanagh and South Tyrone	SF	C	October 25, 1955

BY-ELECTIONS

Election	Constituency	Won by	Awarded to	Date
1832-35	Monaghan (1834)	L	C	July 30, 1834
1835-37	*Drogheda (1835)	L	C	June 29, 1835
	Carlow County (1835)	L(2)	C(2)	August 19, 1835
	Longford (1836)	L	C	May 4, 1837
1837-41	Devizes (1838)	L	C	May 25, 1838
	Carlow Borough (1839)	C	L	July 11, 1839
1841-47	**Newcastle-under-Lyme (1842)	L	C	July 22, 1842
	Bridport (1846)	C	L	April 27, 1846
1847-52	Horsham (1848)	C	L	September 4, 1848
1852-57	**Peterborough (1853)	L	L	August 15, 1853
1859-65	Barnstaple (1863)	L	C	April 15, 1864
1865-68	Helston (1866)	L	C	July 5, 1866
1868-74	Bewdley (1869)	C	L	April 30, 1869
	Galway County (1872)	HR	C	June 13, 1872
1874-80	**Tipperary (1875)	Ind N	C	May 27, 1875
1880-85	Evesham (1880)	L	C	January 6, 1881
1955-59	**Mid-Ulster (1955)	SF	C	October 25, 1955
1959-64	**Bristol, South-East (1961)	Lab	C	July 31, 1961

[1] The dates given are those on which the House of Commons made an order for the Return of Members of Parliament to be amended. In a few cases the Clerk did not attend to amend the Return until a few days later. At Wigtown Boroughs (1874) and Londonderry Borough (1887) the Return did not require to be amended as in the case of Wigtown the member declared elected had been appointed a Judge and the seat was vacant, and at Londonderry the member had also been returned for another constituency but chose to represent Londonderry.

[2] The only case where the result of a petition was reversed by a second petition.

*Lack of property qualification to be elected.

**Disqualified from being elected.

Appendix 14 DOUBLE AND TREBLE RETURNS 1832-1949

Prior to the Ballot Act of 1872, a Returning Officer had no right to give a casting vote in the event of candidates polling the same number of votes. His duty was to return all candidates polling equal votes although they were not allowed to take their seats in the House of Commons until after election petitions had been decided. From 1872 until 1949 a Returning Officer, *if a registered elector in the constituency,* could give a casting vote. Since the Representation of the People Act 1949 if candidates poll equal votes the winner is decided by lot.

GENERAL ELECTIONS

Election	Constituency	Remarks
1841	Cardigan Boroughs	The poll books for two polling places had been lost or stolen and although the votes were not equal the Returning Officer decided to return both the Conservative and Liberal candidates. The House of Commons Committee accepted other evidence as to the contents of the poll books and declared the Liberal candidate elected and that the return of the Conservative candidate was an 'undue' election. (April 18, 1842)
	Thetford	Two-member seat in which the second and third candidates (a Liberal and a Conservative) polled equal votes. On scrutiny one vote was struck off the Liberal candidate and the Conservative declared elected. The return of the Liberal candidate was an 'undue' election. (May 4, 1842)
1847	Montgomery Boroughs	Two candidates (both Conservatives) with equal votes. One candidate decided subsequently to withdraw a petition and not defend his claim to the seat.
1852	Knaresborough	Two-member seat in which three of the four candidates (two Liberals and a Conservative) polled equal votes. On scrutiny one vote was struck off one of the Liberal candidates. One Conservative and one Liberal candidate were declared elected and the return of the other Liberal was an 'undue' election. (April 25, 1853)
1857	Huntingdonshire	Two-member seat in which the second and third candidates (a Conservative and a Liberal) polled equal votes. On scrutiny four votes were struck off the three candidates leaving two Conservatives elected and the return of the Liberal candidate was an 'undue' election. (July 31, 1857)
1859	Aylesbury	Two-member seat in which the second and third candidates (a Conservative and a Liberal) polled equal votes. On scrutiny one vote was struck off the Liberal candidate and the Conservative declared elected. The return of the Liberal candidate was an 'undue' election. (August 2, 1859)
1865	Dunbartonshire	Two candidates (a Conservative and a Liberal) with equal votes. The Liberal candidate decided to withdraw a petition and not defend his claim to the seat.

DOUBLE AND TREBLE RETURNS 1832-1949 (Cont.)

Election	Constituency	Remarks
1868	Horsham	Two candidates (a Conservative and a Liberal) with equal votes. The Conservative candidate decided to withdraw a petition and not defend his claim to the seat.
1874	Athlone	Two candidates (both Home Rulers) with equal votes. After a scrutiny of rejected ballot papers 13 votes were added to one candidate and eight to the other giving a majority of five. The return of the other candidate was an 'undue' election. (April 27, 1874)
1885	St. Andrews Burghs	Two candidates (an Independent Liberal and a Liberal) with equal votes. On scrutiny the Independent Liberal obtained a majority of two and was declared elected. The return of the Liberal candidate was an 'undue' election. (February 18, 1886)

BY-ELECTIONS

Election	Constituency	Remarks
1839	Totnes	Two candidates (a Conservative and a Liberal) with equal votes. The election was however declared void on a technicality — the Returning Officer had failed to give proper notice of the poll.
1878	Northumberland, Southern	Two candidates (a Conservative and a Liberal) with equal votes. As a result of a recount the Conservative candidate was found to have a majority of six and the Liberal candidate decided to withdraw a petition and not defend his claim to the seat.

Appendix 15 VOID ELECTIONS CAUSED BY RETURNING OFFICER IRREGULARITY 1832-1987

GENERAL ELECTIONS

Election	Constituency	Remarks
1868	Wexford	Failed to hold poll after a second candidate had been nominated on the hustings but who subsequently withdrew.
1874	Hackney	Failure to provide sufficient ballot boxes and consequently at two of the polling places no poll was taken and at several others the polling was delayed.
	Haverfordwest	Refused to accept a second nomination without the candidate providing £40 security for the Returning Officer's costs.
	Mayo	Failed to hold a poll after a second candidate had been nominated on the grounds that the candidate had not appointed an election agent.

BY-ELECTIONS

1839	Totnes	Failed to give proper notice of the poll.
1847	Rye	Failed to give proper notice of the poll.
1851	Harwich	Closed poll early.

Appendix 16 SUCCESSFUL CANDIDATES FOUND TO BE DISQUALIFIED 1832-1987

GENERAL ELECTIONS

Election	Name	Party	Constituency	Reason
1841	J. Holdsworth	L	Wakefield	He was Returning Officer for the constituency and although he delegated his duties at the election he was held to be disqualified.
1852	Hon. R.E. Boyle	L	Frome	Secretary of the Most Illustrious Order of St. Patrick.
1865	W. Forsyth	C	Cambridge	Standing Counsel to the Secretary of State for India.
1880	T. Russell	L	Bute	Partner in a firm which held a government contract.
1955	P.C. Clarke	SF	Fermanagh and South Tyrone	Felon

BY-ELECTIONS

Election	Name	Party	Constituency	Reason
1842	J.Q. Harris	L	Newcastle-under-Lyme	Bribery by his agent at a previous election.
1853	G.H. Whalley	L	Peterborough	Guilty of 'treating' at a previous election.
1859	Viscount Bury	L	Norwich	Bribery by his agents at a previous election.
1875	J. Mitchel	Ind N	Tipperary	Felon
1955	T.J. Mitchell	SF	Mid-Ulster	Felon
1961	A.N.W. Benn	Lab	Bristol, South-East	Peer (Viscount Stansgate)